AF378009

Mondrala Press wishes to thank all its friends, fans, patrons, and investors for making this book possible, and especially:

Ms. Randa Dumanian
Mr. and Mrs. Karol and Dagmara Maziukiewicz
*de domo* Sowul

without whose enthusiasm and open hearts this book
could never have happened.

# ABOUT THE AUTHOR

Aleksander Krawczuk (1922-2023) was a noted scholar of Greek and Roman antiquity, a professor at the Jagiellonian University, a former minister of culture, and an author of over 30 popular and widely translated books on the subject of the Antique. For fifty years, his books have enjoyed great popularity among a whole army of devoted fans—many of them people who had never taken interest in the Antique until they picked up one of his books.

What other scholar of antiquity writes popular best-sellers? Yet, at one point, the good professor even hosted an internationally syndicated TV program on ancient Greece and Rome. Alas, due to Russian cultural policies during the Cold War, it was very difficult to publish Polish books in the West. The current effort tries to work off the backlog.

This book appears as part of a project to translate all of the works of Aleksander Krawczuk into English. The following titles have appeared already:

*Seven Against Thebes: Myth and History*
*A Meeting in Oea, or Concerning Plato*
*The Last Olympiad: Twilight of Antiquity*
*Titus and Berenice: Jews, Romans, War, and a Legendary Love Story*
*Rome and Jerusalem*
*The Thirteenth Apostle: Constantine the Great*
*The Devil's Brood: the Sons of Constantine*

Five more titles will appear in 2025:

*Julian the Apostate*
*Pericles and Apamea*
*The Case of Alcibiades, or, Ambition*
*The Tombs of Chaeronea, or, Concerning the Fall of Greece*
*Conversations with Petronius*

Follow the series here: https://www.amazon.com/dp/B0BHF7KVTK

YOUR TRANSLATOR'S SPECIAL REQUEST

Translating and publishing this series of books has been a labor of
love for me. I grew up reading it, and I have always wanted to be able
to share it with my American friends. And finally, here it is.
It will not make me rich, but if you liked the book, would you please
recommend it to a friend?
And if you could give it an Amazon review,
you will be helping others find it!
https://www.amazon.com/dp/2919820494

THANK YOU!

ALEKSANDER'S ANTIQUITIES

# ROME & JERUSALEM

## THE END OF AN AGE

### SECOND EDITION

by Aleksander Krawczuk
translated by Tom Pinch

MONDRALA
PRESS

Originally published in Polish in 1974 as *Rzym i Jerozolima*.

Editing by Mondrala Press
Cover Design by Mondrala Press

ISBN eBook:        978-2-919820-67-2
ISBN paperback:    978-2-919820-68-9
ISBN hardcover:    978-2-919820-69-6

# A NOTE ON THE ILLUSTRATIONS

The illustrations in this book are taken from *The Eleven Caesars*, a series of engravings by hand unknown and published in London by Thomas Bakewell between 1790 and 1799. They themselves were copies of engravings by Aegidius Sadeler II (1570–1629), a Flemish engraver active at the Prague court of Rudolf II. They, in turn, were based on a series of half-length portraits of eleven Roman emperors painted by Titian in 1536-1540 for Federico II, Duke of Mantua.

The imaginary portraits, inspired by the *Lives of Caesars* of Suetonius, were among Titian's best-known works. The paintings were housed in a purpose-built room inside the Ducal Palace in Mantua. Bernardino Campi added a twelfth portrait in 1562. Between 1627 and 1628, the paintings were sold to Charles I of England by Vincenzo II Gonzaga in perhaps the single most famous collection acquisition in European history, and when the Royal Collection of Charles I was broken up and sold after his execution by the English Commonwealth, the *Eleven Caesars* passed in 1651 into the collection of Philip IV of Spain. There, they were all destroyed in a catastrophic fire at the Royal Alcazar of Madrid in 1734 and are now known only from copies and engravings.

The image on the back cover is *Christ Carrying the Cross*—a painting attributed to a follower of Hieronymus Bosch. It was most likely painted between 1510 and 1535. The work is housed in the Museum of Fine Arts in Ghent, Belgium. The woman in the lower left quadrant is Veronica—whose mythical figure is an iteration of Queen Berenice, the right-hand syzygy of Nero.

# TABLE OF CONTENTS

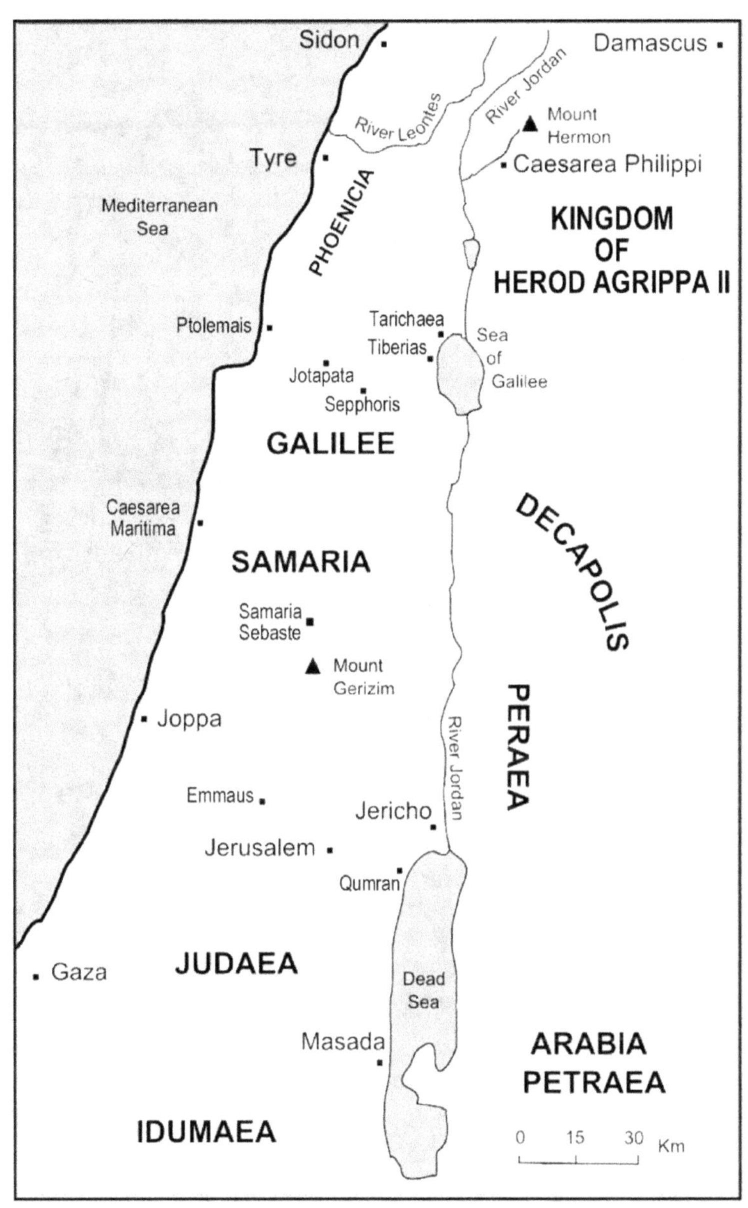



Palestine at the time of the First Jewish War

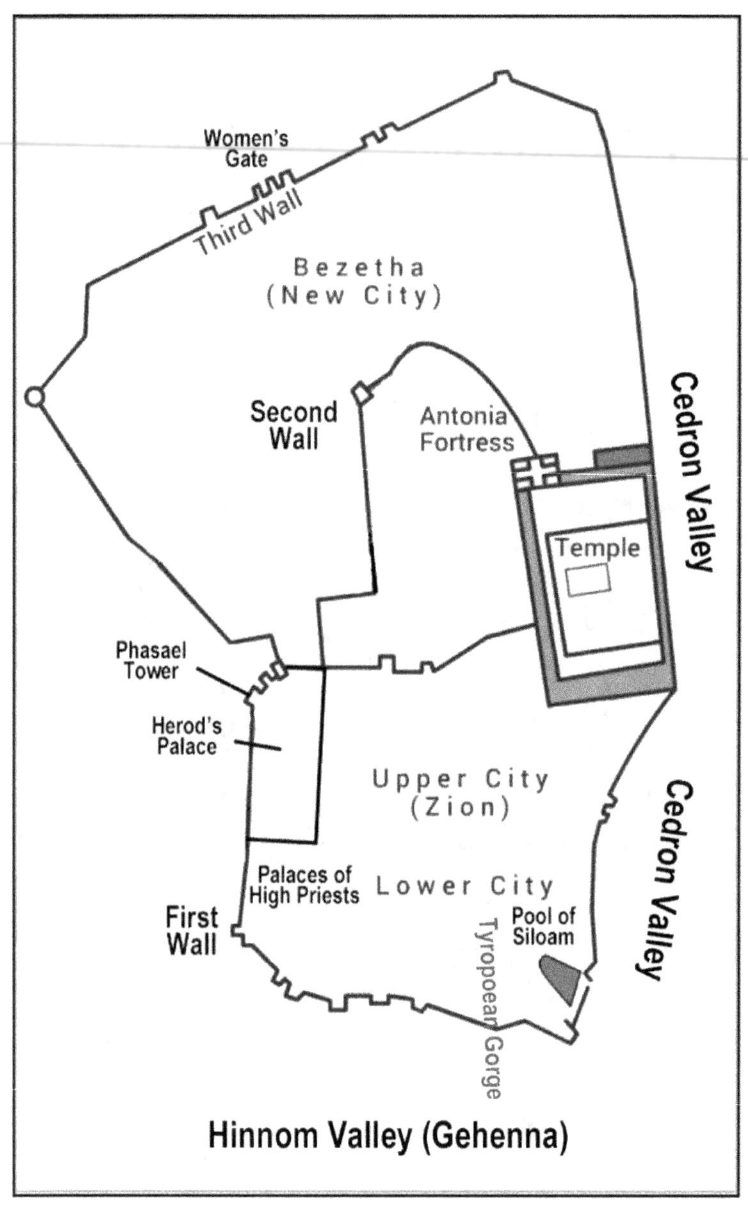


Jerusalem at the time of the First Jewish War

Temple Mount at the time of the First Jewish War

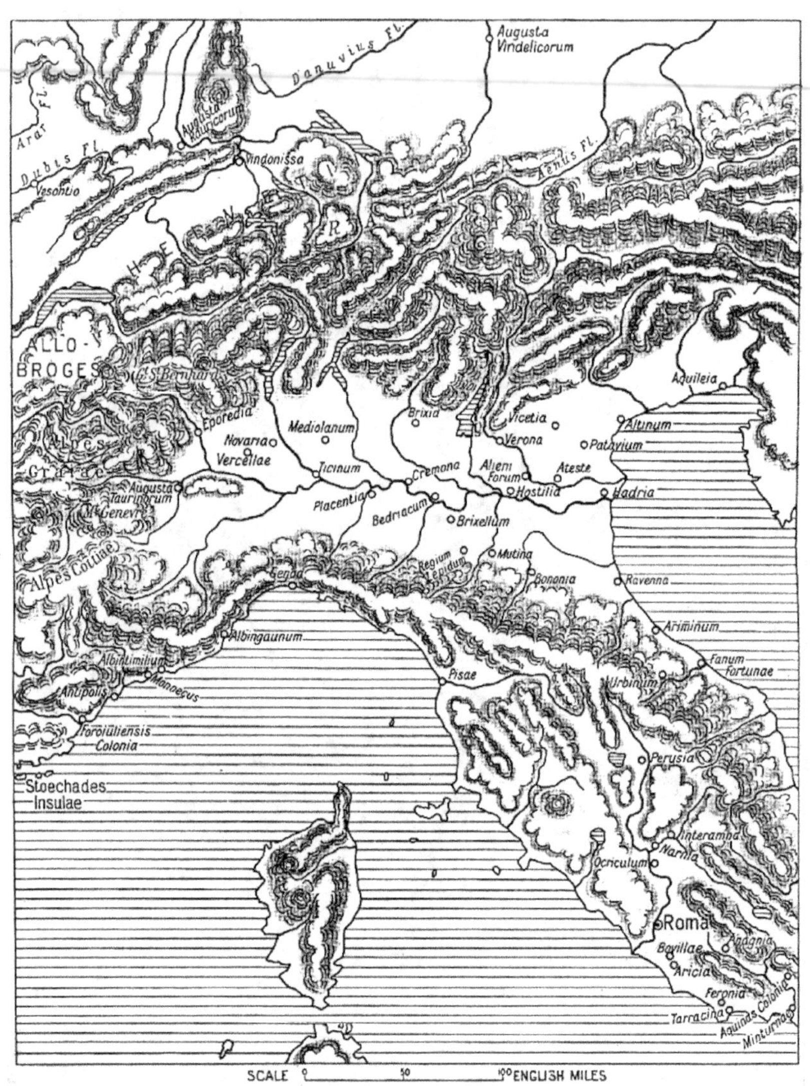



North Italy in AD 69

# SOME NOTES ON THE RHETORIC OF ALEKSANDER KRAWCZUK

*Rhetoric* is what the ancients called it, and went to Greece to study. The word meant as much "structure" as "style." And the structure and style of this book, as of every book of Aleksander Krawczuk, are all of his own.

If they surprise you, it is because, like me, you have grown up reading English-language books on history and, therefore, like me, are expecting one of two kinds of books: either a *narrative* ("one-damn-thing-after-another") or *argument* (like, say, *The Myth of Andalusian Paradise*—you get the point). The former sort is deemed "popular," meaning that we simpletons desire to know what-then, what-then; while the *academicians* prefer a controversy (a way to make waves).

But this book falls into neither category.

1. First, Krawczuk's books are more like a broad overview of a topic, a period, or an idea. We see the topic, as it were, from the eagle's perspective, from very high up, now focusing on this aspect of the subject, now that, and as we do, all of the different elements gradually coalesce into a broad, nuanced, and richly textured picture.

This style of writing does have its English-language equivalents. Barbara Tuchman's *The Proud Tower* is a portrait of an age, a kind of snapshot of the West about the year 1900; Michael Haag's *Alexandria, City of Memory,* does the same for British Colonial Alexandria.

*Rome and Jerusalem* is similar to these books in that it gives us a picture of the Roman Levant at the time of the First Jewish War. It puts the war in the perspective of the great political events on the Mediterranean stage and the major intellectual and religious currents of the period. The device of weaving several stories together, switching back and forth from one place of action to another, from a political narrative to a personal biography to a religious debate, allows us to sense how complex and interconnected everything was—and is.

2. But Krawczuk's reluctance to tell us how these different elements fit together sets him apart. He leaves the interpretation to us. Each of his books has a theme—in *Seven Against Thebes* it was the historical tradition, in *The Last Olympiad*—cultural transformation. In the Jewish Trilogy, the theme is national survival in a changing world. Krawczuk sets about showing certain aspects of the problem, occasionally highlighting them through comparison and contrast with modern people and places, but he offers no conclusions. The reader is presented with the picture and left to make sense of it himself.

The result is that his books remain with us. For weeks and months we find ourselves thinking about the issues and the different interpretations of the text. All the possible interpretations of the enigmatic conclusion of *Rome and Jerusalem* have been with me for decades: the new emperor and the Greek guru walking off, hand in hand, talking about the ways in which they would reform the world, while in Rome Vespasian's men capture the city.

3. Another prominent characteristic of Krawczuk's approach—and rare among professional historians—is to note similarities between the past and the present, pointing out certain timeless and universal aspects of human nature.

This has, as it were, two sides: an obverse and a reverse.

Since so much of ancient history only survives in fragments, forcing us to intuit or conjecture what may have happened, an anecdote from a different time may well help us to do so—this is what men said and did two thousand years later in a similar situation: could something like this have happened in the earlier case, also?

A belief underlies this method: that the past is not a foreign country but is populated by people like us and that we can understand

ii

them no better but also no worse than we can understand our contemporaries. Perhaps the most striking aspect of this technique in the present book is the amount of attention Krawczuk devotes to understanding the possible motivations of the actors—patriots, politicians, soldiers, and priests, who, it turns out, reasoned as we do today.

And, of course, the converse is also true: a story from the past can help us put our present in a clearer perspective. This has been an important part of Krawczuk's reception. It is easy for Poles to see themselves in first century Jews.


4. Finally, Krawczuk's books have a feature that modern historians, striving to sound scientific, generally eschew: that occasional flash of literary brilliance. Few historians will dare to include in their books a fictitious apocalyptic prophecy in the style of Daniel (p. 109), an imagined soldiers' dialogue (pp. 126-8), or this pixish flight of fancy:

> A person inclined to fantasize about syzygies might look for one in the evolution of the legend about different women with the same name. The two alleged Berenices, both cured miraculously, merge in the later tradition into one, and she, in turn, transferred to the city of historical Berenice, transforms into a Jewish princess, alive and famous in the years of early Christianity. And, in spite of everything that her contemporaries said about the historical Berenice, this Berenice of the legend is the kernel of her future rise to the elevated status of sainthood.

> And thus posterity showed Queen Berenice a special grace—while it denied it to Nero; the emperor on whose grave flowers were placed for many years after his death; the ruler loved and awaited by many and resurrected three times; became the Beast of the Apocalypse in the eyes of later generations. Say what you may: this is a manifestation of the law of *syzygy* if there ever was one. And an example of the ultimate Divine Justice.

*Tom Pinch*
*Ardennes National Park*
*Luxembourg*

# ROME & JERUSALEM

Titus

# A CONSPIRACY THEORY

But did Emperor Nero really die? Did he really commit suicide by stabbing himself in the throat? Were those really *his* ashes in the grand porphyry sarcophagus in the tomb of the Domitians at the foot of the Hill of Gardens, just outside the city walls?

Several months had passed since the events of early June 68, and almost everyone in the capital was asking himself such questions. And—incredibly—many answered them in the negative. For whatever reasons, many in Rome did not want to believe that Nero had died. They said: our lord lives, bides his time, and will return soon!

The rumor went that Nero, with the help of a few most trusted freedmen, had staged his suicide, cremated a substitute corpse, and escaped and that he did this to confuse the assassins sent to kill him. Of course, he had had to act that way—he had had no choice—because everyone had abandoned him: some out of fear, others from stupidity. But he escaped and is hiding somewhere in Italy. Or overseas. And he is waiting for an opportune moment to return. But he will return and reassume the reigns of power.

And soon! For it is clear that neither Rome nor the provinces will endure the abomination of the government of senile Galba. As someone rightly said about him: "he might be fit to rule, except last time he looked, he ruled already."

Others yet refused to believe the story of Nero's suicide on other grounds, saying:

"Nero was a coward. There is no way he would have killed himself. And since no one boasts about having killed him and no one demands the bounty set on his head, perhaps Nero is not dead after all?"

Finally, the suspicious asked: "Who has seen the cremation of Nero and the placement of his ashes in the tomb of the Domitians?" (The Domitians' tomb was the emperor's family tomb). "Just think, how very suspicious!" they said, "the supposed witnesses had been *women*: his two nurses, Ecloge and Alexandra, and Acte, a concubine he had rejected many years ago but who still loved him dearly. The three spared no expense to make the funeral as dignified as possible and contributed to it over two hundred thousand sesterces of their own money. Acte probably paid most of it, as she was an extremely wealthy woman thanks to Nero's favor: she had extensive estates, magnificent villas, and swarms of servants.

The three women cremated a body and collected its ashes in a snow-white cloak shot with gold thread—the very cloak Nero had worn at the New Year's celebrations six months before his tragic end. But whose body was it? Was it really Nero's? Only they knew—and they knew only because Nero had trusted them. Could it be that they spent all that money on the funeral in order to give the false impression that the body of the emperor was being buried while he himself was, in fact, hiding somewhere else?

Sporus had also stood by the burning pyre. Once upon a time, Nero had decided to make a girl of him. He ordered him castrated and then married him, formally and ceremonially, as his wife (in Greece, of course, as Rome would not have stood for such kinky business). Later, the boy-girl was present at the scene of the suicide. All this made excellent material for mockery:

"What trustworthy witnesses to the cremation and burial! Three freedmen—a concubine and two wet nurses—and a eunuch!

How can anyone believe such witnesses? The whole thing is a farce, though, admittedly, very entertaining, as befits a great artist."

Such and similar gossip was heard among the people who had suddenly been deprived of the joys of life: blood games, chariot races, song and dance performances. And of the joy of gossiping about palace intrigues, crimes, and orgies—there were no such topics with the new emperor, Galba, the octogenarian killjoy.

Oh, for those wonderful times of their beloved Nero!—they were sorely missed. Fresh flowers were often found on the white altar slab in front of the porphyry sarcophagus in the Domitians' tomb. Often, the flowers were laid by people who claimed that the sarcophagus was empty or contained false remains. Yet, they still wanted to give an outlet to their feelings of attachment to the memory of their beloved emperor.

In the Forum itself, right next to the main Rostrum, images of Nero appeared at night. And his edicts—edicts in which the still-alive Emperor announced in a threatening tone: "I will soon return to take revenge on all those who have betrayed me and my people!"

And it seemed as if Fate itself encouraged such hopes: Galba, the man who had overthrown Nero, reigned for barely half a year. On January 15, AD 69, soldiers of the imperial guard—the Praetorians— murdered him in the Forum. They did this in a coup staged by one of Galba's earliest supporters, Otho. And this Otho had once been one of Nero's closest friends. In AD 58, Nero took his beautiful wife, Sabina Poppea, and sent him into honorary exile in Lusitania as governor of that province, covering more or less the territory of today's Portugal and western Spain. From that distant land on the Atlantic, Otho returned to Rome with the new emperor, Galba. He had helped him come to power, but only in passing, only to start an intrigue against him at the earliest opportunity. He then bribed the Praetorian guard to kill Galba and elevate him instead.

During the same month of January AD 69, a month stained with the blood of Galba, frightening news reached the capital: the armies on the Rhine had rebelled. In the first days of AD 69, they acclaimed as emperor one Aulus Vitellius—governor of Lower

Germania. And so the Empire, deprived of the bliss of Nero's sweet rule, was threatened with divine punishment: the worst of all wars: a civil war. Those who claimed that the moment of his return was at hand weren't completely wrong: were Nero alive, all he needed to do was to show himself, and all would flock to him for safety.

## ON THE ISLAND OF KYTHNOS

And now, as if responding to these calls, in February 69—as bundles of spring flowers—humble violets—were being placed on the altar in the Domitians' tomb—the news came that Nero had revealed himself in the East—somewhere in Greece or in Asia Minor. Yes, that Nero, our Nero, the true Nero: the same face and posture, the same hairstyle, quite long and loose at the back, and even his eyes were the same: grey and attentive, a little nearsighted. Of course, he played the kithara and sang beautifully. That he revealed himself in the Greek East was fully understandable. After all, he had always declared that he loved the Greeks most of all because only they could understand a truly great artist.

In the last years of his reign, Nero had traveled to Greece, reactivating ancient games and visiting holy places, and in AD 66, he restored freedom to the country, which its inhabitants welcomed with sincere enthusiasm. He would, therefore, have had every right to expect a warm welcome among them and whatever support he desired.

It felt good to talk like this in the taverns on the Tiber, safely awaiting further developments, but the cunning and pusillanimous Greeks did not intend to take any risks. They did not rush to help this new-fangled Nero: neither those who believed he was their emperor returned nor those who didn't but thought it beautiful and beneficial of him to return and rule again. No one did a thing to aid him, and in truth—from the very beginning—most thought the man was an impostor. Yes, he did manage to gather about himself a handful of runaway slaves and ordinary rogues, but they were the sort who had nothing to lose, and he promised them mountains of gold once he was back on the throne.

He took over a rickety ship and boldly sailed across the Aegean, aiming for some unknown destination. However, a storm soon drove him to the island of Kythnos in the Cyclades. There, he was delayed for a longer spell. The island lay on an important sea route, connecting Greece with Asia Minor, and long-distance ships called here quite often, even in the winter season, which was generally not favorable for navigation. In particular, many soldiers on leave passed through here *en route* from Syria, Palestine, and Egypt for Italy, for no large-scale military operations were possible in the winter. And this Nero—for what else do we call him?—wooed these soldiers and inducted them into his bodyguard, and whoever refused disappeared without a trace. He also robbed merchants and liberated and armed their slaves.

Our hero, Titus, came close to meeting the (presumed) impostor and almost certainly heard about him—for that February, he was en route from Corinth to the East. He had been traveling to Rome to pay homage to emperor Galba, but when he reached Corinth and heard about the emperor's death, he turned around. His mission had been to assure Galba of the loyalty of the Roman legions in Palestine and to give him an update on the progress of the Jewish War. Galba's death made the mission irrelevant.

And Titus was eager to return to Syria because Queen Berenice awaited him there. Their love was no longer a secret, and many thought that love and not politics had changed the young man's travel plans.

Fortunately for him—and for the pseudo-Nero—Titus had chosen the roundabout route, traveling along the Greek and Asian shores and bypassing Kythnos altogether. So, just as the alleged Nero appeared on Kythnos, the Roman aristocrat, who had often seen the real Nero up close, was already somewhere in Asia and heading for Cyprus.

By chance, centurion Sisenna found himself on Kythnos. He was traveling on a mission from the Syrian legions to the Praetorians in Rome. He, too, had been dispatched in response to the news of Galba's death. His task was to report his legions' acceptance of the events in Rome and to deliver a gift secreted in his baggage. It would have been a great coup for the impostor Nero to gain Sisenna's support. He realized this and spared no effort trying to convince Sisenna to join his cause. Prudent Sisenna pretended to take the masquerade at face value but fled the island at the first opportunity, not forgetting to take his luggage along. From then on, he spread the word everywhere he went about his extraordinary adventure, embellishing the story with every retelling. Thanks to his reports, the case gained publicity in Italy, causing many conflicting emotions. However, before the authorities could decide what to do in the matter, the danger vanished just as suddenly as it had appeared.

It happened like this:

Galba had appointed a new governor of Galatia and Pamphylia, two provinces in Asia Minor, one Calpurnius Asprenas. When Otho took over, he did not withdraw the appointment, and Asprenas set off for his provinces in February. He had with him an escort of two ships from the naval base at Misenum in the Gulf of Naples. Sailing about the boot of Italy, he missed Sisenna and ordered his flotilla to anchor off the shore of Kythnos unawares, paying no attention to the small ship in the harbor.

As soon as he was told what kind of ships these were, the false Nero invited their two captains aboard his ship. He told them who he really was, what misfortunes had befallen him, and how he had cleverly managed to escape certain death in Rome by faking his own suicide and cremation. He mourned the terrible reversal of his fate, as a result of which he had lost everything—power, wealth, even his name!—but he remained the same person, the one and only true Nero, the only legitimate ruler of the Empire. But new opportunities were opening before him, and the empire, so tormented by recent upheavals, awaited his return. And now, fate brought him two Misenian ships!

Referring to the unwavering loyalty that the Misenian fleet had always shown him, the presumptive Nero asked the two captains to convey him to Syria or Egypt. Everything would change for the better the moment he landed there. It was a small risk for them, he said and promised a fabulous reward if the gamble worked out.

It is unclear how he had learned that the Misenian fleet had been loyal to Nero, but it was true that in the last months of the emperor's reign, when the news of rebellion came from everywhere, Nero had tried to form a new legion for his defense out of the Misenum marines. Of course, some rumors of this could have reached the impostor's ears accidentally, but it is difficult to rule out other possibilities, even the most unlikely.

The question also arises: why did the false Nero want to reach Syria or Egypt? Did he expect that the population and legions of those lands would defect to his side? Or perhaps he wanted to escape even further, beyond the borders of the Empire, to Parthia, Ethiopia, or India? We are at the cusp of fantasy.

The two captains heard the dramatic appeal, noted the beautiful promises, and replied that they agreed but had to talk to their men first. They would come back as soon as they gauged their mood. Alas, they did not go to their crews but straight to the governor. Asprenas wasted no time on negotiations. The crews of the two ships, obeying his orders, attacked the "imperial" ship. The impostor was killed on the spot. Asprenas took his severed head with him to Asia and, from there, sent it to Rome, where people finally had the time to investigate who this Nero of Kythnos had been. There were various theories. Some clues suggested that he had been one of Nero's freedmen. Other clues seemed to lead to the shores of the Black Sea. But soon, momentous events shook Italy again, and the curious story of the Neo-Nero became an insignificant footnote.


## THE BEAST OF THE APOCALYPSE


But the people of Rome did not forget Nero. Not even the sight of the severed head of the Nero of Kythnos ended the persistent rumor that Nero was alive and about to return. Ten years later, a new self-proclaimed Nero appeared in the East, and ten years after that, another. Yes, for twenty years after his porphyry sarcophagus had been deposited in the tomb of the Domitians, Nero kept coming back. Is there better proof that the emperor was truly popular among the masses? No one would have come up with the idea of pretending to be Nero if he did not think he might thereby gain widespread support. In the subsequent five centuries of the Empire's existence in the West, no other emperor was resurrected so many times. No name has caused so much anticipation in some and so much fear in others.

Because, of course, not everyone shared the general longing for the happy times of Nero. Many people in Rome—and in the provinces—recalled his reign with horror. They heard these repeating reports of the imminent return of the tyrant/matricide with fear that caused a lasting psychosis which, in time, left a permanent mark on the entire European civilization, mainly thanks to a certain mysterious book from the time.

Most scholars think that, in its present form, the *Book of the Apocalypse*, that is, *The Revelation of Saint John*, dates to the reign of Emperor Domitian, i.e., the end of the first century and therefore, about the time when the third self-proclaimed Nero appeared.

However, quite a few researchers share the view that at least some parts of *The Revelation* are older and were written during the rule of Nero or soon after his death—that is, in the days of the appearance of the Nero of Kythnos. Whatever the case, it seems logical that the writings of the first generations of Christians would contain some mention of their first great persecutor. Therefore, anyone who encounters the following words at the end of chapter XIII of the *Apocalypse:*

> Here is wisdom. Let him that hath understanding count the number of the beast: for it is the number of a man, and his number is six hundred three score and six[1]

must ask himself whether or not they may relate to Nero.

---

[1] *Revelation* 13:18

But another passage seems even more specific. It comes in chapter XVII, in which Rome is represented as a woman sitting on a scarlet beast, a beast full of blasphemous names and having seven heads and ten horns:

And there came one of the seven angels which had seven vials, and talked with me, saying unto me, Come hither; I will shew unto thee the judgment of the great whore that sitteth upon many waters:

With whom the kings of the earth have committed fornication, and the inhabitants of the earth have been made drunk with the wine of her fornication.

So he carried me away in the spirit into the wilderness, and I saw a woman sit upon a scarlet coloured beast, full of names of blasphemy, having seven heads and ten horns.

And the woman was arrayed in purple and scarlet color and decked with gold and precious stones and pearls, having a golden cup in her hand full of abominations and filthiness of her fornication:

And upon her forehead was a name written, Mystery, Babylon The Great, The Mother Of Harlots And Abominations Of The Earth.

And I saw the woman drunken with the blood of the saints, and with the blood of the martyrs of Jesus: and when I saw her, I wondered with great admiration.

And the angel said unto me, Wherefore didst thou marvel? I will tell thee the mystery of the woman and of the beast that carrieth her, which hath the seven heads and ten horns.

The beast that thou sawest was, and is not; and shall ascend out of the bottomless pit, and go into perdition: and they that dwell on the earth shall wonder, whose names were not written in the book of life from the foundation of the world when they behold the beast that was and is not, and yet is.

And here is the mind which hath wisdom. The seven heads are seven mountains, on which the woman sitteth.

And there are seven kings: five are fallen, and one is, and the other is not yet come; and when he cometh, he must continue a short time.[2]

Is the beast that was, but now exists and does not exist at the same time, having come out of the abyss—is that not the resurrected Nero? And is he not the sixth king, ruling currently after the five who have already fallen? It would seem that way if we count (as many commentators do) from Caesar onwards. It is true that Caesar was not really an emperor and ruled only by virtue of dictatorial powers, but to the inhabitants of the provinces—the most likely readers of the *Apocalypse*—the difference was probably academic. That Caesar could decide everything by himself, like any autocratic ruler, and that, after his death, he was declared a god, and that all subsequent rulers of Rome bore his name as part of their full title—up to and including Nero, who was indeed the sixth in that order, the sixth and indeed the last of the Julio-Claudian dynasty—all of that seems to support that interpretation because it all makes the passage a typical *vaticinium ex eventu*, i.e., "a prediction after the fact." And, viewed in this light, who is he who has not yet come but when he comes will stay only a short time? This, of course, would have to be Galba: he ruled for just six months. By this interpretation, then, the *Book of Revelation* must have been written shortly after January 15, 69 AD, i.e., during the reign of Otho, and most likely under the influence of the news of Nero's reappearance in the East, perhaps in February or March of that year.

But regardless of how we interpret the symbolic figures and numbers, one thing seems certain: Nero, the first persecutor, is the most important, perhaps even the fundamental element of the apocalyptic vision and the prototype of the Antichrist. When *The Book of Revelation* was written, only relatively small groups of people, scattered in various cities of the Empire, thought of this emperor with such hatred and heard with such fear the rumors of his return. For many, perhaps even most, he was either indifferent or downright sympathetic. However, as Christ's followers grew in number and importance, the terrible image conveyed in the words of the *Apocalypse* captured the collective imagination.

---

[2] *Revelation*, 17:1-10

# LOOKING DOWN AT ROME FROM MONTE PINCIO

The Domitians' tomb at the foot of the Hill of Gardens—today called Monte Pincio—fell into ruin over the centuries. Its decorations, marbles, and even its bricks were recycled. There is no trace left, not even of its foundations. The porphyry sarcophagus containing Nero's ashes has disappeared.

(It is not without significance that the sarcophagus was made of porphyry. This dark-red stone was imported from Egypt. Although it had already been used for statuary under Claudius, it came into general use only under Nero, especially during the construction of his Golden House.[3] The sarcophagus was, in fact, carved in Nero's favorite stone, and the decision to use it may have come from Acte. Whatever happened to the sarcophagus, the snow-white marble of the altar before the sarcophagus probably decorates one of the Roman churches today).

But even in the Middle Ages, people still remembered where the tomb of the Domitians had stood and whose remains were buried there: the remains of the Beast of the Apocalypse. Residents of nearby houses pointed to a huge tree—it was a walnut—growing right next to the ruins; they complained that malicious demons resided in it. Therefore, at the end of the 11th century, Pope Paschal II ordered the tree cut down, and in order to banish the dark powers from the site forever, he built a church at the foot of the hill, a church called today Santa Maria del Popolo. In the second half of the 15th century, Pope Sixtus IV rebuilt it in a much more impressive, three-nave form and added a dome. The interior was gradually enriched with sculptures and paintings by many excellent artists, among them Raphael and his

---

[3] Domus Aurea (Latin, "Golden House") was a vast landscaped complex built by Nero largely on the Oppian Hill in the heart of ancient Rome after the great fire in 64 AD had destroyed a large part of the city. Extensive gold leaf decoration that gave the palace its name was not the only extravagant element of its decor: stuccoed ceilings were faced with semi-precious stones and ivory veneers, while the walls were frescoed.

students. This church is today one of the most beautiful monuments of Renaissance architecture in Rome.

Anyone who stands on the terrace of the Pincio Hill today sees before her the vast panorama of the city of emperors and popes. At her feet lies the very ornate, oval Piazza del Popolo (named after the church) with the spire of an Egyptian obelisk in its center. A long street, called in ancient times Via Flaminia, crosses the square and extends beyond the city limits of ancient Rome. Currently, its section within the city center is called Il Corso, and at the place where it touches the square, stand two small domed churches both dedicated to the Virgin: Santa Maria In Montesanto and Santa Maria Dei Miracoli. But directly in front of her, the tourist has the third dome of this area, the dome, roof, and bell tower of Santa Maria del Popolo.

And when she looks up, she can see the gigantic dome of St. Peter's Basilica in the distance. The magnificent tomb of the Domitians, in which Nero was buried, stood very close to the place where the terrace square now extends over the square. An old tradition holds that the body of the apostle Peter, crucified on the orders of Nero, was buried not far away, in what was once a suburban street named Via Cornelia, directly under what is today the dome of Saint Peter's.

As the crow flies, less than three miles separates the two sites.


## THE SCIENCE OF SYZYGY

Our old friend, Clement,[4] speaks:

And that very Peter taught me and several other beloved students gathered around him in Caesarea Maritima:

---

[4] Clement, the hero of an early Christian novel now often referred to as Clementine Literature, has appeared in an earlier volume of this trilogy, *Titus and Berenice.*

'The world is built in such a way that all phenomena exist in pairs of opposites: things, concepts, and persons. They are opposite but interconnected. Greeks call such pairs *syzygies,* or things yoked together. [5] To give the simplest and most obvious examples, these are day and night, light and darkness, sun and moon, life and death, knowledge and ignorance. Only man can choose between right and wrong in any given syzygy, between truth and appearance, beauty and ugliness.

'However, in order not to make that choice—and therefore the merit of choosing it—too easy for men, these pairs appear to us in such a way that the baser, inferior, and illusory element of each pair obscures in our eyes its greater and more virtuous partner. And so, we have the temporal world constantly before us to make us think that it is tangible and real, while we can barely imagine Eternity because it is infinite. Similarly, ignorance always appears more true than true wisdom.

'Examining carefully how the law of syzygy operates, we must first observe that it is most perceptible in the case of prophecy. The present moment is like a mother who gives life to her children, while Eternity receives them like a father. Hence, we have two kinds of prophets. There are *worldly soothsayers* who prophesy falsely. They always appear before *the prophets of truth* do—who actually know the future because they have been received by the Father and are His righteous sons.

'If only everyone understood that! Then, no one would be deceived by Simon the Magus, the man who is sowing so much confusion now but really is the servant of the left-hand god, weak and evil!

'All syzygies were brought into existence in such a way that the one on the right is stronger and was created first, and only then the left and weaker one. Thus, the heavens were created before the earth. But in the human world, it is the opposite. The weaker element of a syzygy appears before the stronger one; therefore, among the sons of adam, first came the unjust Cain, and the just Abel only second. There are many examples of this rule, especially among the prophets

---

[5] Syzygy /ˈsɪzɪdʒi/ (from Greek *syzygia* "yoked together")

and the patriarchs. With this in mind, it is easy to establish that Simon, who was first to go among the Gentiles as a prophet, is only darkness before light, ignorance before wisdom, sickness before health. He bears false witness because it must be so. And when the end of this world draws near, the same will happen again: first, the Antichrist will appear and will deceive many, and only after him— the Messiah.

'But he who does not understand the science of syzygy will find it difficult to grasp who my predecessor, Simon, really is. Therefore, many honest people believe him, even though no one knows him. They love him even though he hates everyone. They accept him as a friend, although he is, in fact, a sworn enemy of each. They welcome him as a savior, but he only brings death. They see the light in him, and he destroys them like fire!'

After hearing this, I dared to ask how we might recognize Simon's true nature. To this, Peter replied:

'There lives not far from here, in Tyre, a Phoenician city, a certain woman named Justa, a Canaanite woman. She has a daughter named Berenice. The girl had once been seriously ill for several years and was possessed by demons. So when Our Lord came to her area, Justa followed him everywhere, begging him to take pity and heal her daughter. But he refused for a long time, repeatedly saying to her that bread intended for one's children should not be thrown to dogs.[6] Until finally, one day, the mother shouted:

"Yet even dogs are allowed to eat leftovers which fall uneaten from the table!"

'And it so happened that soon thereafter, Berenice regained her health. Then, both women turned away from their old gods and embraced The Law with all their hearts.[7]

'At this, Justa's husband, a pagan, immediately drove them out of the house, and she, wanting to secure male protection for herself in

---

[6] In other words, the miraculous healing of Jesus should be reserved for the Jews.

[7] The Jewish Law, i.e. Judaism

16

her old age, bought two little boys, kidnapped somewhere in distant lands, and put up for sale by a slave trader. They were brothers, perhaps even twins, as evidenced by their striking resemblance to each other. She raised them lovingly as her own sons, and they grew up loving her like their mother. Now, when these two boys grew up and were able to go about freely, they joined Simon the Magus for a while, about whom there was then so much commotion in Samaria, Galilee, and Phenicia. They became his closest and most trusted students, for they were bright and enterprising young men. But after they learned the sorcerer's secrets, they became frightened and abandoned him. They are now here with us and will be happy to tell you everything they witnessed firsthand.'

And he pointed to Aquila and Niketas.

And what we heard from their mouths was truly astonishing, even unbelievable. First, they told us about Simon's parents, who had come from Samaria. Then, where the sorcerer had been educated and how he had risen to prominence among Dositus's disciples. They detailed the tricks by which he had managed to depose his master, take his place, and win over the woman named Helen or Selene.

The brothers assured us that Simon was indeed capable of performing miracles. Statues obeyed him, moving as if alive. He walked on and even wallowed in glowing coals and levitated in the air at will. He turned stones into bread and took on the shape of various animals, becoming a snake or a goat. With his breath, he opened locked doors, broke iron shackles with his thought, and made heavy objects in the house float up and swing under the ceiling like dry leaves on water.

What was I supposed to think about all this?


## THE RED AND THE WHITE

After the passage of so many centuries, should we find it easier or more difficult to answer Clement's question?

Of course, the easiest thing would be to pass with an indulgent smile over the strange laws of syzygy and the extraordinary miracles of Simon the Magus. In the former case, we are dealing with the product of a naïve and rather entertaining attempt at philosophizing, [8] while in the second—with the superstitious belief in black magic. Is it worth studying this kind of literature, which is neither original nor even artistically inspired? It may be of interest only as a witness of its time because it shows the mentality of the people among whom the new religion of Christianity was born.

But its testimony is authentic. The preceding chapter summarizes a chapter from the second book of an old Christian novel, *Homilies*. We have discussed it in our last volume on the occasion of the discussion of *Ennoia*—a universal principle supposedly incarnated in the person of Helen or Selene, the girlfriend of Simon the Magus. And though the oldest preserved copies of this book date to a much later period, most scholars think it was written in the second century ad—less than a century after the events it describes. One of the preserved copies, in Greek, is called *Homilies*, i.e., "Sermons," while the other, Latin, is called *Recognitiones*, i.e., "Recognitions." Together, they are referred to as *Clementine Literature*, after its narrator-hero, a Roman citizen named Clement, son of Faustus.

Clement lost all his loved ones when he was young; first, his mother, Matidia, disappeared when, under the influence of a mysterious prophecy, she went on a long journey to the East with Clement's twin brothers. A little later, Faustus left in search of them and likewise disappeared without a trace. Finally, Clement also left Italy—but not in search of his family because he did not believe that they were still alive, but in search of a foreigner named Barnabas. He had met him accidentally in Rome and was so impressed with his teachings that he decided to sail to Palestine to follow him there.

They reconnected in Caesarea. There, Clement met Peter and was drawn into the great controversy between him and Simon the

---

[8] Russian philosophers like Vladimir Solovyov (1853-1900) would resort to "syzygies" in modern times.

Magus. From this point on, the main purpose of the novel is to present the apostle's views on various philosophical and religious matters. Interestingly, those views deviate on many points from what we consider the main teachings of the Church and clearly reveal that the work was written among Judaizing Christians and Gnostics.

Thus, *Clementine Literature*, although seemingly naive in places, is one of the most interesting monuments of ancient religion. Some of its elements are related to very old beliefs, and others relate to beliefs and legends that live on today. And therefore, let us look at the story in more detail, starting with the syzygies.

The word *syzygy* appeared in the Greek language in very ancient times, describing married couples or two animals placed under a common yoke. Later, it was used for pairs of people, objects, and concepts which were somehow similar to each other. Its interesting use arose in astronomy, where it was used to describe two stars related to each other in such a way that when one appeared in the sky, the other simultaneously set. Peter would have been entitled to use such an example when describing the concept of syzygy.

But where do we look for the sources of the doctrine the *Clementine Literature* puts in the mouth of Peter? Who was the first to come up with the idea of paired but opposed concepts? Looking for Greek sources, we must go back several centuries to the theories of Heraclitus and Empedocles. The first seemed to think that all change in the world resulted from a constant conflict of opposing forces, which were subject to one law. The second imagined a universal strife between love/attraction and war/repulsion, affecting the four basic elements and thereby causing the world to fluctuate. However, there are obvious differences between these ancient Greek concepts of what we might call "proto-physics" and Peter's Law of Syzygy because the latter emphasized the interdependence of the two members of each pair.

More interestingly, we can point to another source of the idea: Iranian religion, which had consistently explained all cosmic and psychological processes in terms of a dualism: a struggle of two hostile but mutually interconnected forces of good and evil, light and darkness, order and chaos, Ormuzd and Ahriman. Iranian beliefs spread widely throughout the ancient world in various forms—it is enough to recall the cult of Mithras, so prevalent in the middle period of the Roman Empire. In Judea, however, many concepts originating from Iran had been adopted much earlier—first, during the period of Babylonian captivity and then during Persian rule over Palestine.

Iranian influence was very noticeable in the views of the sect of the Essenes, who lived in monastic communities on the Dead Sea. Among the writings of this sect, discovered in the caves of Qumran, we found a treatise presenting the future war between the Sons of Light and the Sons of Darkness, a very Iranian vision of the world.

Also Iranian was the belief in the existence of hierarchies of angels and demons. It had taken root among Jews in general and Essenes in particular. The view that at least some of the teachings of "Clementine Peter" arose under the influence of Iranian religion is supported by many details. Thus, Peter calls Simon the servant of the left-hand deity, a figurative expression typical of the symbolism of Iranian beliefs. Also, a typical Iranian syzygy is the male/female opposition, and the *Homilies* present it in a very Iranian form: the feminine being evil and vicious, the male being righteous and good:

> What is masculine is all truth, and what is feminine is all error. What is born of these two is partly error, partly truth. The feminine covers the white male seed with its blood, as if with red fire, thus employing an external element to increase its otherwise weak strength. It rejoices in the temporal flowering of the body and, through short-lived pleasure, destroys the elemental force of rational thought. It inspires sinful lust and thereby misleads the soul, which is the bride, away from her bridegroom, Truth. And every man is like a beautiful bride whose mind will be enlightened when the white word of a true prophet fertilizes him.

Of course, we encounter similar contemptuous judgments about the left and the feminine in other cultural circles (Daoism comes to mind), but what matters to us here are not the conclusions drawn from this opposition but the imagery itself. For example, notice how white and red are contrasted. The former is male, pure, creative, and prophetic, while the latter is a symbol of femininity, desire, blood, and destructive fire.

## JUSTA THE SYRO-PHOENICIAN

Yet, such sharp words of condemnation for everything that is feminine appear only in the theoretical parts of the *Homilies* and especially in those strange speculations on syzygies, while the women who appear in the novel are taken seriously and treated with respect. And thus, here is the pious Justa and her daughter Berenice. The former is a character well-known to us from the gospels. She is the woman from Tyre, a pagan, who managed to convince Jesus to heal her daughter. This story is often quoted in scholarly treatises on the origins of Christianity, which draw attention to the harsh—even contemptuous—attitude with which Jesus originally dismissed the supplicant. Combined with other such scenes and statements, this seems to suggest that in the early period of Christianity, the Good News[9] was intended only for orthodox Jews. Only they were recognized as beloved children worthy of miracles and mercy, and all non-Jews were dogs, which had to satisfy themselves with leftovers at best.

However, neither Mark (Chapter VII) nor Matthew (Chapter XV), who tell the story, give us the names of the mother and daughter. The first of them refers to her as "a woman from Tyre" and a "Hellene," which in this instance denotes her as pagan rather than as Greek; and only later is she defined in terms of her ethnicity: "a Syro-Phoenician woman by birth." Matthew, on the other hand, limits himself to saying that she was a Canaanite woman, which at that time meant a resident of Palestine who was not a Jew. *Homilies* repeat that information but also give us the names of both women.

The question arises, of course, whether the author of the novel

---

[9] Greek εὐαγγέλιον meaning "good news" is the source of *evangelion* (Gospel), *evangelist, evangelical,* etc.

based these names on some tradition richer than the one preserved in the Gospels or whether he just made up the names, as is the custom of many writers, not only ancient. Neither possibility can be ruled out. In any case, the choice and combination of the two names is interesting because even if they had been made up, it did not happen entirely arbitrarily and not without some deeper intention.

The first name, Justa, is, of course, Latin. It means "Righteous" or "Just." We often see it as a nickname among the Romans, and it may seem surprising in a Syro-Phoenician woman who probably did not speak the masters' tongue. Yet, the name appeared often in the first and second centuries both among Jews and their sympathizers because it was considered the Latin equivalent of the Hebrew name Zadok, with approximately the same meaning. The popularity of the name is confirmed by literary texts and inscriptions.

Thus, in the times of Nero and his immediate successors, a certain Jew in Galilee, i.e., in the land bordering Tyre, was called Justus. He was a wealthy and influential man and had received Greek education. He played a somewhat ambiguous role at the beginning of the uprising against the Romans, but he survived the conflict thanks to the protection of the ruler of the lands bordering Lake Gennesaret, King Agrippa II.

Many years later, the same Justus published a history of the Jewish War in Greek. It has not survived to our times, but we know that it criticized an earlier work on the same topic and was very critical of the attitude, activities, and truthfulness of its author, Josephus Flavius. Painfully affected by the critical—or maybe just honest?—work, Josephus responded not with a rebuttal but with an autobiography. It justified his conduct and praised his military deeds but did not omit any opportunity to speak ill about Justus.

Those matters are less important to us here. What is important is that in the first century, the name Justus appeared in northern Palestine, borne by someone who was not a Roman. Interestingly, Josephus himself gave that name to his own son.

In the New Testament, the name Justus appears as an epithet of three persons: someone named Barsabbasha in Jerusalem, someone named Titius in Corinth, and finally, of a certain Jesus, who bravely aided the imprisoned apostle Paul. All three were either Jews or "God-fearers"—gentile sympathizers of Judaism.

Although these issues may seem insignificant, we are right to take note. They illustrate that the old Christian novel, from which we draw our material, renders well the climate and practices of its age.


## THE MANY BERENICES

But significantly more interesting is the other name given in *Homilies*—the name of Berenice. It triggers several interesting reflections.

In the years in which the action of this novel takes place, that name was borne by another woman: beautiful and famous, and famous not only within Palestine but also in Rome. She was the great-granddaughter of King Herod the Great, the sister and "almost-wife" of King Agrippa II, and later, the beloved of Titus. And given her fame and her reputation, it is astonishing that the Christian tradition should seize upon her name—the name of a sinful woman (though one exemplarily pious)—to name several of its heroines. And yet, the Christian tradition gave her name to the demon-possessed daughter of Justa in Tyre. It also gave it to the woman whose sudden healing from chronic bleeding is described in the Gospels (even if the gospels do not give her name). Matthew, Mark, and Luke give an account of her, differing only in some unimportant details.

This is how Luke presents it in Chapter VIII:

But as he went, the people thronged him.

And a woman having an issue of blood twelve years, which had spent all her living upon physicians, neither could be healed of any, came behind him and touched the border of his garment, and immediately, her issue of blood stanched.

And Jesus said, Who touched me? When all denied it, Peter and they that were with him said, Master, the multitude throng thee and press thee, and sayest thou, Who touched me?

And Jesus said, Somebody hath touched me: for I perceive that virtue is gone out of me.

And when the woman saw that she was not hid, she came trembling, and falling down before him, she declared unto him before all the people for what cause she had touched him, and how she was healed immediately.

And He said unto her, Daughter, be of good comfort: thy faith hath made thee whole; go in peace. [10]

This story contains several elements significant for our understanding of the mentality of the time. For example, the power to perform miracles was seen as a kind of energy located in certain individuals so that its bearers immediately felt its loss. Similar stories appear in other texts from the same period.

But we are also interested in what isn't in the story. There is no mention of where the action takes place, where the woman came from, or what her name was. And this created a rich field for legend-making.

Far to the north of Lake Gennesaret, near the sources of the Jordan and surrounded by a bucolic countryside, lay a half-Greek city called Caesarea Philippi (to distinguish it from the other Caesarea by the sea). As early as the 4th century AD, and probably even earlier, people pointed out a house in this Caesarea Philippi, a house which had once belonged to the woman from the gospel story. In front of its gate stood two bronze figures. Eusebius, bishop of the other Caesarea, Caesarea Maritima, had seen them with his own eyes at the beginning of the century. He left us the following description in Book VII of his *History of the Church*:

> On a high pedestal stands a bronze statue of a kneeling woman stretching out her hands in supplication. Opposite her stands another figure in bronze. This depicts an upright man. He is wearing a wide cloak, beautifully draped, and is stretching out his hand towards the woman. At his feet, some unusual plant seems to

---

[10] *Luke* 8:43-48

be growing out of the pedestal. It climbs up to the very hem of his bronze cloak. People say that the plant is a medicinal herb, effective against all diseases.

But Christianity did not embrace the cult of images and statues until the beginning of the 4th century! Indeed, in the beginning, many followers of the new religion thought that the veneration of any likenesses of any living creature was a sin because it violated the second commandment:

> Thou shalt not make unto thee any graven image, or any likeness of any thing that is in heaven above, or that is in the earth beneath, or that is in the water under the earth.
>
> Thou shalt not bow down thyself to them, nor serve them: for I the Lord thy God am a jealous God, visiting the iniquity of the fathers upon the children unto the third and fourth generation of them that hate me;
>
> And shewing mercy unto thousands of them that love me, and keep my commandments.[11]

Mindful of these words, Eusebius tries to justify the surprising fact that the local Christians considered the man's figure in Caesarea Philippi to be an image of Jesus:

> It is no wonder that those who were once pagans made these objects after experiencing the miracles of Our Lord. We know that they also preserved portraits of Paul and Peter and even of Christ himself! It seems that early Christians were sometimes not careful enough not to venerate such images, thus keeping their old pagan customs.[12]

This is a very interesting sentence for any historian of religion. Today's scholars tend to characterize this phenomenon in a similar manner, though in slightly different words: over the centuries, Christianity gradually adopted what it at first considered an essential feature of paganism; willy-nilly, it gave way to the powerful urge of an ancient, universal tradition dear to the heart of the common man.

---

[11] *Exodus* 20:4-6

[12] Eusebius, *History of the Church*, VII 19:1-3

In the case of the statues in Caesarea Philippi, we are dealing with something even more significant and almost symbolic in its meaning. Probably all researchers today agree that these were pagan votive figures and that they almost certainly represented the god of doctors, Asclepius, and a woman who attributed her healing to his grace. Over the centuries, such pious and often very expensive tokens of humble gratitude—statues, bas-reliefs, inscriptions—were widely displayed in honor of various deities in all the lands of the ancient world, and thousands of them have survived to this day. The custom itself survived the death of paganism. And often, like in this case, the Christian legend became entwined with older or foreign images, giving them new names and new interpretations—to the glory of the new religion. This was all the easier because the Greek word *soter* appeared so often in Greek dedicatory inscriptions and temple monuments. In pagan contexts, the word meant "savior," "benefactor," and "healer," and in the Christian context—the Savior, that is, Christ.

Pagan influences in Caesarea Philippi were exceptionally strong, both among the city's population and at the court of its ruler, who resided here for several dozen years, from the mid-first century until its very end. The king was, of course, Agrippa II, Berenice's brother. He expanded the city wonderfully, and in honor of Nero, to whom he owed so much, he renamed it Neronias. In the summer of AD 67, Vespasian, the commander-in-chief of the Roman army suppressing the uprising in Judea, stayed here for twenty days. His son Titus was with him, and his affair with Agrippa's sister, Berenice, began here.

A legend has been preserved in the *Acts of Pilate*, sometimes also called the *Gospel of Nicodemus*, a work dating back to the 4th century. It claims that during the trial of Christ before the tribunal of Pontius Pilate, a woman named Berenice (in the Latin version: Veronica) presented herself as a witness. Unable to get any closer, she shouted from the back of the room:

> "I suffered from bleeding, but I touched the hem of His robe, and what had lasted twelve years with me stopped immediately!"

But the Jews replied:

"According to our Law, a woman cannot be admitted as a witness!"

Some versions of this legend gave the woman a princely status—true, not as the princess of Caesarea Philippi, but of Edessa, further to the north, a displacement easily explained because Edessa was one of the main centers of Christianity at the time. And according to an even later story, probably dating to the 6th century, this Berenice owned a miracle-working portrait of Christ. The seriously ill emperor Tiberius found out about it and ordered the picture to be brought to Italy. When he saw it, he recovered, converted, was baptized, and punished Pilate. And finally, already in the Middle Ages, the best-known legend of Veronica arose out of these elements: the woman who placed a kerchief on the bloody face of Christ as he was led to Golgotha. And—lo!—the impression of Jesus's face was preserved on the fabric forever. Only then did the naive, folk etymology of the name "Veronica" arise—a name which, in reality, is just a Latin transformation of the original Greek form, *Berenice*. But the new etymology proposed that the name was a combination of two words, one Latin, *verus* (true), and one Greek, *eikon* (image), which combined meant a true likeness.[13]

Three paintings by Hieronymus Bosch have survived, depicting the same scene in different ways and in various arrangements: Christ carrying the cross. The one currently in the museum in Ghent is considered to be the best of them all. The main element of the composition are human heads, almost all of them caricatured or distorted with ugly grimaces. According to many, this work, carefully thought through in every detail, is one of the last works of the master, perhaps even the last. In the crowd of ugly, vulgar faces deformed by animal excitement and hate, the viewer detects only two beautiful, calm, and sad faces: a dark-haired, bearded man in the middle, carrying a cross, and a young woman standing slightly to the side. She has a blue turban on her head, from which hang golden pendants, probably symbols rich with meanings, but her dress is black,

---

[13] E. Dobschutz, *Christusbilder*, Leipzig 1899, v. VII: *Die Veronika-Legende.*

and a black ribbon ties the turban. The woman closes her eyes, and with pale lips full of silent despair, she turns away from the man surrounded by the executioners and bending under his burden. And thus, we see her fair, elongated face in profile. In front of her, she holds a white scarf with a dark imprint of the face that appears just to the right. What connects these two—or three—faces is the dignified expression of the expectation of imminent death.

A person inclined to fantasize about syzygies might look for one in the evolution of the legend about different women with the same name. The two alleged Berenices, both cured miraculously, merge in the later tradition into one, and she, in turn, transferred to the city of historical Berenice, transforms into a Jewish princess, alive and famous in the years of early Christianity. And, in spite of everything that her contemporaries said about the historical Berenice, this Berenice of the legend is the kernel of her future rise to the elevated status of sainthood.

And thus posterity showed Queen Berenice a special grace—while it denied it to Nero; the emperor on whose grave flowers were placed for many years after his death; the ruler loved and awaited by many and resurrected three times; became the Beast of the Apocalypse in the eyes of later generations. Say what you may: this is a manifestation of the law of *syzygy* if there ever was one. And an example of the ultimate Divine Justice.

## WHEN DO GODS PUNISH EVIL?

One day, some twenty years after Nero's death, four men were taking a stroll in the portico of the temple of Apollo in Delphi, strolling and talking animatedly. One of them was Plutarch, the second was his brother, the third was his son-in-law, and the fourth was a close family friend. They did not hide their outrage. They had been touched to the quick by the arrogance of an Epicurean to whom they had just spoken. He had stated brutally that there clearly could not exist such thing as divine justice since various criminals prospered until the end of their days. Having said this, he left them ostentatiously without waiting for their reply. He thus made it clear that he rejected all contrary arguments out of hand.

Not surprisingly, the four men felt it was their sacred duty to attack the problem immediately. It confounded—as it was to continue to confound for the millennia to come—not only philosophers, theologians, and moralists but also ordinary men. For even simple people constantly asked themselves—themselves and others—the embarrassing question: if there really do exist all-knowing and just gods, then how comes it that so many criminals escape punishment? Indeed, everyday experience clearly showed to them—just as it shows to us—that ruthless individuals, contemptuous of divine and human law, routinely reap abundant harvests of their wickedness in the form of wealth, power, and fame.

The four men took the challenge very seriously. And because their opponent had left, they tried to recreate his argument and then find its weak points. At the same time, they honestly admitted and addressed every difficulty raised by their answers. They wished to proceed in this sensitive matter as impartially as possible, even though all four were pious men and deeply believed in the power, goodness, and fairness of the immortal gods. Plutarch reported the course of their discussion in detail in a philosophical treatise most often called in English *On the Delays of the Divine Vengeance*,[14] even if a better rendition of the title would be *On Those Whom the Gods Punished Late*.

But what conclusion did the men reach? Plutarch does not say He does not even claim that the four were able to agree on a particular solution to their problem. Nevertheless, a careful reader will easily guess that such a conclusion was suggested by a certain story, which Plutarch quotes at the very end of the discussion, noting that he, in

---

[14] Plutarch, *De Sera Numinis Vindicta*

turn, heard it from one of his friends.

The story concerns the journey of a seemingly dead man into the afterlife and the things he saw there. This idea seems naive to us today, for it has been recycled time and again in literary and para-religious works of many eras. Nevertheless, Plutarch's story deserves a closer look for several reasons. First of all, certain parts of it are a literary masterpiece of fantasy writing—and remind us just how much brilliant literature the Greeks and Romans have left us, literature which remains barely known today. We have been admiring several aspects of the ancient world for centuries and completely overlooking whole regions of it—regions of untamed fantasy, morbid delusion, fears, nightmares, and dreams. Why? Probably because such works and images are fundamentally contrary to what we usually associate with classical civilization: the snow-white marble of order, moderation, and rationality.

Just as importantly, Plutarch's story illustrates a certain stage of the development of ideas, ideas that have since become deeply embedded in the system of European religious thought. By reading the essay carefully, we can, on the one hand, discover motifs of earlier thought—Platonic, Orphic, and Pythagorean—and, on the other, sense the imminent arrival of future ideas, presented here as it were in their embryonic form, ideas which will in time produce works of art of rare beauty. Which ones, anyone who listens to the words of Plutarch—or rather, Thespesius—will easily guess.


## THESPESIUS IN THE AFTERLIFE

A certain Thespesius from the city of Soloi in Cilicia[15] lived so extravagantly that he frittered all his wealth away within a short time. By the time he came to his senses, it was too late. From then on, he did not hesitate to take any steps necessary to get back on his feet: he was

---

[15] Now Soli in Turkey

ready to do anything for profit. He never acquired much wealth but certainly acquired a nasty reputation. The answer he received from the oracle of the hero Amphilochus[16] did the most damage to his name. Thespesius, through someone else's offices, had inquired of the oracle whether he would ever fare better in life. Amphilochus replied: "You will do better only after your death!" Everyone understood these words to mean that only death could help Thespesius because nothing in this life would ever be able to improve him. And it so happened that after some time, he died as a result of an accident: he tripped, fell, broke his neck, and gave up the ghost, although he did not receive any visible external trauma.

After three days, when everything had been prepared for the funeral, the apparently dead man suddenly woke up of his own volition and rose from the bier. Then, having regained strength, he completely changed his life and behavior. From then on, his countrymen were unable to point to anyone who conducted himself more diligently, served gods more devoutly, treated his enemies more severely, or loved his friends more faithfully. Naturally, many people wanted to know the reason for his extraordinary transformation, for it was widely believed that it could not have occurred without some profound cause. At last, giving in to numerous requests, he revealed the whole truth to his loved ones:

> The moment my soul was separated from my body, I found myself in the situation of a helmsman thrown out of his boat and into the depths of the sea. However, I soon rose slightly upwards. I now had the impression that I was breathing with my whole being, and I looked around without any effort as if my entire soul had opened like an eye. However, I did not see any of the objects that had surrounded me before. I was in a completely different world. I saw huge stars, separated from each other by immeasurable spaces and shining with such amazingly intense light and color that I could float

---

[16] There were several of these, but the most famous was located in Mallus, Cilicia. Amphilochus had been the son of Amphiaraus and Eriphyle and the younger brother of Alcmaeon. He participated in the Second Expedition of Seven Against Thebes.

on their rays, like a ship moving with wind on the calmest sea.

Then, I saw the souls of the dead ascending from below. They resembled bubbles of fire rising through the air. Then their shells cracked open, and tiny human-like shapes emerged from them. But not all souls moved in the same way. Some popped out with astonishing speed and headed straight for the sky. Others spun about in circles like spin tops, now tipping a little, now straightening again, making uncertain and confused movements.

I did not recognize most of them. However, I noticed two or three that seemed familiar, so I approached them and greeted them politely. They didn't hear or understand my words. They gave the impression of being completely unconscious, senseless, and terribly frightened. They shrunk away from touch or even gaze. At first, they wandered around alone, but after a while, they met others in the same condition, became tightly intertwined with them, and only then, all together, they started to cast about in various directions, making incomprehensible sounds: I heard cries, and wails, and groans.

But the former souls—I saw them very clearly—soared high above on the pure light of heavens. There was a glow coming from them. They shunned those thrashing in confusion but willingly approached each other, full of gentle kindness. I got the impression that they expressed sadness by shrinking and joy by spreading themselves open like a flower opening its petals.

And then a soul of one of my relatives approached me, a relative whom I did not know well, for he had died when I was still a boy, and said:

"Do not be afraid. You have not yet crossed the threshold of true death. Your mind alone has been brought here, summoned by divine decree, but the other faculties of your soul remain firmly anchored to your body on earth. You can easily see that this is the case because the souls of the truly dead do not cast a shadow!"

When I heard this, I made a great effort to concentrate, and looking around, I noticed that it was indeed as the soul had said. I alone was accompanied constantly and everywhere by a delicate, shadowy outline, while other souls shone brightly, and their interiors were transparent. And as I continued to observe them, I began to notice very significant differences among them. Some shone with a light that was gentle, constant, and even, like that of the full moon, while others seemed to have scars, marks, and fissures running through them. Some souls, spotted and downright eerie, were marked with the black zigzag, the hideous pattern of vipers. And still others had deep cracks that reached all the way to their centers.

My relative explained:

"The supreme avenger of all evil is Adrrasteia, daughter of Zeus and Fate. No criminal—whether great and mighty or minor and inconspicuous—can escape her by force or deceit. Three goddesses reporting to Adrasteia make sure of this. The first of them, Poine, or *Pain*, takes hold of some criminals while they are still alive, still locked in their bodies, and punishes them through the instrumentality of their temporal bodies. However, such punishment is mild by nature and leaves much that needs to be corrected later, for those in whom evil is more deeply rooted require more drastic treatment. After death, their spirit is handed over to Dike, *Justice*. She tortures them but rejects the incurable. These last are pursued by the third--the fiercest—goddesses, Erynia or *Fury*. They flee her in blind panic. But she catches every last one of them and throws them into the abyss. And it is a terrifying sight to see this abyss even from a distance. Why, it is frightening to even think about it!"

Then he spoke as follows:

"Punishment dealt out to criminals during their lifetime is like a certain barbarian custom. The Persians, you see, tear the clothes, diadems, and ornaments off the condemned and then whip these inanimate objects while their owners stand by watching this "punishment." But all along, they cry before their king, moan, and beg for mercy. And this is how it would be with us, too, if we were punished in our earthly life alone, for such sufferings inflicted on our property or on our bodies do not harm the soul and do not touch the roots of evil. Basically, they only affect our imagination, our superficial sensations, our easily deceived senses.

"Now, whoever comes here from the world of the living not yet fully purified is seized immediately by the goddess Dike. His soul—now stripped of its material shell and completely exposed—cannot escape punishment, nor hide anywhere, nor disguise its sins in any way, for it can be seen everywhere and by all in all its ugliness. Dike first shows such a soul to his parents, if they were honest people, and then to his offspring. So, both generations can see exactly how disgusting the soul is, how unworthy of their blood and lineage. But if the parents and offspring of the soul were also evil, the soul must now see how they are punished, and at the same time, they see the soul's own torment. And you should know that a sinful soul is subjected to very long and elaborate torture. Every vice, every trace of crime, is removed from it through it. And these tortures are as much more intense than the mere physical torments suffered in our earthly life, as waking is more intense than sleep.

"The scars, cracks, and poisons left on the soul by various passions are less permanent in some people, while in others, they are more deeply rooted. Just look at the colors of these souls! So varied, so mixed up! What is dark and dirty in them testifies that the man acted ignobly during his life, sinning with greed and pettiness. The blood-red is a sign of cruelty and violence. The blue-gray—of physical pleasures. Malevolence and envy produce dark violet stains.

"For you see, below, on earth, each sin stains us differently, and the soul's own desires and passions thereby transform it. The soul, in turn, influences the appearance of the body. But here, the end of suffering comes only when, after complete purification, the soul begins to shine with a steady and uniform glow. However, recurrences of passion do occur during treatment. Sometimes, old desires come back, and are always accompanied by violent convulsions and tossing. These side effects usually pass quickly, though in some rare cases, they can last a long time. At last, after undergoing multiple tortures, some souls achieve perfection. But others are dragged back into the bodies of living beings by the weight of their stupidity, laziness, and lust. It's high time you saw it with your own eyes!"

Having said which he led me into a mysterious space without borders.

# THE GROTTO OF BACHUS AND
# THE CRATEROS OF DREAMS

The rays of starlight floated us gently forward, and we soared straight and purposefully like eagles do on extended wings. At a certain moment, however, we found ourselves near a vast and deep pit, and then suddenly, the force that had previously held us up so reliably disappeared. I noticed that other souls also experienced something similar. They gathered in flocks, like birds. They circled here and there but always along the edges of the pit, and none had the courage to fly straight across, from one edge to the other.

And yet the interior of this chasm was not terrifying at all! On the contrary, as I soon realized, the pit was indeed incapacitating, but this entirely to its divine charm. It resembled Bacchus' grottos, decorated with greenery and flowers of all kinds. A light and gentle breeze carried a delightful scent from its depths. Like wine, it intoxicated anyone who breathed it in even once. Therefore, the souls, drunk with pleasure, rejoiced openly. There was a truly Bacchic mood everywhere. My guide said:

"This is the place from which the god Dionysus emerged into the world. This is where he started his way to the sunny summit of the gods on Mount Olympus. Later, he elevated his mother, Semele, there. This place is called *Lethe*, or *Oblivion*."

But he did not let us linger in this strange place of pleasure, even though I wanted very much to do so. He dragged me away by force and lectured me:

"Pleasure causes the mental principle of the soul to atrophy and waste away and solidifies and strengthens everything that is irrational and material in the human soul. It brings to mind the memory of the joys of the body and awakens the desire to return to life on earth."

Thus we continued along our radiant path and covered as much of it again. It was then that I saw what, from a distance, looked like a huge vessel, a *crateros* for mixing wine. Various colors poured into it in streams. One was whiter than snow or the foam of the sea, another as red as the reddest band of the rainbow. Seen from a distance, each glowed in its own color. But as we came closer, the vessel turned out to be a deep black hole, and the colors of the streams became strangely dark, and their glow dimmed, all except white. And I saw three demons sitting in such a way that they formed a kind of triangle. They constantly stirred the streams of light so that they flowed in certain proportions. The guide explained:

"This is where Orpheus came looking for his wife's shadow. But he misremembered everything he had seen here and gave false reports of the place to men back on earth. Among other things, he said that Apollo shares the oracle of Delphi with the Goddess of Night. But the Lord of Light has no communion with darkness—it is impossible! What you see here is the oracle of the Night and of the Moon. Such an oracle does not exist anywhere on earth, it has no fixed abode there. Yet, it does manifest itself among men on earth. How, you ask? Why, in the form of nightmares and hallucinations! So here you see how such visions are mixed and dispersed in all directions. They contain some element of truth, yes, but that truth is mixed up with a variety of illusory colors."

He went on:

"I do not know whether you can see the Delphic oracle of Apollo from here because your soul is still earth-bound, and its bonds may not allow you to rise sufficiently high."

Still, he tried to raise me up and show me the light beaming from a divine tripod. He said that the stream passed through the womb of the goddess Themis and flowed against the cliffs of Mount Parnassus in Delphi. But I could not see any of this because the glare of the light blinded me completely. However, as I passed by, I heard a female voice. It announced various matters in rhythmic verse. It also prophesied (it seemed to me) the time of my death.

Someone said:

"This is the voice of Sibyl. She sings while orbiting the face of the Moon."

I wanted to hear her voice still more, but the powerful momentum of her movement threw me back, like the impact of a huge sea wave. Only a few words reached my ears and said something about Mount Vesuvius and a conflagration that would destroy the city of Puteoli. And also, a couplet about the emperor reigning at the time: "He is a good soul, but he will fall ill suddenly and lose the world!"

# INTERPRETATIONS

The introductory part of Thespesius' narrative opens before us like a panoramic painting by a master fantasist: a study of bright colors and strange shapes. It tells the story of suddenly waking up in another world, of the splendor of the stars that suddenly become close, of the appearance and paths of souls clothed in various forms and shining with various colors.

In the second part, we first join in a flight through the expanse of radiant starlight and then fly over a pit that turns out to be a graceful Grotto of Bacchus. This part of the piece is probably an even more striking idea than the first. It joins together a typical description of the sort of place the Mediterraneans have always found attractive—a shady and cool rock garden, where, among rich and lush greenery, crystal clear springs burst forth—and a vision of souls circling in flocks like birds around its edges for the very breeze from the grotto intoxicated them like wine.

However, artistically speaking, the third part is the most brilliant. A vast *crateros* of dreams appears before us. We hear Sibyl's voice, loud and clear but only in snippets. The description speaks of constant movement, constant shimmering of lights and colors, continuous shapeshifting of images that overlap and transform into ever-different, unexpected shapes. And it all seems to happen before our eyes.

No element remains constant. The narrative talks about dreams but is itself like a dream: elusive, ambiguous, full of strange, seemingly random symbolism. Naturally, we do not grasp all the allusions of the story today. For example, we can only guess that it contain a hidden polemic against the teachings of the Orphic sect. We're better able to intuit some allusions to old myths—for example, the myth that before Themis and Apollo took over the oracle at Delphi, it was ruled by the Goddess of Night. And we can only assume that the text carries other hidden meanings, lost to us forever.

We also find here an idea of rare originality: Thespesius describes a great black hole into which multi-colored streams of light flow, and his guide explains to him (and us) that the place is an oracle that really does not exist anywhere, in any of the worlds, for the *crateros* in which the streams mix is itself only an illusion and sends forth only illusions. If we had to imagine the source of dreams, this is perhaps what it would look like, but it exists only in our hearts and minds.

Nevertheless, says the same allegory, dreams contain an element of truth, for white means truth, while all the other colors denote illusion. And when we gaze from a distance (like Thespesius does at first)—that is, before we analyze the language of our dreams— they seem to us like a colorful but senseless tangle of random elements. Only when we come closer—that is, after we consider the content of our night visions carefully—do we notice how the illusory lights and colors fade away, and all that remains is what is really important: the white of truth. And this truth can be understood and interpreted by interpreters of dreams, whom the ancients called *oneirocritics*.

But what is this black hole that, when viewed from a distance, resembles a large vessel for mixing wine, called by the Greeks *crateros*? Though this will sound surprising—it is the shadow of the Moon!

The allegory should be understood this way:

Thespesius's entire journey takes place in the sublunary space, on the border between it and the Empyrean Sky—the ethereal sphere of the stars. It is there, and not in the darkness of the underground, that the souls of the dead reside—although different souls reside in its different areas. That is why we heard at the beginning that the stars seemed larger and yet, at the same time, separated by huge distances. Souls rose from below, i.e., from the earth, and rushing upwards through the air, they had the shape of fiery bubbles.

The Bacchic Grotto then is a shadow that the earth casts onto the sky. This shadow is a symbol of earthly delights that cause the intoxicated souls to lose their natural lightness and fall back towards a new birth on earth. This is the Pythagorean doctrine that the human soul can migrate from one body to another.

And now we come to the fourth vision in Thespesius's story. It is permeated by a sense of horror and is quite like what Dante will see many centuries later when he visits Hell and Purgatory. And like the vision from the Middle Ages, these descriptions of the tortures of the damned are full of primitive sadism.


## THE LAST CIRCLE


We then turned to those who suffered punishment. At first, it was just an unpleasant sight, but as we went in deeper and deeper it became monstrous. Surprisingly, I met many dear friends, acquaintances, and relatives there. They endured constant torment and pain, complaining, moaning, and crying. And finally, oh horror of horrors, I saw—my father! His soul crawled out from some cavernous crevice and stretched out its hands desperately toward me. He was covered with wounds and ulcers. Those who guarded him did not allow him to remain silent. He had to confess the reason for his suffering. He had committed a heinous crime against guests staying at his house. When he found out that they had gold with them, he poisoned them. He managed to hide his crime while he lived on earth, but here, in the afterlife, his crime had been known from the beginning. He also told me what tortures he had already suffered, and now they were about to lead him to further torment. Terrified and shocked, I dared not beg for pity for my father. I turned around and tried to run away.

Alas, turning around, I did not see my gentle and familiar guide! Instead, I saw before me a terrible vibrating swirl of demons, horrible to behold, who now began to drive me forward, forcing me to continue on the trajectory laid out for me.

At length, I turned in that direction, and moving on, I saw that those whose crimes had been brought to light and punished on earth while they were still alive did not have to endure long and severe torments here, because only the irrational, emotional part of their souls had to be purified. Whereas those criminals who had gone through their entire earthly existence enjoying the appearance and reputation of respectability had to bare the interiors of their souls now, suffering tremendous pain. The demons flayed them, showing that beneath the smoothness of their skin, they were rotten to the core, for their evil lay deep within the rational layer of the soul. I also saw the irretrievably damned, closely entwined in twos or threes, biting each other like vipers, suffering now the pain with which they had once so happily afflicted others.

There were also three pools there: one of boiling gold, one of liquid icy lead, and the third full of molten iron. Demons like blacksmiths stood over them, taking hold of individual souls and immersing them in these pools. These were the souls of those who had been driven to all manner of wickedness by insatiable greed. And I saw that as soon as such a sinner's soul, dipped in the pool of gold, began to glow with its light, it was suddenly immersed in the pool of ice-cold lead, and when it cooled there and solidified into a frosty blue, it was taken just as suddenly into the sharp heat of the molten iron, where it immediately blackened and shrunk so horribly that it changed its form And then it was suddenly thrown again into the lake of boiling gold.

This process was repeated without end, without rest, and without mercy.

But the most severely tormented were those souls who already believed themselves free and safe because they had already suffered. They floated up with the feeling of blessed relief but were captured suddenly and subjected to torture again! These were the souls of the criminals whose guilt and punishment had been passed on to their offspring. When the soul of such an heir, already tormented for the sins of its ancestor, met the cause of its misfortunes, it attacked him with fury and relentlessly chased him with monstrous screams. He, of course, would try to flee or hide from the attacker, but immediately, the guardian demons appeared and took him back to the place of torture, and he, knowing full well what awaited him, howled horribly with fear. There were souls about whom dozens of condemned descendants hovered like swarms of bees or flocks of bats, squealing and hissing with immense hatred.

Finally, I saw the place where certain souls were prepared for rebirth. And this was what the demons did, resembling diligent craftsmen in their work, for they had a difficult job: they had to reshape the souls so that the souls may fit the bodies of various animals. They used various terrifying tools in their work because, due to the different shapes of the souls and their destined bodies, it was necessary to flatten some parts of the souls, grind smooth others, or cut others off altogether. In short, the soul was being reshaped to fit the conditions of its destination.

And there I saw Nero's terribly tortured soul. It was pierced through and through with red-hot nails taken straight from the fire. It had been sentenced to a great transformation, for—a voice explained to me—it would soon be reborn in the shape of a viper, an animal that comes into the world by eating through the womb of its mother. In this way, the famous matricide would soon be murdered by his own offspring. But at that moment, there suddenly appeared a blinding light, and a loud voice was heard saying :

"No! Make him into a different, gentler creature! The one whose voice can be heard in muddy ponds. Nero had already suffered on earth for his crimes; and he deserves some mercy from the immortal gods because he gave freedom to the best and most pious nation of all over which he ruled!"

This is what I saw up to that point. I then tried to turn around and flee, but when I did turn, I went numb with horror. Unexpectedly, a tall and handsome woman arose before me, and taking me by the hand, she said in a terrible voice:

"Come closer so that you may see and remember everything!"

Simultaneously, she brought close to my face a long, glowing reed, the sort that painters use when they want to capture their images. But she was interrupted by a second woman, and at that moment, I was lifted by a violent blast of wind. I felt a strong tug as if someone had suddenly loosened a tight rope. I tumbled down into my body and opened my eyes.

I was lying on my bier, prepared for the grave.

## CONCERNING THE LAST CIRCLE

Only Hieronymus Bosch could have illustrated the last part of Thespesius's story because he, alone among all the masters of painting, had seen the same scenes of torture conceived in a similarly sadistic imagination. And what he had seen, he immortalized in grim and grotesque visions of *The Seven Mortal Sins*, *The Garden of Earthly Delights*, and above all, in *Hell* and *The Last Judgment*. He and Plutarch had equally vivid imaginations—and strangely similar.

Oh, how fruitful it would have been to show Bosch this story—a story which Thespesius narrates in barely several words but which evokes so many powerful images, such as a workshop of demonic craftsmen, where human souls are processed using various tools so that they might enter animal bodies. Bosch and Plutarch evidently shared a similar sense of humor, too. Here, Thespesius (though, more likely, Plutarch) ends the macabre review of tortures with a humorous accent: a tyrant and a matricide, who was about to become a viper, is unexpectedly pardoned (in a sense): he will be born again, yes, but not as an evil viper, but as a frog croaking harmlessly in puddles. Because, of course, this is how we should understand the words about "the gentle creature whose voice can be heard in muddy ponds."

And hidden within this commutation of punishment— something understandable to us from our own legal practice—there

Nero

lies couched a transparent but malicious allusion to the artistic ambitions and public performances of the actor-emperor. And then, immediately in the next sentence, the humorous idea finds a serious justification: it is appropriate to take pity on the criminal because he gave freedom to the Hellenes, a people chosen and beloved by the gods.

Thus, as you can see, a fond memory of Nero persisted in Greece for many years after his death: a memory so fond and so widespread that even those who knew perfectly well the crimes he had committed and sincerely condemned them were inclined to moderate their judgment.

There is another striking thing in Thespesius's account: while passing through various regions, he met thousands of souls, including many of his friends. However, he mentions only one figure by name—the Emperor Nero. This fact is quite surprising when we compare it to other stories of the afterlife. How many shades of famous men and women passed before Odysseus when he fed the dead with dark blood at the entrance to Hades! How many people Aeneas saw when he descended into the underworld! How many more was Dante to see! This practice of the authors is fully understandable: after all, who would not want to know how our recent eminences are doing in hell and what tortures the tyrants of today, praised by all in public, were destined to suffer in the afterlife?

In this, by bringing out only one public figure into the light—the Emperor Nero—Thespesius shows surprising restraint. How do we explain it? There could have been all kinds of reasons, but the most obvious seems to be this: Nero's name gained particular prominence at the time of the writing of the dialogue. And the explanation of that prominence is probably simple: the cause was probably yet another of the re-appearances of Nero.

Plutarch wrote his dialogue after the appearance of the second false Nero. That Nero, we remember, surfaced ten years after the Nero of Kythnos. Using that date—February of AD 69—and adding ten years to it, we can pinpoint in time the strange adventure of Thespesius.

Just as we can pinpoint in time the strange journey of a certain medieval poet who, having lost the straight and narrow, found himself in a dark wood over a thousand years later [17]

## THE EMPEROR AND THE INTELLECTUALS

If we accept the internal evidence of Plutarch's dialogue, Thespesius visited the other world after Nero's death, i.e., after June 68 AD, but before the eruption of Vesuvius—for Nero was already dead but the Sibyl was only announcing the coming of the cataclysm. That took place, as we know, on 24-26 of August AD 79. In fact, we can date the writing of this dialogue even more precisely: all we need to do is figure out who the emperor is—"the reigning one"—about whom Sybil says: "He is a good soul, but he will fall ill suddenly and lose the world!"

Now, between June 68 and August 79, Rome had five emperors: Galba, Otho, Vitellius, Vespasian, and Titus. Of these five, only the last two died a natural death—meaning not by a sword but as the result of natural causes. But neither Plutarch, nor any Greek, nor any contemporary intellectual would have called Vespasian "a good soul"—contrary to the opinions which subsequently gained currency among later historians—and this for two important reasons.

First of all, they blamed him for depriving Greece of what Nero had given her: freedom. This generous act of Nero, announced by him during the Isthmian games of AD 66, was to lead the heavenly voice to implant the soul of the matricide into the body of a frog rather than a viper. (Although we can be fairly certain that the tyrant himself, had the choice depended on him, would have preferred to become a venomous snake rather than a skittish and unarmed resident of muddy waters).

Vespasian annulled Nero's fancy four years later, in AD 70, to

---

[17] *Inferno, Canto I,* Dante Alighieri (1265–1321): "Midway upon the journey of my life/I found myself within a forest dark,/For the straightforward pathway had been lost."

45

the immense and unconcealed chagrin of the inhabitants of Hellas. He justified his decision by the fact that in her cities, there had arisen, within those four short years, all sorts of petty and scandalous quarrels between various factions wherever Roman supervision was lacking. It was most likely one reason for the decision. However, the most important reasons for withdrawing the favor were, beyond any doubt, financial and the fear that the freedoms granted to Greece would encourage other provinces to make similar demands.

How much outrage this caused is best illustrated by the reaction of Apollonius of Tyana. The sage initially supported Vespasian and (if we believe our sources) held many long conversations with him at the beginning of his rule (AD 69-70). However, once he learned that Vespasian deprived Greece of her freedom, he never wanted to meet the emperor again, and in his letters to him, he wrote openly:

"You enslaved Greece. You think you possess more than Xerxes, but in fact, you have less than Nero. For Nero knew how to renounce something he already had in his hand!"

And also:

"Since you hate Greeks, whom you turned into slaves, though they had enjoyed freedom, why do you need me, also a Greek?"

And finally:

"Yes, Nero liberated Greeks for fun. But you did not impose your yoke in jest!"[18]

There was another reason why Vespasian could not enjoy the sympathy of his contemporary writers and thinkers. In the first months of his reign, he ordered all philosophers to leave the capital and exiled two of them—the most stubborn and loudest—to uninhabited islands. We should note that the edict, though much criticized at the time, was not a malicious whim. In fact, it was not about *all* philosophers but about a specific type of philosopher, namely the self-proclaimed preachers of radical stoicism which was much in vogue at the time.

---

[18] Philostratus, *Life of Apollonius of Tyana,* V 41

To the delight of the crowds, they criticized the imperial system, and especially the emperor's powers. In its place, they praised the full and unrestricted freedom of the individual as the highest social good. Prudently, they did not spell out in detail what this freedom might consist of in practice. Mucianus, Vespasian's friend and probably the second most powerful man in the Empire, a blue-blooded aristocrat of great learning—and reading—characterized the type:

> They are full of noisy boasting. All it takes to become one is to grow a beard, arch the eyebrows, throw a cloak over the shoulders, and eschew wearing sandals. (It is very important to be barefoot in this business). In an instant, the fellow becomes a philosopher and begins to shout loudly: Behold, I am wise, brave, just! Each of these crackpots shows off a snorting pride, even though, they say, he can neither read nor swim. The whole trick lies in looking down on everyone else.

> They call a man of noble birth a wimp, a plebeian "mean-spirited," a handsome man "handsome," and someone not very handsome "honest;" a rich man is obviously an insatiable glutton, and the poor man has to have the temperament of a slave!

In fact, Vespasian himself did not care about their criticism, and challenged by one of them, he said:

"It seems to me you're looking for a martyr's death. Yet, you should know that I have never killed a dog just because it barked at me."[19]

The emperor was prudent and knew that any opposition movement, even the most empty and ridiculous, can quickly gain strength once it acquires its own martyrs—the steadfast witnesses of its truth. At such times, a drop of blood can become a seed from which hosts of fanatical followers grow, and the bloody glow of a legend can glorify and illuminate a whole movement. Therefore, it was enough—Vespasian reasoned—to send away the most rebellious stoics to distant

---

[19] Cassius Dio, *Roman History*, LXVI 13.

places, where their speeches against tyranny would be heard only by the waves lapping on the shore and the shrieking seaside birds.

But back to our story: since it is obvious that Plutarch would never have called Vespasian a "good ruler," the only emperor left is Titus—the only one of the five emperors who would have deserved Plutarch's appellation of "good." Sibyl's next words, overheard by Thespesius, also point to him since they state clearly and with some emphasis that he will lose everything as a result of sickness. This statement, put into the mouth of the prophetess, belies the view that Titus died by poison, which many believed at the time. It is easy to guess the reason that had aroused such suspicions: the emperor died in the prime of life—he was barely above forty. His sickness lasted only a few days, and its end was dramatic.

## HOW TITUS DIED

At the beginning of September AD 81, Titus—apparently completely healthy but strangely depressed—was watching games in one of the Roman circuses. His retinue noticed at a certain point that tears welled up in his eyes unexpectedly, for no particular reason.

The emperor offered a sacrifice to the gods, but the sacrificial animal ran away from the altar, which was always considered a bad omen: the gods were unwilling to accept an offering from the suppliant, for his fate had already been sealed. There was also a report of a thunderclap out of the blue—a thunder not preceded by lightning. Even a dream about such a phenomenon—all fortune tellers agreed—would have presaged misfortune, let alone such thunder in reality!

Soon afterward, the emperor left the capital, full of anxiety and expecting the worst. He went to the mountains, to the Sabine country, where his family had had its roots and where they still had private estates. But at the first stopover, while in his bath, he suffered a sudden attack of fever—or at least, that's what Plutarch says in one of his works.

He made the rest of his trip in a litter. At a certain moment, he opened its curtains, gazed into the heavens, and, as if complaining to someone, he uttered words overheard by those nearby and commented on in Rome for a long time afterward:

"My life is slipping through my hands, though I am without fault. Or at most with one."

But there, he stopped and revealed to no one what he had on his mind.

He died on September 13 in the same villa where his father, Vespasian, died two years earlier. The cause of death was apparently the treatment administered on the orders of his brother, Domitian: he had been covered with snow to lower the fever that burned his insides.

This is how we can reconstruct the course of the disease based on the accounts of Plutarch, Suetonius, and Cassius Dio. But, as we have said, there also circulated a completely different story about the cause of the young emperor's death. Among those ancient authors who firmly claimed—contrary to the Sibyl of Thespesius—that Titus was poisoned—was the biographer of Apollonius of Tyana, Philostratus. He writes that Apollonius predicted such a death to the future ruler and even indicated the type of poison.

It happened in a private conversation in the city of Tarsus and, therefore, could only have been reported by Apollonius. The biographer of the sage always strove to glorify his hero and imagined the scene like this:

As soon as they were alone, Titus asked whether he could ask about something very important. Apollonius replied immediately:

"Go ahead and ask. And the bolder, the more important the business."

To which Titus replied:

"My question concerns my life. I'd like to know against whom I should be on guard. I ask this even though I understand that it makes me look like a coward!"

But Apollonius shook his head and replied gravely:

"Not at all. By asking this, you merely show that you are prudent, as befits someone who plays in the dangerous game of high politics."

Saying this, the old man raised his eyes to the sun and swore by its divinity that he had intended to address this matter even if Titus had never asked. He then said:

"The gods have ordered me to warn you that during your father's lifetime, you should especially fear those who are most hostile to you both."

Titus smiled and replied:

"This is obvious. But after his death?"

"After his death, be on guard against your relatives!"

"But what death should I fear?"

"Remember Odysseus! You know that his death came from the sea."[20]

If we take this reference literally, Titus was supposed to be on guard against a member of his family who might try to kill him with the bone—or perhaps the sting—of the common stingray, as one of the myths said Odysseus died.

However, the circumstances of Titus' death were different, for he certainly did not suffer the slightest wound, not even a scratch. So, how should we understand the words of Apollonius? Philostratus goes on to claim that the emperor was poisoned with the venom of a creature called the sea hare.[21] It is a snail with four antennae on its head; two of them, always upright, look like the ears of a hare, hence the name of the beast. Its only defense is a secretion—bluish, reddish, or purple—which it releases in danger to surround itself with an impenetrable cloud. The secretion is poisonous, although not as

------

[20] Philostratus, *Life of Apollonius of Tyana*, XXXII
[21] *Anapsidea Aplysia*

potent as the ancients believed. They thought that even its smell caused vomiting, flatulence, and miscarriages in women. Just imagine how dangerous it was, they thought, to eat it!

The only creature that could eat the sea hare with impunity, the ancients said, was a fish called "mullus" in Latin,[22] a tasty and much sought-after treat, but even it usually sickened after such a meal. But man, after eating the sea hare, soon began to smell fishy, which was the first symptom because the venom brought death not immediately but gradually, after many days, making it extremely difficult to identify the poison. Nero had used this venom, men whispered, to remove people whom he did not want to kill openly.

Now, it seems that the biographer of Apollonius invented the presumed warning after hearing some rumors concerning the causes of the emperor's death. In this, he differed from Plutarch, who used the authority of Sibyl to dispel such gossip: the emperor had died a sudden but natural death.

Titus assumed the throne on 24 June AD 79. The eruption of Vesuvius buried Pompeii at the end of August of that year. It follows that Thespesius saw the afterlife in July or August 79, eleven years after the death of Nero, who had had to suffer that many years of heavenly torture only to be reborn in the form of a frog and undergo further and perhaps even more severe punishments.

## APOLLONIUS AND THE LION

Had Nero not committed such heinous crimes, he would perhaps still have faced rebirth on earth, but perhaps in a much nobler form than a frog. Such a conclusion seems to follow from the story of Apollonius's extraordinary adventure in Egypt. These are the words of the sage:

> There was a beggar who wandered about the country, leading a lion on a string like a miserable dog. And the animal, though very

---

[22] Red mullet

frightening in appearance, humbly fawned not only on him but on everyone who dared to approach.

And it followed his owner across the towns and villages of Egypt, begging for scraps and even entering the most venerable temples, for their priests consider lions ritually pure. And indeed, the beast behaved nobly, never licked the blood of sacrificial animals, never reached for their meat when they were skinned and quartered after the ceremony. Instead, it ate bread, honey cakes, and dried fruit; and meat only if it had been cooked. Strangest of all, it didn't refuse wine when it was poured into its bowl. But it never got drunk! You could say it knew its measure.

Well, it so happened that one day, I was sitting in one of the temples, all alone, immersed in meditation, as is my custom. Suddenly, I heard noise and laughter, and after a while, I saw the man come in with his animal, surrounded as usual by a crowd of the curious. And behold, as soon as the lion saw me, it tore itself free, trotted over, and put its heavy head in my lap. It whimpered pitifully and groveled. You'd swear it was asking for something like never before. People gathered around and started laughing, saying:

"How pushy! Begging for alms! He's been well trained!"

But I looked carefully into the animal's eyes, thought for a while, and said:

"Not so. You are mistaken. The lion does beg, but not for alms. It wants me to tell you that the rational soul of a man is locked in its body. And not just any man! Here lies before you in the form of a four-legged beast, the great Pharaoh Amasis, ruler of Egypt, who once reigned from the capital city of Sais."[23]

And as soon as it heard these words, the lion roared piteously and lay on the ground. Human tears flowed from its eyes. I stroked its shaggy head gently and said to the crowd:

"We must send him to the temple in Leontopolis. For since, by the will of the gods, the king of men took on the form of the king of

---

[23] The future Pharaoh Amasis appears as a character in Witold Makowiecki's novel *Out of the Lion's Maw*, Mondrala Press, 2022

beasts, it would be a shameful thing of us to allow him to collect alms for a beggar, now that we know who he is!"

As soon as the news of the extraordinary discovery spread, Egyptian priests gathered together to honor the ancient pharaoh who had returned to them so unexpectedly. They offered him due sacrifices, decorated him with colorful ribbons and wreaths of flowers, and then led him in a procession across the country. They sang solemnly to the music of flutes hymns to the glory of gods, and the lion strode ceremonially as befits a true ruler used to receiving tribute.[24]

# THE METAMORPHOSIS OF AMASIS

This story, like all the stories collected in Philostratus's biography of Apollonius, serves mainly to glorify the sage's supernatural skills. In this case—his gift of clairvoyance and his ability to understand the speech of animals. To us, the story seems naive, perhaps even silly. And yet, it is more than just a testimony of the mentality of that era. There are other reasons why we should make a note of it. Namely, the story was carefully constructed from carefully selected historical elements.

And so, first of all, who was this pharaoh Amasis?

His name in ancient Egyptian was something like *Yahmose* and meant "Born from the Moon." He lived in the 6th century BC. He came from a very poor family, entered the army, and gradually rose to such high positions that he was able to seize the throne and depose the rightful pharaoh, Apries. He first imprisoned him, then executed him, and then—honored him with a magnificent funeral. From then on, he reigned wisely and fairly over his people for over forty years and remained in their memory as their last truly outstanding ruler before the conquest of the country by the Persians. The Greeks also spoke of him with great respect for many generations because they had received many favors from him. With his aid and permission, Greek merchants

---

[24] Philostratus, *Life of Apollonius of Tyana*, VI 32.

founded the first permanent colony in the Nile Delta, the city of Naucratis. Many temples in Greece received rich gifts from him. The temple of Apollo at Delphi—the very place where, seven centuries later, Plutarch was to tell his friends about the vision of Thespesius—received a thousand talents of silver, an astronomical sum. It was commonly said that all this happened thanks to his beloved wife, a woman of Greek descent. But the pharaoh also tried to achieve certain political goals in this way.

Herodotus, who visited Egypt about eighty years after the death of Amasis, when the country was already under Persian rule, was able to record many stories about the "Moon-born," stories still current in the oral tradition. Two of them are worth quoting since they characterize the man. Although they may seem trivial to us today, they do contain an important thought.

Amasis could not boast of illustrious ancestors, and many dignitaries from old and powerful families treated him haughtily even after he donned the double crown of the Two Kingdoms.[25] But he showed exemplary patience, correctly predicting that punishments would only cause a wave of resentment and would not remove the cause of contempt. He finally found a way to humble those who disrespected him. He had a golden bowl in which the palace guests washed their feet. He ordered it melted down and recast as a statue of a divinity. He then placed it in such a way that all those passing by had to venerate the image. After some time, he gathered his critics and said, pointing to the statue:

"This was once a bowl in which you washed your feet and into which you spat, or worse. And now you bow humbly before the same metal! Remember that I, too, experienced a similar transformation. I was once an ordinary, simple man. But now it has pleased the gods to make me your ruler, and it is your duty to serve me!"

Amasis devoted his morning hours to the matters of state and spent afternoons and evenings on feasting, fun, and games. Some criticized it. They said that a pharaoh, a god incarnate, should always

---

[25] The red crown of Upper Egypt and the white crown of Lower Egypt.

behave with dignity. He replied:

"Remember that an archer strings the bow only when it is to be used. Then, he unstrings it immediately. For he knows that a bow strung taught and left that way would soon become completely useless."[26]

Amasis had to enter an animal body to atone for rebelling against his legitimate ruler and depriving him of his throne and life. And to pay for all the feasting and fun, he was obliged to make a living by begging, being led on a string through the common throng. But because the same Amasis had cared for the good of his subjects, he was graciously allowed to take the form of the noblest of quadrupeds, and he eventually met a savior who recognized him, freed him from further wandering, and had him taken to Leontopolis.

"Leontopolis" means "The City of Lions," and its name derived from the fact that an Egyptian god, represented in the form of the king of animals, had been worshiped there for many centuries. But there were two such in the Nile Delta. Which one is the Leontopolis of the story? We can guess easily: in this case, it is certainly the Greater Leontopolis. It was the capital of a district in the center of the delta. How do we know?

A lion called by the Greeks *Misis* or *Mios* was worshipped in its temple—both names are a corruption of its Egyptian name, *Mahes*.

No systematic excavations have been carried out in this town, but many small items have turned up, and among them, many cult figurines of various deities. Most were statuettes of a man with a lion's head, on which rested the solar disk because Mios, like all lions in general, was considered a special form of the god Ra. A certain papyrus text Greek called the Lord of Leontopolis "light, fire, flame, terror and lightning, Lord of darkness and gales."

The temple kept a live lion, and when it died, its carefully mummified body was placed in a tomb along with all his predecessors identified with Osiris. And then immediately, a search commenced throughout the country for the lion's successor which might meet

---

[26] Herodotus, *Histories*, II 172—173.

certain traditionally observed conditions regarding body size, color, and mane. In other words, everything happened analogously to another, and much more famous, sacred animal—the sacred bull Apis of the city of Memphis.

The Greek names of the Lord of Leontopolis suggest how the story arose that Apollonius discovered Pharaoh Amasis in the form of a lion: to the Greek ear, all four names—*Mios, Misis, Mahes,* and *Amasis*—sounded similar. It is also obvious that the description of the ceremonial escorting of the lion to the temple is simply a real-life image of the processions that led each newly discovered *Mios* to Leontopolis amid the singing of hymns and prayers.

And thus, the biography of Apollonius, even in its most naïve fragments, again proves to be a good source for our understanding of the world of antiquity since it reflects, however unintentionally, many of its aspects. And this is why the anecdote—though it has led us away from the main plot of our story—was worth mentioning here even though the sage from Tyana will appear in our story again. But also in order to show how maliciously the empire of the first century fantasized about its rules, ordering them into the bodies of different animals. The Pharaoh-lion eats honey cake and eagerly (but moderately) sips wine from its bowl. The criminal emperor, but also an artist, becomes a frog. These grotesque ideas will return centuries later to the pen of a poet of the cloudy north:

> This winged swarm of moths flashing about us now
> Once extinguished every ray of education.
> Following the Judgment Day, darkness will swallow them.
> But for now, damned to eons of wandering,
> Though they hate all light, into light they are compelled to fly.
> For the spirits of darkness, this is their greatest torment!
> Look at that tiny butterfly decked out in colorful robes,
> He was once some kinglet or oligarch
> And with the great outspreading of his wings
> He darkened whole cities, whole districts.[27]

---

[27] Adam Mickiewicz, *Dziady* ("Forefather's Feast") lines 1213-1223

What follows next is familiar to every Pole.

And now we will return to the business from which we have wandered. And we will do so by way of the Lesser Leontopolis.

## ONIAS'S TEMPLE

The other Leontopolis lay on the eastern branch of the Nile. It had a temple in which not one but two lions were worshipped. The lions symbolized the deities Shu and Tefnet, a brother-and-sister pair who were also husband and wife. They were the children of Atum, the great lord of nearby Heliopolis. As a couple, they were commonly referred to as *ruti* and piloted the Heavenly Barge of Morning and Evening—that barge with which the souls of the dead had to merge by the use of special prayers in order to soar freely above the mortal earth.

This is how things had stood in ancient times, under the old Egyptian pharaohs. In time, the temple fell into disuse, and around 160 BC, the Macedonian King of Egypt, Ptolemy VI, gifted its grounds to a foreigner named Onias.

That Onias was a Jew, a descendant of an illustrious family of High Priests. He had fled from Judea when the Syrian king Antiochus, then the ruler of the whole of Palestine, gave custody of the Temple of Jerusalem to another family, one more submissive to his will. Long an enemy of Antiochus, Ptolemy gave a warm welcome to the Judean exile. And the exile, in turn, wishing to repay the king for his hospitality, proposed an extraordinary plan:

Since Antiochus had desecrated the Temple of Jerusalem, it seemed right and proper to erect a new Jewish temple elsewhere, outside of that king's reach. And if so, then why not do it on Egyptian soil? Ptolemy would thereby win over all the Jewish opponents of Antiochus: why, many Jews would leave Palestine and settle on the Nile precisely *because* here they would be allowed to serve their God in peace and in accordance with the Law.

Ptolemy decided that the plan made political sense and granted to Onias that unused plot of land in Leontopolis. Construction work began immediately, with the support of at least some members of the Jewish diaspora—a diaspora very numerous in Egypt. The temple itself was built in the shape of a tower, 60 cubits high. An altar was set up for the offering of animals, modeled on the altar of Jerusalem. Superb liturgical robes were prepared. Only the seven-branched candlestick that had stood in the Temple of Jerusalem was absent. In its place, a giant lamp, forged of pure gold, was suspended from the ceiling on a golden chain.

The temple grounds were surrounded by a wall of fired brick, and the gate was framed with stone pylons like those of Egyptian temples. The cost of the maintenance of the temple and of the daily offerings was covered by the income of a plot of arable land graciously granted by the king.

The very location of the temple in Leontopolis went against the ancient Judean tradition, which held that legitimate sacrifices to the God of the Jews could only be made in one place—in the Temple of Jerusalem on Temple Mount—and that only houses of prayer (synagogues) could exist outside the holy city. This political claim of Judea aside, many Jews were afraid that the new center of worship might cause religious division, dilute the sense of Jewish unity, and reduce those revenues of the Temple and of the city of Jerusalem— which they earned from the Jews of the Egyptian diaspora.

As it happened, the hopes of Onias and his king did not come true, and no mass migration from Judea took place: Judea soon regained full independence, the Temple of Jerusalem was reconsecrated and functioned successfully for several decades, well into the Roman times. And yet, the colony of Leontopolis lived on for many generations, and its memory has survived to this day in the Arabic name of the place: *Tel-el-Yehudiyeh*—Jews' Hill.

Numerous remains of the settlement persist in the form of inscribed tombstones. Today, they repose in the museums of Cairo, Alexandria, Louvre, and Saint Petersburg.

The inscriptions are in Greek, and the names of the deceased are sometimes Greek (Aristobulus, Alexander, Onesimus, Glaukias, Theodora, Arsinoe, Demas, Nicanor, Hilarion, Philip, Dositheus, Nicomedes, Elpis); sometimes Hebrew (James, Joseph, Judas, Samuel, Jesus, Nathan, Onias, Barchias, Rachelis, Joannes, Eleazar (that is to say, Lazarus), Sabbataeus, Sambaios; and sometimes formally Greek, but really Judean: Salamis (Salome), Marin (Mary), Irene (a translation of Salome, meaning Peace).

Here is a typical epitaph from Leontopolis:

"Eleazar, noble and popular, aged thirty. (Died) year Two of Caesar, 20th Mehir".

By our reckoning, Lazarus died on 14 February 28 BC. (The "Caesar" of the inscription is Octavian, who later became Emperor Augustus).

Another inscription, missing its first line, is more eloquent:

"You, who loved your brothers, who loved your children, who were kind to all, goodbye! May the earth cradle you gently. She died aged about 45. Year 19, which some people reckon as Year 3, the 5$^{th}$ of Pachon."

This double dating allows us to establish that the woman whose name we do not know died on April 30 35 BC, during the reign of the infamous Queen Cleopatra VII, the last ruler of independent Egypt, the beloved of Antony.

Several longer inscriptions survive:

"O passerby, cry for me, a mature girl. I lived a blissful life in luxurious chambers. I had my whole trousseau ready for my wedding, but I died prematurely. Instead of a marriage bed, this gloomy grave awaited me. When the clatter of wedding knockers rang out, it announced my death. Like a rose in a garden full of dew, Hades suddenly snatched me away. Passerby, I was only twenty."

The opening and closing lines of the inscription are versified. Other inscriptions are all in verse:

Passer-by, I am Jesus, son of Phameios.
I descended to Hades at the age of sixty.
Mourn for me, all of you, me, who

Has suddenly departed into the abyss
To dwell hereafter in darkness.
Cry also you, o Dositheus!
You, of all, should shed the most painful tears
For you are now my successor since
I have died without issue. All of you,
Who gather here, weep for unfortunate Jesus!"[28]

## THE LAST FORTRESS AND THE END OF ONIAS'S TEMPLE

This collection of epitaphs from a small settlement in the Nile Delta shows how strongly Hellenized Egyptian Jews became, and not only those living in the capital of the country—Alexandria. Also here, in a provincial town, modest Jewish colonists spoke Greek and bore Greek names, and when they said goodbye to their loved ones, they tried to imitate—if clumsily—the poetry of Greek tomb inscriptions. I wanted to record all of this here because the phenomenon will allow us to understand certain developments we are about to encounter.

But what was the eventual fate of Onias's Temple and of the faithful who worshipped there?

As we will learn in subsequent chapters, Titus captured and burnt the Temple of Jerusalem at the end of August AD 70. Daily sacrifices continued right up to the end—amid the clash of weapons and the torrents of human blood. And then they ceased forever. But even after the fall of the capital and the destruction of the temple, the insurgents continued their struggle since they still held three fortresses in the south of the country. The last to fall was the almost inaccessible—Masada, the eagle's nest of King Herod the Great, perched high above the Dead Sea. This happened only in AD 73, after a very long siege.

The Romans, commanded by the governor of Syria, Flavius

---

[28] J. B. Frey, *Corpus Inscriptinum Semiticarum*, II 1936, Rome 1936, pp. 37—438, Josephus Flavius, *The Jewish War*, VII 10, 2.

Silva, surrounded the mountaintop with a chain of fortifications but soon realized that they would not be able to starve the defenders, who had inexhaustible supplies of food in their warehouses and of water in their cisterns.

Large stores of grain, olive oil, wine, and dates were said to have dated to the times of King Herod the Great himself, almost a hundred years earlier, preserved perfectly thanks to the dry and clean desert air. People said that the king had ordered these supplies to accumulate and kept expanding and reinforcing the stronghold to ensure protection for himself from two dangers that constantly threatened him: on the one hand, he was afraid of his people, for whom he was a tyrant, and on the other hand, of Queen Cleopatra, who did not hide her intention to annex Herod's lands and demanded them from Antony. And thus the political complexities of a century earlier now favored the defenders of the last independent piece of Judea.

The besiegers eventually completed massive earth ramps and pushed their siege engines up the steep approach from the west. On May 1, AD 73, powerful blows of their battering ram broke down one section of the wall, but the defenders immediately built a wooden barricade in the gap. The legionaries tried to set it on fire, but this was prevented by a contrary wind. Only when the wind changed direction did the beams catch fire. Meanwhile, night had fallen, and Silva postponed the final assault until the following day. But on that day, to the great surprise of the legionaries, no one defended the walls, and a great silence prevailed over the fortress. The cohorts—protecting themselves by a wall of shields—cautiously entered the spacious courtyard of the fortress and stood silent, their mouths agape: they saw a sight that terrified even the toughest men. Everywhere lay piles of corpses—men, women, and children—still warm and drenched in blood, although there were no signs of struggle anywhere. After a while, two women emerged from an underground hiding, leading five little children. Only they survived the tragedy of Masada's last night, and only they could explain what had happened:

The insurgents, fully realizing the utter hopelessness of their position and inflamed by the passionate speech of their leader, Eleazar, decided that none of them would be taken alive. The men first killed their women and children, and then they chose ten from among themselves by lot. Those ten killed all the others quickly and efficiently, as each put his neck under the sword without resistance. Then, these ten selected one to kill the rest, and, in the end, he himself committed suicide.

The Romans counted nine hundred and sixty corpses within the fallen fortress. Since then, Masada has remained dead, abandoned forever. But to this day, visible remains of the fortress and of the Roman earthworks survive in the rocky wasteland.

Not by accident did the spring of AD 73 bring the destruction of the last outpost of armed resistance in the land of Judea and of the last Jewish temple where sacrifices to the God of the Jews were still being offered—the Temple of Leontopolis, in Egypt. And here's how the two were connected:

Before the Romans took control of Judea, many rebels fled the country and made their way to Alexandria. There were many extremists among them, the so-called *Sicarii*, i.e., "dagger-men," for they eliminated their opponents by assassination. These men attempted to trigger an anti-Roman uprising in the Egyptian capital. They believed that a war in Egypt had as much chance of success as in Palestine, given the hundreds of thousands of Jews in Alexandria and as many as a million in the entire country. Indeed, Egypt housed, at the time, the largest Jewish population in the world after Palestine.

But the elders of the Jewish community in Egypt realized very quickly what was afoot and what mortal danger the plot posed to their community. A failed rebellion in Egypt would destroy the Jews of Egypt just as it had laid low the Jews of Judea. They took decisive action and squashed the planned rebellion in the bud: they arrested six hundred plotters and delivered them into Roman hands. A similar fate befell those who, as the arrests began, managed to escape from the city and flee for southern Egypt.

Josephus, who was generally very averse to the extremists—he considered them to be the cause of the tragedy of his people—in this case, did not hide his respect, indeed admiration, for the toughness these men displayed during interrogations when they were forced to offer sacrifices to the statue of the emperor. The historian wrote in Book VII of *The Jewish War*:

> Their stubbornness, their madness—or maybe someone will call it their spirit?—made a huge impression on everyone. For none of them broke, and none stooped to worship the emperor. They survived all tortures. Nothing could break their faith. It seemed as if they saw pleasure in suffering, and their bodies did not feel the agony of torture or the heat of the fire. But little boys were the most astonishing, for none of them could be forced to call the emperor his master! Such was the power of the spirit that filled their frail bodies!

This happened in AD 71 or 72. The then-prefect of Egypt, Julius Lupus—he seems to have been the son of that officer of the Praetorian Guard who killed Caligula's wife and daughter, for which he was sentenced to beheading by Claudius[29]—immediately notified Rome about the disturbances in his province and soon received a reply: Emperor Vespasian ordered the closing of the temple in Leontopolis. It's easy to see why the emperor issued his order. He was afraid that the temple of Onias, the only place in the world where Jews still made sacrifices to their God, might appear to continue the tradition of the destroyed Temple of Jerusalem; that it could become a new center of Jewishness not just on the Nile, but in the whole world. To carry out the order, Lupus went to Leontopolis personally, seized the liturgical utensils, thus preventing further sacrifices, he thought, and closed the temple.

He died soon thereafter, in the spring of AD 73. He was succeeded by Paulinus, who again had to deal with the cult of Leontopolis—apparently, some services were still taking place. The new prefect took the matter seriously. Not sparing harsh punishments, he forced the priests to give up all vestments and treasures, had the temple bricked up, and forbade even as much as approaching the

---

[29] See the preceding volume of the trilogy, *Titus and Berenice*

building. Josephus, writing several years later, reports that the town soon became completely deserted. The only evidence that the Lord's temple once existed there are the grave inscriptions quoted above and the Arabic name of the place. But perhaps the world needed to see the destruction of this temple to understand one thing: that in the life of every nation, the invisible spiritual bond matters more than the loftiest building or the most efficient organization. A bond invisible, elusive, and therefore often overlooked, but distinct, indestructible, and immortal.[30]

## MEANWHILE IN ROME

Alas, no Roman seems to have understood this. He would have looked with pride at his capital, vast, populous, and ever more splendid. Virgil spoke of it in his sonorous poems, saying that it surpassed all other cities like a towering cypress rises above the creeping bush. From the Palatine ruled his emperor, one and only. He had the Senate at his side. He commanded fearless legions and efficient administrators, and ruled a great many rich provinces. To his mind, could an empire exist without a gorgeous capital, without soldiers, without vigilant, reliable administration, or without splendid monuments to its glory?

At the end of the winter of AD 69, Sisenna, who had so luckily escaped from the hands of the impostor Nero on the island of Kythnos, found himself approaching the capital on the Tiber full of confident joy. He was about to feast his eyes on the most sacred places of Rome, stand before the emperor, and almost certainly receive a reward that would delight his heart. He would receive it not only for the hardships and dangers he had coped with so skillfully but also for delivering safely to Rome a symbol of brotherly unity of the Imperial

---

[30] Words written under Russian occupation on about the two hundredth anniversary of the First Partition of the Polish Commonwealth (1772).

Galba

army.

Sisenna probably entered Rome at the beginning of March. He entered not by Via Flaminia but by one of the roads from the south—because his ship had landed on the shores of Italy either in Brundisium or somewhere in the Gulf of Naples, like all ships arriving from the East. And though he was probably too busy in the first days of his stay in the capital to visit the tomb of the Domitians, he must have quickly realized that the cult of Nero was alive and well and the new emperor, Otho, clearly wanted to be considered the heir and successor of Nero.

You see, when on the evening of January 15, after they murdered Galba, the Praetorians, and the crowd accompanied Otho to the Palatine in a joyful procession, unexpectedly, from all sides, erupted triumphant cheers, first just a few and rather shy, then taken up by the crowd and chanted in thunderous unison:

*"Salve Otho Nero! Imperator Otho Nero!"*
The same thing happened in the following days, and the emperor tried to pretend that he didn't hear those thunderous acclamations. Perhaps—says Tacitus—because he was afraid to prohibit them? Or was it because he felt ashamed to encourage them? Nevertheless, in his first official letters to the provincial governors, in which he announced his assumption of power, he signed his name in just those words: "Otho Nero."
Every resident of the capital could see that old portraits and statues of Nero, removed during the reign of Galba, reappeared in many private houses. Otho now asked the Senate to permit, by way of a special resolution, that the statues of Sabina Poppaea, Nero's wife be restored to public spaces. The argument was simple: four years earlier, after her tragic death, the Senate ha deified her, that is, included her in the pantheon of officially recognized Roman deities. Nothing revoked that resolution since, so Poppaea was still entitled to the title of *diva*, that is, "divine," and should receive the honors she deserved. For all the piety of the argument, many thought that Otho took this action not out of respect for this woman—once his wife but then taken away from him by Nero—but for other reasons, for the emperor also

restored to their former rights and privileges all the freedmen and former officials of Nero deposed by Galba.One of Otho's advisors in all of this was Senator Galerius Trachalus. The year before, he had held the consulate by the grace of Nero, and now, the excellent orator that he was, he composed public speeches for the new emperor. It was significant that a private person was entrusted with preparing the official speeches of the emperor: this practice, too, was an imitation of Nero's. Here is what Tacitus writes about it:

> Older people who have had the chance to compare the past and the present say that of all the emperors, Nero was the first to borrow someone else's eloquence. For the dictator Caesar had competed with the greatest rhetoricians in skill, and Augustus had an easy and fluent speech worthy of a ruler. Tiberius also knew the art of public speaking, using words sometimes full of penetrating intellect and sometimes purposely ambiguous. Even the disorder of the mind of Gaius Caesar [Caligula] did not distort the power of his rhetoric. Also Claudius, whenever he made a speech—if he had given it enough thought—did not lack a certain sense of sophistication.[31]

Among the first documents that Otho signed was the grant of fifty million sesterces to finish the construction of Domus Aurea, Nero's beloved work, which the frugal Galba had stopped immediately upon coming to power.

And at last—and this, too, was widely commented upon—Otho announced his intention to marry Statilia Messalina, Nero's last wife. He would be her fifth husband.

Of course, the current ruler of Rome did all this not out of selfless sympathy for the man who had kept him away from the capital for ten years but out of calculation. He wanted to show to the public, and especially the population of the capital, that he firmly distanced himself from the policies of Galba. He also wanted to capitalize on the public affection for Nero. Tacitus, then about ten or fifteen years old and perhaps already permanently residing in Rome, confirms this.

He says:

---

[31] Tacitus, *Annals*, XIII 3

It was believed that he tried to honor the memory of Nero in the hope of gaining the support of the commoners.[32]

(The historian held an undisguised contempt for both the senatorial class and for the lower orders).

Of course, Otho could not go too far in that direction. He knew perfectly well how hostile the senators and the equites had been to Nero. The two estates had been the principal victims of Nero's terror, which is why, in time, they all came to conspire against him and finally brought about his destruction. And in the face of the coming civil war—and each day brought new reports of the approach of Vitellius's army—Otho had to seek the favor or at least neutrality of influential people. So, he tried to show that he would not imitate Nero's ruthlessness or extravagance in his private or public life. He understood well that, in the eyes of the upper classes, acting as a singer and a chariot driver had harmed Nero no less (and probably even more) than the bloody murders of real and imagined conspirators. A despot can never openly admit his weaknesses. He will be forgiven all cruelties and crimes but never—ridicule.

In Lusitania, Otho had established his reputation as an efficient and energetic administrator, and now he implemented wise policies, preaching the gospel of internal peace, harmony, and cooperation. The mainstay of his power were the Praetorians, so he showered them with favors and privileges. Yet, at the same time, he protected from their vengeance Marius Celsus, who had remained faithful to the cause of Galba to the end. If the new emperor punished anyone, it was only those who were universally hated.

Foremost among them was Sophonius Tigellinus.


# TIGELLINUS

Nero's Praetorian Prefect, the evil spirit of the later years of his rule,

---

[32] Tacitus, *Histories*, I 78

and the real perpetrator of many of the crimes attributed to the emperor, had come from the dregs of society. He owed everything to his ruler, but in his hour of need, was the first to abandon him. Already under Galba, there were calls to punish him for his various misdeeds under Nero, but he saved himself thanks to the intercession of powerful friends, who feared that their involvement in his crimes might also come to light. At length, Galba found it politically expedient to abandon the matter. But as soon as Otho took power, the calls arose again, not just in the corridors of power, but everywhere and at every opportunity, in forums, circuses, and theaters people raised the cry: "Death to Tigellinus!" And Otho was happy to throw the toad to them.

Tigellinus was taking the waters at Sinuessa, a town two hundred miles south of Rome, at the borders of Campania. He was searching for a cure for what was probably gout, but at the same time, he desported himself with a swarm of young and willing women. It was later said maliciously that he had kept a ship in the harbor, ready to go to sea at the drop of a hat to take him to parts unknown straight from an orgy (or maybe even without interrupting one). But as it happened, the tribune sent by Otho appeared at the gate of his house without warning, and there was time to escape. Tigellinus reached for the arguments that had never failed him before. He offered millions but was refused. He managed to delay a little, groped his girlfriends some more, and finally started shaving and—cut his throat with his razor.

And yet, only two years earlier, during Nero's Greek journey, the same Tigellinus had taken part in an unusual wedding ceremony in the role of the father of the bride.

The bride was Sporus, a boy, castrated and made a girl on Nero's orders, presumably, because his face resembled that of Sabina Poppaea, the beloved first of Otho, then of the emperor. The ceremony was performed in accordance with all legal requirements, formally and solemnly. Greeks, as always theatrically inclined but prompt to wisecrack, celebrated the event in a sublime mood, wishing the young couple that gods may soon bless them with numerous offspring. Sporus was now addressed as Empress and Mistress. He was introduced to feminine society by a lady from the highest Roman aristocracy, the rich and influential Calvia Crispinilla. She also took charge of his wardrobe and makeup.

## CALVIA CRISPINILLA

What was Crispinilla's position at Nero's court? A title given to her by Tacitus says it all: *magistra libidinum*, i.e., the Mistress of the Pleasures of Love.[33] Petronius portrayed her in his *Satyricon*. That work, written during the reign of Nero, is full of malicious allusions to various figures, which we do not always understand today. Its author belonged to Nero's closest circle, where he was referred to as *arbiter elegantiarum*—the authority on savoir-vivre, as we would say today, and knew many secrets of the palace. One of the preserved fragments of the novel features a certain Quartilla. Note the similarity of her name to that of Nero's Mistress of Pleasure. She demonstrates her experience and skills in a surprising way:

> Then Psyche approached her and whispered something in her ear. To which she responded:
>
> "Yes, Yes! How good that you reminded me! Why not deflower our Pannychia now since such a great opportunity presents itself?"
>
> Immediately, a girl was brought in, pretty enough but not a day older than seven. They all started to clap their hands and hooting, and a wedding took place without delay. I was terrified. I started yelling something to the effect that neither her intended, Giton, an extremely shy boy, could cope with such debauchery, nor was the girl old enough to endure what a woman must suffer.
>
> But Quartilla was indignant:
>
> "And do you suppose she is any younger than I was when I first had

---

[33] Tacitus, *Histories*, I 73

70

a man? May Juno hate me if I remember ever being a virgin! Already as a baby, I played around with my peers. Later, when I began to walk, I took on older boys, and I am still going strong. Surely, this must be the origin of the proverb: who as a child carried a calf will lift the bull!"

I shut up, afraid that they might do even worse to harm to my brother.

Meanwhile, Psyche had already covered the girl's head with the red wedding veil. Already, the degenerates had decorated the marital bed, lit the wedding torches, and formed a procession. Quartilla jumped up, fired up by the general excitement.

She grabbed Giton by the hand and pulled him to the bedroom. The boy, truth be told, did not resist at all. Neither did the girl look saddened or terrified.

As soon as the children lay down and the curtain of the door was drawn, we all squatted at the threshold. Quartilla was the first to stick her nose through the opening, which she brazenly widened, and she observed the children's play with lustful interest. She then pulled me to look in as well. And because as we watched, our faces came close together, she began to smack her lips suggestively and kept covering me with furtive kisses.[34]

We are led to think that Calvia Crispinilla's temperament and practices were similar.

An interesting side note: following Nero's death, Crispinilla fled overseas to the province of Africa. There, she tried to convince the commander of the local legion to rebel, allegedly intending to stop grain deliveries to Rome as vengeance for its betrayal of her master. However, the scheme failed, and she soon returned to Rome, still under Galba: apparently, she had enough powerful friends to guarantee her safety. When Otho took over, there were demands to punish her as well. However, the emperor remained deaf to these appeals—perhaps because he highly appreciated Crispinilla's ingenuity in the field of the art, which he himself had practiced

---

[34] Petronius, *Satyricon*, 25

zealously in his youth?

Moreover, even now, although he generally avoided excesses and was devoted to the matters of state, he did not deny himself certain pleasures and he took Sporus into his inner circle. Perhaps because the boy reminded him of Sabina Poppaea, too?

Or to prove a worthy successor of Nero in everything?

## THE JOINED HANDS OF THE DISJOINTED EMPIRE

Now, various noble slogans appeared on Otho's coins. Anyone who held a denarius with his image could read some beautifully sounding words. Alas, all were pious wishes rather than statements of fact, things like *Pax Orbis Terrarum* ("Peace on Earth") or *Securitas Populi Romani* ("The Safety of the Roman People"). It is worth noting that the latter slogan already appeared on some coins under Nero: a conscious continuation of certain propaganda motifs.

In truth, the emperor spared no effort to make these proud announcements a fact. Above all, he wanted to avoid the greatest threat of all at all costs—the war with Vitellius. He sent him letter after letter. He promised mountains of gold, amnesty, honors, whatever form of retirement Vitellius might choose himself, as long as he laid down his arms and renounced the title his legions had given him illegally. Vitellius, of course, responded with similar offers and promises. Each considered himself the rightful emperor of Rome, and each was prisoner of facts on the ground, their supporters, and their troops. Neither could go back now or resign under any circumstances, even if he sincerely wanted to.

As was to be expected, the letters became increasingly sharper and more threatening until, at last, they descended into mutual accusations and common insults. The emperors accused each other of gross misconduct in their private lives, real and imagined, and there was no shortage of material to work with. Each also tried more effective means by—sending assassins. Those sent by Otho were quickly identified among the soldiers in Vitellius's camp, where everyone knew each other, while those sent by Vitellius hid among the multilingual crowd of the capital and calmly waited out the whole affair without even trying to accomplish their task.

Meanwhile, the legions from the Rhine never interrupted their march. Soon, the news of their rapid crossing of the Alps was received in Rome and—of the terrible atrocities they committed against the Italian cities that attempted to resist them. One of Vitellius's generals, Caecina, carried out a bloody "pacification" of the land of the Helvetii in today's Switzerland because the local magistrates had tried to delay a delegation from the Rhine army traveling to the army of the middle Danube.

Given this situation, the court of Otho received the centurion Sisenna with particular joy. He had come from the East as a bearer of truly good news ahead of the upcoming battle. Of course, it was already known in the capital that the four legions in Syria, under the command of Licinius Mucianus, and the three legions in Judea, under Flavius Vespasian, had sworn allegiance to Otho. But now, Sisenna brought to Rome a visual proof of the loyal feelings of the Syrian army. It was a metal object, probably silver or bronze, depicting two hands joined in a brotherly handshake. This was a traditional Roman symbol of unity and consent, known to us from many coins of the imperial period. The intertwined hands sometimes hold a banner with a legionary eagle and are usually accompanied by short but eloquent inscriptions such as *concordia exercituum* ("Agreement among the Armies"), or *Fides exercituum* ("Loyalty of the Armies"). Moot it is to say that—as it happens in every era—this monolithic unity of the army was celebrated in official propaganda most intensely precisely when the actual mood of the legions of the Empire was completely its opposite.

But now Sisenna was bringing the Praetorians a symbol that the legions in Syria had ordered to be made and had sent spontaneously. It was, therefore, an authentic expression of their attitude towards the units in the capital. The in effect said: "We approve of your choice of emperor and will defend it." It is easy to imagine what complications could have arisen if this symbol of brotherhood had fallen into the hands of the false Nero on the island of Kythnos! The Impostor could have taken advantage of it by spreading the word that he had the army of the East behind him.

The ceremonial handover of the symbol most likely took place in the main square of the Praetorian camp in the presence of the emperor himself.


Otho was thirty-seven years old. He was of medium height and had a good figure. He had slightly bendy legs, but when he appeared in public in the capital, the folds of his toga kept them out of sight. (The legs looked worse in a military camp, where only short tunics were worn). However, only household members and initiates knew that the emperor had thinning hair, for he always appeared before strangers in a perfectly fitting wig. His predecessor, Galba, had also worn a wig, but he had been forty years older.

Otho shaved daily from his early youth, and no one had ever seen him with facial hair. To soothe skin irritations, he regularly applied masks made of moist bread. He borrowed this idea from the ladies of the time who worried much about keeping their skin fresh. But even in their case, the satirist Juvenal ridiculed this type of cosmetic procedure. He maliciously depicted how a wife shows herself to her husband as a revolting monstrosity because her face is covered with swollen bread, and she smells of an ointment invented by Sabina Poppaea.

> Let the longing lips of your unfortunate spouse
> Stick to the hideous goo! You will go to your lover
> Neat and freshly bathed, but when will you ever want
> To appear beautiful and alluring at home?[35]

It was also said that Otho was the first among refined gentlemen to rub his feet with scented oils, in which his childhood friend, Nero,

---

[35] Juvenal, *Satires*, VI 461—464

imitated him. All this, as well as his frequent use of the mirror, was considered evidence of extreme effeminacy. It would soon turn out that this judgment was shallow and false.

The centurion Sisenna assured the emperor that he could count on the army of the East, which wholeheartedly supported him as its rightful commander-in-chief, but we can be pretty certain that he did not enlarge on the fact that the Eastern legions had taken their oath indifferently and mechanically. They had grown used to accepting obediently all decisions made in the capital. Besides, in this case, they had no alternative because the news of the rebellion of the army of the Rhine and the impending civil war arrived only later. Had the troops of Syria and Judea known about it before taking the oath, they would probably have acted more prudently, delaying their oath and waiting to see what transpired in the West. Or perhaps they would have put forward their own candidate.

## PREPARATIONS FOR WAR

Speaking to Sisenna, Otho did not have to pretend to be of good cheer: he really looked to the future with great confidence. He had two-thirds of the provinces behind him—as well as most of the legions: not only the legions of Syria and Judea but also those of Egypt, north Africa, Asia Minor, and above all, the powerful army of the Danube. Only the Western provinces had sided with Vitellius: the two Germanies, Gaul, and Britain, and, lately though not without reservations, Spain.

Everything now depended on whether it would be possible to bring the troops from the Danube in time; they were the closest and could effectively block the path of Vitellius's advancing legions. Otho's forces in Italy were relatively small: nine cohorts of the Praetorians, several so-called urban cohorts, and a legion newly formed from the soldiers and crews of the fleet of Misenum. (This last began forming under Nero but was only now officially inaugurated, that is, received its eagles, battle banners, and number along with its name—

*Prima adiutrix*, i.e., "the First (perhaps Foremost) Rescuer" ).

Alas, the emperor had been forced to divide those troops. He had sent the navy together with a large corps of Praetorians to southern Gaul to defend it against the advancing enemy. And he sent five Praetorian cohorts, a cavalry squadron, *Prima adiutrix,* as well as two thousand gladiators to northern Italy. These units were to hold the main crossings of the Po.

They had to rush because Caecina had already crossed the Alps despite the snow and ice of winter. The emperor was supposed to leave the capital two weeks later. He had with him the rest of the Praetorians, scouts, as well as some veterans re-drafted into service and a few thousand marines. The fighting spirit among the soldiers and officers was excellent. This, however, could not be said about the civilian population in the capital.

It was the natural course of things that war preparations aroused nervousness, confusion, and anxiety in the city. Soon, food shortages arose, followed by a wave of higher prices, which especially affected the poor. For the first time in a century, the horror of war stood at the gates of the capital.

And a war all the more absurd because, in the eyes of the Romans, both protagonists—Otho and Vitellius—were basically the same: neither cared about the public good, a political program, or some noble ideal; each was simply after personal power. This only increased the people's fond longing for their lost Nero. In moral terms, the current rivals were not better than him, but Nero had reigned legally as the rightful heir of Augustus and had given the empire fourteen years of peace.

And then, to complete the measure of misery, a cataclysm struck the city.

# THE GREAT FLOOD

The sudden flooding of the Tiber greatly worsened the situation in the capital. The river carried away the oldest Roman bridge, built centuries earlier from whole tree trunks and so ingeniously that not a single nail had been used in its construction. The waters of the Tiber spilled everywhere. They reached areas that had never been flooded before, broke into houses so suddenly that many people drowned in their beds or at their tables in taverns. Worse still, after the waters receded, numerous residential buildings started to collapse as their weak foundations were washed away. (The blame for this lay primarily with dishonest developers who built houses for the poor cheaply and hastily). Grain granaries standing right on the river were swept away, raising bread prices yet again. There was a real threat of famine. As usual in the era, it was widely believed—and loudly stated—that this was a bad omen for Otho because the river appeared to block Via Flaminia—his route to the north. Interpreters of dreams, always numerous in the capital, said that "cloudy and agitated waters seen in dreams announce an impending catastrophe. They warn against travel. If they break into the house, they presage violence that will cause massive damage to both the building and its inhabitants. This is what such dreams mean." Now imagine how much more potent a warning such an event in real life offered on the eve of a great military expedition, just before the leader too to field.

Unsurprisingly, ther bad omens foreshadowing a catastrophe were widely reported, developments dangerous and unusual. In Etruria, an ox spoke with a human voice. In Rome, the reins slipped from the hands of the bronze statue of the goddess of Victory. (This statue stood on a chariot in the vestibule of the Capitoline temple). On Tiber Island, the statue of the divine Julius Caesar turned all by itself, from west to east, and it happened on a clear and completely windless day.

On March 14, the emperor bid the Senate goodbye. He entrusted the venerable fathers with the care of the state during his absence. And in order to win over the support of the body, he ordered—as he was leaving!—that the estates of all senators exiled under Nero and later pardoned under Galba should be returned to their rightful owners, as long as they hadn't already been sold. Then, he delivered a speech at a public rally. He said everything that could be expected in such a situation. So he talked long and strong, saying that he had the whole Empire behind him and the unanimous support of the people and the Senate. He condemned his enemies and made it clear that the cause of the war was not the lawlessness of the legions of the Rhine but their lack of understanding of the merits of the case.

The people listened attentively and noticed immediately that the emperor never said one bad word about Vitellius. Some asked whether this was due to Otho's personal restraint or to the calculations of the speech writer. They meant Galerius Trachalus and suggested that unsure of the outcome of the upcoming struggle, he preferred not to close certain avenues to himself.

At last, on March 15—the Ides of March—Otho left Rome. Tacitus testifies that the emperor received friendly ovations along the streets from the crowds wishing him victory, but the people have long been accustomed to flattering every ruler, so they cried loud and willingly, although neither love moved them nor fear forced them to do so. As Tacitus says: "the mere pleasure of servility was reward enough."

The emperor rode north along Via Flaminia. He didn't care about the omens. He even ignored what had to be pointed out to him if he hadn't noticed it: that the 15 of March inaugurated a series of mourning ceremonies in praise of Attis, the beloved of the Great Mother of the Gods. The legend had it that on that day, Attis, when still a child, had been thrown into riverside reeds to die. He was eventually saved but the worshipers of the goddess, celebrating the annual feast, carried bundles of reeds into the city, intoning mournful hymns.

Otho himself was a follower of the Egyptian goddess Isis and ignored this omen just as he had ignored all the others because he only believed in stars, and his astrologer had assured him of victory.

Upon leaving the city, he passed the Hill of Gardens and the Domitians' tomb where Nero's sarcophagus stood. The procession progressed very slowly, because up to the twentieth milestone, the road was covered with mud, silt, and rubble of houses destroyed by the recent flooding.

There were certainly Christians among those watching the progress of the imperial troops. Although still small, their community had revived since Nero's persecution of five years earlier. They were now focused on the upcoming celebrations of the passion of their Savior, though, living as they were in the heart of the Empire, their lives were of necessity intertwined with the great political events of the day. And in those days of March, they had to recall the words of their Messiah: "If a kingdom be divided against itself, that kingdom cannot stand. And if a house be divided against itself, that house cannot stand."[36]

And no kingdom and no house seemed to them more divided than the Roman Empire.

## JOHN OF GISCHALA AND TITUS

But not only Rome was in the throes of an internal crisis. The situation was very curious: just as in the West two Imperial armies were approaching each other to clash in the now inevitable fratricidal battle; so in the East, while another Roman army was enclosing within its iron grip the heart of another country, the defenders of that country, instead of concentrating all their efforts on resisting the invading army,

---

[36] *Mark* 3:24-25

struck out at each other with swords in truly mad blindness, wasting away their own resources, human and material, and wasting their land.

It the summer of AD 68, Vespasian, as soon as he had received the news of the death of Nero, interrupted all action in Judea and withdrew to his base of operations in Caesarea Maritima. However, he left strong garrisons close to Jerusalem, the center of the Jewish uprising: the Xth legion was stationed to the east of the city, in Jericho, and the Vth legion to the west, in Emmaus. The insurgents now held only a tiny rectangular area: it included a part of Judea proper—the lands around the capital—and Idumea, which is the country west of the Dead Sea. And on its eastern shore, they held only the fortress of Machaerus.

In the spring of AD 69, power in Jerusalem lay in the hands of John of Gischala,[37] a leader of the fanatical Zealot party. He had arrived here a year and a half earlier, in the fall of AD 67, having barely escaped with his life from Galilee. We should recall how it happened because the event characterizes both John and his opponent, Titus.

In the summer and early autumn of AD 67, Vespasian conquered almost all of Galilee. In Jotapata, he captured the commander of the rebels of that region, Joseph, who later took the nickname Josephus Flavius and was to become a historian of the war. Only Gischala continued resistance in the northern reaches of Galilee, where he incited the inhabitants to fight at all costs and directed his forces with great energy. The Roman commander sent his son, Titus, with a unit of a thousand horsemen to attack him.

Although surrounded by a wall, the settlement was small, and the Romans could easily have taken it by storm. Titus, however, wanted to avoid unnecessary bloodshed. He knew well that most of the inhabitants were simple farmers who had sided with the rebels either in the heat of the moment, or under the pressure of their peers, or even out of fear. He also realized that his soldiers, once they broke into the town, sword in hand, would murder everyone within it

---

[37] Jish or Gush Halav in upper Galilee

without mercy, guilty or innocent. So he had it announced to the besieged that he would spare their life and property as long as they capitulated immediately. He understood their love of freedom but could not tolerate blind stubbornness. Their cause was lost, and the rest of Galilee was already in Roman hands. Their walls would not protect them because he, Titus, had taken much stronger fortifications by storm. These words were very typical of Titus. He had shown much courage and determination in battle but was fed up with the constant slaughter. Josephus attests to it based on what he had seen firsthand.

Meanwhile, the insurgents forbade the residents of the town to hold any talks with the Romans, and John himself responded to Titus's proposals, pretending to accept them almost unconditionally:

"I admit that your argument is valid. You convinced me. I am ready to give up and will persuade all the others to do the same. But I beg you for a small delay. Today is the Sabbath, and the Law categorically forbids us from undertaking any activities on this day."

Titus, already familiar with Jewish customs, accepted this request and set up camp at some distance from the city; he trusted the Jewish leader enough not to surround the town. But as soon as night fell, John secretly led his men and their families out of the town and moved south to Jerusalem. On the way, it turned out that the women and children slowed down their march. So the commander ordered them left behind, and when he heard their crying and lamenting, he said:

"We must first save the men capable of fighting. If we stay here, we will all die miserably and uselessly. But once we find ourselves out of danger, we will find a way to take revenge on the Romans should they harm you in any way."

At this, his men ran forward, abandoning their women and children in the wilderness in the middle of the night.

When the following morning, as had been agreed, Titus stood at the gates of Gischala, its residents came out begging him for mercy. But he did not enter the city; learning of John's escape, he sent cavalry to chase after him. They did not manage to capture the leader but captured and killed many of his followers and took the women and children, three thousand people in total. (This number seems to be greatly exaggerated—like most numbers given by Josephus).

The young Roman general, although hurt by the whole affair and ashamed that he had been tricked so easily, refrained from taking revenge on the people of Gischala. Before entering the settlement, the soldiers first demolished a piece of the defensive wall, which was the common practice then and symbolized the capture of a city, but no one was punished for helping the insurgents. The inhabitants themselves proposed to Titus that they would find and hand over those of John's supporters who were still hiding among them, but the general rejected this offer, justifying his refusal in a way that gives him credit:

> I fear that the process of rounding up the presumed insurgents would be used by some for their own vile purposes. The excuse of cooperating with me would serve them as an opportunity for base revenge and the settling of personal scores. They will bring me peaceful and innocent people so that I can condemn them and execute them. No. It is better for real criminals to live in fear of future discovery than for us to live with the knowledge that we have killed innocent men because such a miscarriage of justice, once made, cannot be rectified. Perhaps those in the hiding will finally come to their senses when they realize that their past crimes have been forgotten.[38]

These words uttered in distant times, deserve attention in our era, which has witnessed the practice of the completely opposite principle, which could be formulated as follows:

> Better punish a hundred entirely innocent men than to let one guilty escape!

---

[38] Josephus Flavius, *The Jewish War*, IV 9, 11.

# JOHN OF GISCHALA IN JERUSALEM

Meanwhile, John managed to reach Jerusalem with a handful of his supporters. Once there, he quickly rose to prominence among the Zealots. Their ranks consisted mainly of the peasantry, driven to Jerusalem by the war, most of them young men without prospects, who, brash and loud, having nothing to lose and confident in their numbers, resorted to terror against all who disagreed with them, accusing them of conspiring with the Romans. They caused the death and imprisonment of many leading personalities. They took the office of High Priest from the Jerusalem aristocracy.

Using as their excuse the theory that the High Priest should come from the line of Zadok, they demanded that the new religious head be selected by lot from among all the descendants of that family. Fate chose a certain Pinehas. He was a simple man, a stonemason by profession, with no education of any kind; he was to be the last High Priest of the Temple of Jerusalem. And thus the last two temples of the Jews—both the Temple of Jerusalem and the Temple of Leontopolis—came to be ruled before their fall by priests descended from the High Priest of the times of kings David and Solomon.

However, it soon turned out that the aristocracy was not powerless. One of the former High Priests, Ananos, incited the people to take up arms against the Zealots. Hand-to-hand fighting broke out in the streets, and many died on both sides. Although the Zealots stood bravely, they were driven into the inner courtyard of the temple. There, they were surrounded by armed opponents posted in the outer courtyard—the Court of the Gentiles. Ananos did not allow an attack on the inner court because that would have meant the destruction of its beautiful gate—the so-called Gate of Nicanor—and the defilement of the inner sanctum.

Interestingly, John of Gischala seems to have stayed on the sidelines during this conflict and even managed to join Ananos's entourage, enjoying his trust and serving as an intermediary between the two sides, even though in reality, he sided with the Zealots. On his advice, they turned for help to the inhabitants of Idumea, a region to the south of Judea. The Idumaeans had a reputation for passionate attachment to the Jewish faith but also as rude ruffians and robbers. They were now told that Ananos and his supporters had betrayed the Jewish cause and were scheming to hand Jerusalem over to the Romans. Two days later, a bunch of armed Idumeans stood at the gates of Jerusalem.

Suspecting that they were there to aid the Zealots, Ananos denied them entry into the city. This only confirmed the Idumeans in the belief that the aristocracy were plotting treason and had to be overthrown. Even the words of the former High Priest, Jesus, speaking to them from the battlements, did not change their mind. They camped before the city and awaited nightfall. At night came a violent thunderstorm and torrential rain. Taking advantage of the noise, darkness, and rain, the Zealots besieged in the temple sawed through the bolts of the Gate of Nicanor, ran stealthily through the deserted streets, and opened the city gates. No one saw them, no one heard the grinding of saws and the stamping of feet. The Zealots now led the Idumeans to the temple precinct, and together, they descended on the men of Ananos sheltering in the porticos of the outer courtyard. These last, taken by surprise, were unable to put up a coherent defense and fell into such panic that many jumped off the wall into the valley below, suffering injuries and death. Meanwhile, the victors spilled out into the city and began to pillage the houses of the rich. Two former High Priests were among the first to die: Ananos and Jesus. Their killers did not allow their bodies to be buried but stripped them naked and left them to be devoured by dogs. Many others died, some after horrible tortures in the dungeons. Rarely were judicial procedures resorted to.

But soon, the Idumaeans realized that the Zealots were not quite selfless and that they had tricked them into doing their dirty work. They released many of the prisoners and left the city. The Zealots watched them depart with satisfaction: from now on, they alone would rule Jerusalem. John of Gischala became their leader and instituted a program of persecution of all prominent figures not associated with his movement.

These events took place in early AD 68. That spring and summer, Vespasian captured major insurgent centers in Palestine and began his march on Jerusalem. But when he learned from refugees about the situation in the city, he slowed down his advance. He told his staff officers surprised by this sluggishness:

"These stupid Jews are killing each other. Let them. Let them bleed and weaken. And let us not attack too hastily since our appearance at the city gates might cause them calm down and join forces. Let's be patient. Time is on our side. Let them murder each other."

Meanwhile, in early July, came the news of Nero's death. Given the uncertainty that caused, Vespasian decided to suspend all operations and wait for orders from the new emperor, Galba. He and the army immediately took the oath of allegiance to the new ruler. Then, Vespasian pulled back to Caesarea Maritima leaving only the Vth Legion in Emmaus and the Xth in Jericho. Then autumn came, and at the end of January, they learned that Galba had been murdered by the Praetorians, and Otho had become the new emperor. They took the same oath again, only this time with the new emperor's name, and began to prepare to march on Jerusalem. The time seemed ripe for the final blow because the house of Judea was now, biblically speaking, even more deeply divided than theretofore: a dangerous rival of John of Gischala had appeared in the capital, far more dangerous than the High Priest Ananos had been.


## SIMON SON OF GIORA IN MASADA AND HEBRON


The news of the death of Ananos caused Simon, son of Giora, to take up arms, even though he was neither a friend nor even a supporter of the murdered High Priest. On the contrary, Ananos had once chased him out from his native district of Accrabene[39] in northern Judea, accusing him of acting too arbitrarily as the leader of the local rebels. Simon then moved with his people and their families to Masada—the same Masada that was to fall five years later, in the spring of AD 73. He found the fortress already held by a unit of the *Sicarii*—the most radical of the Zealots. They allowed Simon into the lower part of the fortress, keeping the upper, completely inaccessible part, for themselves. The newcomer from Accrabene soon found approval in their eyes because of his courage, ingenuity, and cunning: he seemed a perfect leader in a war of subterfuge. The *Sicarii* now invited him to join them, but he refused. He accused them of lacking sufficient fighting spirit and enterprise because they clung to Masada and did not undertake any sorties against the Romans. He was not going to laze idly behind the walls of the mighty fortress and watch indolently as the Romans advanced ever deeper into the heart of Judea.

Which he proved as soon as he heard of Ananos's death. He had respected and obeyed the High Priest. Why should he obey his killer, John of Gischala, a vigilante from Galilee usurping the role of the leaders of the revolt? Why should he, Simon, stay away from in the great events in Jerusalem, and remain locked up in a mountain fortress in the middle of nowhere? The time of confusion favors the bold!

So, Simon left Masada and went into the mountains. He gathered around him landless peasants and runaway slaves. At the head of this mob, he descended into the cultivated valleys, and he began to rob and pillage the local population, all in the pious name of opposing the Romans. Always mobile, he appeared now in Accrabene, now in the heart of Idumea. He stockpiled treasure and supplies in inaccessible caves and his followers grew along with his reputation.

He seemed an embodiment of a particular kind of folk hero popular in all ages: he carried out daredevil exploits, eluded pursuit, and escaped from all danger unharmed. He was terrible to his enemies, severe to the rich, and friendly to the poor. The Zealots soon realized how dangerous his reputation was, so they sent a large force to capture

---

[39] Josephus seems to place Accrabene on the border of Judea and Samaria

the "bandit," which is what they now called him, though they themselves were called the same not only by the Romans but also by conservative Jews—Josephus Flavius, for instance. They were confident of success, even though they had only had to deal with the timid and helpless townspeople of Jerusalem, who were terrified of the very sight of weapons. As could have been predicted, they got into a fight in unfavorable conditions, suffered severe losses, and retreated to Jerusalem. But Simon did not immediately attack the city walls, realizing that his forces were still too weak. He decided to conquer Idumea first. The Idumeans, led by their elders, successfully repelled his first few attacks, but on the day of the decisive battle, an unexpected split emerged among them. And when some joined Simon, the rest scattered in panic, each to his village and farm. Shortly thereafter, Simon captured the city of Hebron. From there, he plundered the surrounding countryside.

## SIMON SON OF GIORA AT THE GATES OF JERUSALEM

Having learned from this bitter experience, the Zealots were now reluctant to meet Simon in the open field and instead staged an ambush: they managed to capture Simon's wife with her servants. With this prize, they returned to the city triumphant, convinced that the "bandit" would have to start negotiations: it was evident how much he loved this woman. But they were to be disappointed. Simon did come to the gates of the city but—not to negotiate. Josephus says figuratively that he seemed like a wounded beast of prey. He couldn't reach the men who had kidnapped his wife, so he attacked and destroyed everyone he encountered in his path. Anyone who stepped outside the gates—to get vegetables or firewood, no matter how old or insignificant—was immediately captured and subjected to horrible tortures. Simon gave the impression that in his fury, he would gladly eat the bodies of his victims. Some of those he captured returned to the city with their hands or feet cut off. They were told to frighten the people into abandoning the Zealots: the maimed messengers were told to deliver the threat of their executioner:

"Simon had sworn an oath before the Living God that if his wife is not returned to him immediately, he will break into the city and murder everyone within it, no matter what sex or age, no matter guilty or not."

Finally, he achieved his goal: his wife was returned to him. He then withdrew from the city and went back to Idumea, plundering it and stripping it bare. Many Idumeans fled in terror to Jerusalem. Simon followed them and soon found himself under the walls of the capital for the second time. He returned to his tried and tested method of terror: he captured, tortured, and killed anyone and everyone who left the city, even if they were just farmhands going out into the fields. He did not do this out of cruelty alone: he wanted to open the gates of Jerusalem and sensed that the population, shaken to the core by the siege, frightened and intimidated, would eventually accept him as their ruler and abandon John of Gischala, who was clearly unable to provide security. Although the thought seemed crazy at first, it was not unrealistic, all the more so because the Zealots committed various crimes in the city and, therefore, unintentionally acted to Simon's advantage.

In Book IV of his *Jewish War*, Josephus Flavius describes the conditions in Jerusalem at that time. He is certainly exaggerating, for he hated John with all his heart. Nor was he an eyewitness to the events, as he had been in Roman captivity since the summer of AD 67, probably in Caesarea Maritima. But his account still has its value, illustrating—even though in caricature—the willful blindness, perversity, and madness of those extraordinary days:

> The Zealots inside were worse than the enemies without. They were worse than the Romans and worse than Simon. Among the Zealots, the Galileans stood out for their arrogance and evil. They were the mainstay of John's power, and he repaid them by allowing them to do whatever they wanted. Their lust for plunder was insatiable. They robbed the houses of the rich for fun, killed men and raped women, ate and drank everything, and stole everything else. At the

same time, not facing a threat from any quarter, they grew feminine: they curled their hair, put on women's dresses, doused themselves with perfumes, and even put makeup on their eyelids—supposedly to emphasize their beauty. And they imitated not only the clothes but also the behavior of women. In their promiscuity, they invented forbidden types of love. They treated the city like a brothel, polluting it with the abomination of their indecency. Dressed like women, they walked with a mincing step but murdered like men, sometimes drawing a sword unexpectedly from under their cloak to stab an unsuspecting passerby. And so, the inhabitants of Jerusalem fled from the tyranny of John, only to fall into an even bloodier tyranny of Simon. All escape routes were cut off for those who wanted to flee to the Romans. [40] [41]

So the testimony of Josephus, a member of the wealthy and aristocratic classes, once a leader of the uprising in Galilee, but by then already holding the view that continuing the war against the Romans was sheer madness. And it wasn't just people like him who were terrified by the events in the capital. The small Christian community, consisting mostly of poor simpletons, had already left the city for the half-Greek town of Pella in the Decapolis. When the news of the fratricidal bloodletting reached them, they heard it in sincere pain but also with a sense of satisfaction: the city that had not wanted to recognize the true Messiah and contributed to the death first of Jesus, and a few years later, to that of his brother James, was now caught in a terrible procession of crimes and on its way to total destruction. That tiny handful of Judeo-Christians certainly thought and spoke about the whole situation in words similar to those used by the author of *The Book of Revelation*: horror, evil, abomination, a woman riding a beast, clothed in purple and scarlet, shining with gold, precious stones, and

---

[40] Josephus Flavius, *The Jewish War*, IV 9, 11.

[41] The feminine dress and make up and violent behavior of the Galileans seems reminiscent of the *kabuki* phenomenon among Japanese city men during the warring states period (1457-1567), who demonstrated their hostility to the established order by wearing women's clothes or their caps backwards and picking random fights in the street. No doubt a sociological phenomenon that deserves further research. (Translator's note).

pearls, holding in her hand a golden cup, full of abominations and fornication.

# JERUSALEM, APRIL AD 69

But that was only the beginning of the misfortunes of the city. Hatred bred more hatred. Indeed, it may have seemed to people witnessing these events that the ghost of the murdered High Priest Ananos walked abroad demanding vengeance.

Idumaeans, of whom many had remained in the city, felt a tribal aversion for the Galileans and were goaded by their behavior, proud and self-confident as if they were the righteous rulers of the city. As for the Zealots, the Idumaeans could not forgive them for how perfidiously they had used them to overthrow and murder Ananos. Old Jerusalemites fueled these attitudes and mutual hostility. The middle class had had enough war and bloody excesses of the extremists. Many were secretly hoping for a settlement with the Romans just to restore peace and secure good government.

And then, for some random, trivial reason, street fighting broke out between several factions. Some Zealots were chased to the palace of a princess named Grapte. She belonged to the royal family that ruled the country of Adiabene on the upper Tigris.[42] Members of this family had accepted the Law about forty years earlier, and they have generously supported the people of Jerusalem and its temple ever since. And now John of Gischala had made his headquarters in the palace of Grapte and deposited his treasury there. Having captured the building, the Idumeans began plundering it while John managed to escape with his men and occupy the quadrangle of the Temple. His Zealots planned to defend themselves there—just as they did when Ananos besieged them. But at that time, they occupied only the inner courtyard, and this time, they tried to hold onto the outer courtyard

---

[42] Corresponding more or less to today's Mosul and Erbil in Iraq.

as well: more ground with fewer men. The besiegers, taught by the sad experience of those events, did not intend to leave John in control of the inner Temple. And, after much arguing, they decided, with a heavy heart, to call for help: the Idumaeans, the townspeople, and the priests decided to invite Simon, son of Giora, into the city, and they sent the former High Priest Matthias to extend the offer.

In April AD 69, Simon entered Jerusalem.


## ROME, APRIL AD 69


On 19 April 69, Rome celebrated the feast of the goddess of fertility, Ceres. The feast had started on April 12 and lasted seven days, and it was customary to celebrate the last day with chariot races. Huge crowds gathered in the the Circus Maximus, and the rest of the city became deserted. Suddenly, among the crowds that filled the steep seats of the audience, the news broke—it was brought to the dignitaries sitting in the boxes by breathless messengers, running in one after another—one from the Palatine, the other from the Praetorian barracks—that Otho had been defeated and died three days earlier. They also reported that the prefect of the city, Flavius Sabinus, the brother of Vespasian, had already sworn in his troops in the name of the new emperor, elevated by the Rhine legions, Aulus Vitellius.

The crowd heaved. There was a dull murmur that gradually grew into an uproar of excitement, and at last, as if on a signal, applause broke out and continued for a long time. Thousands and tens of thousands of mouths began to chant the customary words:

"Imperator Vitellius! Emperor Vitellius!"

This was how the new ruler was greeted by the same people who, only a week earlier, gave a passionate ovation to Otho as he left the capital. They wished him then a quick and complete victory over his vile adversary, the enemy of the Roman people and the state. Now they gave the same ovation to his conqueror.

The games were not interrupted. No official would dare to

issue such an order, knowing that it could lead to bloody riots because the people truly loved only their idols—the charioteers—and their passionate feelings were not really invested in political power struggles but in the rivalry between different circus factions. Still, on the same day, images of Galba, dressed with laurel and flowers, appeared in the temples. This was supposed to mean that the gods had avenged the murder committed by Otho on his predecessor. No one seemed to recall the insignificant and minor fact that the Rhine legions had proclaimed Vitellius emperor when Galba was still alive and it was their rebellion that precipitated Otho's coup. And soon, a heap of flowers rose up by the pool of Curtius in the Forum, where Galba had fallen on January 15.


Let's recall that January scene:

The crowd accompanying the Imperial litter scattered immediately as soon as they heard the sound of horses galloping in from the direction of the Praetorian barracks. The porters threw down the litter in such panic that the old and infirm Galba fell out onto the pavement next to the Pool of Curtius. While he was still down, a soldier stabbed him in the throat since a magnificent cuirass protected the emperor's chest. And immediately, his body was frightfully defiled, men cutting off his privates and lopping off his head.


That very same day, April 19, AD 69, the Senate met to grant to Vitellius all the dignities, titles, and privileges of his predecessors. Resolutions of appreciation and thanksgiving for the victorious army were adopted, and an official delegation was sent to the new emperor with profuse congratulations.

Meanwhile, more detailed information about the last hours of Otho's life began to arrive in Rome.

Otho

# THE LAST HOURS OF OTHO

The Emperor committed suicide on the morning of 16 April 69 in Brixellum, today's Brescello. The town lies on the middle Po, south of the river. Otho's troops had suffered a heavy defeat two days earlier at Bedriacum. That was on the other side of the river, near Cremona, on the road to Mantua.

In preceding skirmishes, Otho's cohorts had inflicted heavy losses on the enemy. They fought very bravely, especially in the battles of Placentia and Cremona, even though only a part of the loyal Danube army had managed to arrive in time to give them aid—its main core was still only approaching the theater of operations.

Nor was everything lost at Brediacum. Otho's troops suffered huge losses, true, but they were neither eliminated nor lost their fighting spirit: they wanted to continue fighting at all costs. There were also reports that the main body of the Danubian army was approaching and that their advance cohorts had already crossed the Maritime Alps, were behind enemy lines, and were already fighting and winning first skirmishes.

And yet, despite all this, the emperor took his own life. How should we think about that act? How do we explain it? Among modern scholars, the view prevails that the emperor had acted in a cowardly fashion. That he suffered a nervous breakdown, couldn't stand the test of the hour, and betrayed his cause and that of his soldiers. However, when we study ancient accounts we must conclude that Otho's motives were manly, even heroic.

The father of Suetonius—the biographer of the first twelve Caesars still widely read today—was present at Brixellum during those dramatic events. Suetonius himself attests to this in his *Life of Otho:*

> One participant in that war was my father, Suetonius Letus, a tribune with a narrow hem in the Thirteenth Legion. [43]

To clarify: the XIII legion, with the nickname *Gemina*, that is,

---

"Twins," was part of the army of the Danube and had its permanent camp near Poetovio, today's Ptuj in Slovenia. From there, the legion had rushed to the aid of Otho. And the narrow purple hem was the mark of an officer from the equite estate (people from the senatorial class wore tunics with a broad hem).

Suetonius continues:

> My father told me that Otho hated all wars. So much so that at one time, he became visibly numb with horror when, during a party, someone mentioned the deaths of Cassius and Brutus. He would not have gone against Galba—so my father claimed—if it had not been for his strong conviction that the matter could be brought to an end without a fight. Then, after the battle of Bedriacum, the sight of a private drove him to take his own life. The soldier had brought the news of the defeat, but no one believed him. Some accused him of lying, others of cowardice and running away from the battlefield. At this, the soldier pierced himself with his sword at the feet of the emperor. And he, seeing this, shouted: "No! I will not endanger such honest and noble men!" [44]

So much the biographer speaking on the authority of an eyewitness. Plutarch, who also wrote a life of Otho, describes the episode differently. Here is his version:

> First, uncertain reports came from the battlefield of Bedriacum. But then a handful of wounded arrived; these were the unmistakable harbingers of disaster. Still, Otho's friends did everything they could to keep up his spirits. They urged him to remain calm, determined, and courageous. The morale of the soldiers was excellent. None of them thought about retreating or leaving the ranks; nobody proposed to go over to the enemy or made any move to save himself. Everyone stood at the gate of Otho's quarters. When the emperor finally came out to them, they grabbed his hands, shouting and begging, and fell at his feet.
>
> Crying, they asked him not to leave, not to abandon them to the mercy of the enemy. They offered him their bodies and souls. They

---

[44] Ibid.

swore that they were ready to fight for him to their last breath. It was then that one of them pulled his sword from its scabbard and shouted:

"For you, emperor, all are ready to do this!" and he stabbed himself in the heart.

But even his life was in vain. At that moment, no one could convince Otho or dissuade him from the resolution he had already taken. With a calm expression on his face, he looked around and said:

"I believe today is a much happier day than they day when you made me emperor. Only now can I truly appreciate the greatness of your spirit. But do not deprive me of something even greater—the opportunity to give my life for so many great Romans! If I am worthy to rule the Empire, it is also fitting that I do not spare my life for the sake of it. I understand perfectly well that the victory of the Rhine legions is neither complete nor lasting. The Danube army is only a few days' march away and is already descending towards the Adriatic. Asia, Syria, Egypt, and the army fighting in Judea are all on our side. The Senate is with us, and we have the women and children of our enemies in our hands as hostages.

"But this war is not in defense of Italy against Hannibal, Pyrrhus, or the Cimbrii! Here, Romans attack Romans. In this way, we are both damaging our common homeland. And therefore, it does not matter whether we win or lose. What good is a victory if it brings misfortune to the homeland?

"That's why I have decided that it is more proper for me to die than to reign. I do not think that I can be as useful to the Romans by conquering as I can be by offering myself as a sacrifice for peace and harmony. Nor can I give Italy a better gift than to spare her another such a gloomy day!" [45]

Tacitus presents the scene in a similar way but makes no mention of the soldier's suicide. And yet, that fact is absolutely certain! It was confirmed by an eyewitness, i.e., Suetonius's father, as well as by the well-informed Plutarch. It is also mentioned by a later historian,

---

[45] Plutarch, *Life of Otho*, 18

Cassius Dio, who had many original documents at his disposal. Therefore, Tacitus's omission of this incident was probably intentional and significant and is characteristic of the writing technique of the great author. Apparently, he decided that including the scene would come across as melodramatic and unbelievable. Yet, his version of Otho's speech is similar in content to what Plutarch gives us, even if it is stylistically different and more rhetorical. According to him, the emperor's first words were:

> My life would be too dearly purchased if I bought it with your spirit and your courage!

It is clearly a paraphrase of the words heard by Suetonius's father. Then, Tacitus has Otho express very masculine and Roman thoughts, formulated in a very artful way:

> The more hope you breathe into me to keep me alive, the more beautiful death seems to me. We have tested each other, my fate and I. Do not count the brevity of time: it is more difficult to take a proper measure of happiness that one will enjoy but for a short time. This civil war was started by Vitellius. The armed struggle for power emerged from that quarter. But it is in my power to end it. Posterity will judge Otho with this in mind. Let Vitellius enjoy the company of his brother, his wife, and his children! I require neither vengeance nor consolation. Others may have held power longer, but no one will lay it down as bravely as I do.
>
> Should I be indifferent to the fact that so many young Romans, so many brave cohorts, will fall one after another, thereby weakening the state? Rather, I shall go away knowing that you were prepared to die for me and but will live. But let's not hold back any longer, I—your salvation, and you—my decision. It is a testimony of pusillanimity to talk much about ultimate matters. And let the fact that I do not whine be proof of the strength of my resolution. Only those who want to live complain and accuse gods and men. [46]

All our sources agree about what happened next, and the minor details where they vary only round out the story.

---

[46] Tacitus, *Histories* II 46-47

# OTHO'S DEATH

The emperor remained calm. He said goodbye to the people around him, honoring them with a hug or a kiss, according to their office and age. He upbraided those who had tears in their eyes. He strongly encouraged his dignitaries to leave Brixellum as quickly as possible because by remaining with him, they risked incurring the wrath of the victor. He even saw to assigning wagons and ships to the departing men and preparing permits and passes for them. When issuing these orders, he also remembered those who were not in the camp, many of them in Mutina, some distance behind the army.

Then, Otho locked himself in his rooms. He burned all his own writings and all the letters he had received from people who too earnestly declared themselves as his supporters—he burned them for fear that they might be used against them. Then he wrote two letters: one to his sister with words of consolation, the other to Statilia Messalina, Nero's widow, whom he had intended to marry, asking her to dispose of his ashes. He then divided among his household staff all the cash he had with him, and he did so fairly, to each according to his merits, and not at all in the usual wasteful manner of those who no longer attach importance to money but want to leave the best possible memory of themselves. In turn, he turned to his nephew, the teenage Salvius Cocceianus. The boy was terrified, so he comforted him, praising him for his affection but rebuking him for showing fear. He said:

"Vitellius will certainly not be so inhuman as not to reward my decision to yield to him. He will see that I deserve his gratitude. Surely, he will spare my family. After all, I do not capitulate in a desperate situation but do so completely voluntarily for I still have troops ready to continue the fight. I have gained enough glory for myself and position for my descendants and need no more. Since Julius Caesar, I am the first to hand over imperial power to a new family voluntarily. So go boldly into life and never forget that Otho was your uncle. But do not be too attached to my memory, for that could be dangerous."

These words proved prophetic—especially the last sentence. Vitellius spared the boy's life. However, twenty years later, another emperor, Domitian, sentenced Salvius Cocceianus to death because he dared to celebrate the anniversary of the birth of his uncle Otho—even though Otho had warned him not to cultivate his tradition.

Otho was now left alone. He rested. Perhaps he would have taken his life already then, in the afternoon of April 15, if a sudden noise, screaming, and clash of weapons had not suddenly reached his ears. It was reported to him that his soldiers attacked the departing senators and dignitaries, trying to hold them by force, showering them with insults and threats as traitors and cowards. There was a danger of lynchings.

Otho sighed and said:

"Let us have another day of life."

He went out, scolded the ringleaders of the disturbance, and returned only once he made sure that peace and order were restored. He commanded that the door to his room be left open, and late into the evening, he received all who needed to see him. Then he drank a cup of cold water, took two daggers, tested their blades, and selected one. He closed the door, lay down, and soon fell asleep. His servants could hear his even and calm breathing. He woke up at dawn and summoned the freedman to whom he had entrusted the care of the departing senators. The man reported that everything was fine and that they all had received everything they had requested. When Otho heard this, he answered him kindly but in a tone of command:

"Now leave me and show yourself to the soldiers if you do not want to be accused of helping me die."

When the freedman closed the door behind him, the emperor took out his dagger, set it with the point up, held it firmly with both hands and pressed down upon it with his whole body so that it went in under the left nipple and right into the heart. He groaned loudly and painfully, but only once. The servants listening anxiously at the door immediately raised a shrill cry of lamentation, which, taken up by the guards and cohorts, soon spread throughout the entire camp. The Praetorian Prefect, Plautius Firmus, was one of the first to break down the door and burst into the room. The emperor was still alive. He gestured vaguely as if trying to cover the wound while pointing to it.

He was buried that very same day, 16 April AD 69.[47]

## THE GRAVE AND THE REPUTATION OF OTHO

In his last conversations, Otho asked to be buried as soon as possible. He was afraid that if his corpse were to fall in the hands of the victors, soldiers would cut off his head and defile it, just as three months earlier, with the silent consent of Otho, the head of Galba had been mistreated, and just a month earlier, the head of the self-proclaimed Nero, killed on the island of Kythnos.

The Praetorians carried his bier on their shoulders. They wore full ceremonial armor. After they placed the body on the pyre, many cried, some hugged the corpse while others pushed through the crowd to touch the hand of the dead emperor. And then they lit the fire. As the pyre blazed, several soldiers committed suicide, stabbing themselves with their own swords. Similar incidents repeated over the next few days among the Praetorian Guard, in a kind of collective psychosis which was difficult to understand even for the contemporaries. For even though the Praetorians had brought Otho to the throne, surely he reigned too short to win their hearts. Besides, it was clear that no large-scale retribution was to be expected from Vitellius.

Plutarch says:

"They buried Otho's ashes in an ordinary grave, striking neither for its appearance nor for the rhetoric of the epitaph. While in Brixellum, I saw this modest monument and the inscription on it. It reads: *Dis Manibus Marci Othonis*—"To the Shadows of Marcus Otho."[48]

---

[47] Tacitus, *Histories*, II 48—49; Plutarch, *Life of Otho*, 16—17; Suetonius, *Life of Otho*, 11

[48] Plutarch, *Life of Otho*, 18.

Upon his arrival at the scene in May 69, victorious Vitellius saw the grave with a different eye. He said aloud, not hiding his contempt for the defeated man:

"He got the monument he deserved!"

They handed him the dagger with which Otho had killed himself. He ordered it sent to Cologne on the Rhine and deposited in the temple of Mars. It was a symbolic gesture: on January 3, when the legionaries proclaimed Vitellius emperor amid tumultuous demonstrations, someone brought him a sword kept in that temple; it had supposedly once belonged to Julius Caesar, and the new claimant to the throne had it paraded through the streets of Cologne. Now, he returned the favor to Mars by sending him the blade that had dispatched his rival.

We should add that most of his contemporaries thought about Otho's voluntary death with admiration and respect. It was commonly said that by taking his life, he had acted like a true Roman. Even Tacitus, generally very harsh to all the rulers of his era, wrote magnanimously:

> Thanks to his two deeds, of which one was the most shameful and the other the most wonderful, Otho earned for himself both bad and good fame in posterity. [49]

The shameful act was, of course, his overthrow of Galba. That this was a common opinion is confirmed by Suetonius, who ends his life of the emperor with the words:

> Many people condemned him when he lived, but after he died, they praised him. They now said that he had killed Galba not so much to seize power as to restore freedom to the Republic. [50]

And twenty years later, the poet Martial dedicated the following epigram to the memory of the unfortunate emperor:

> As the scales of the civil war were turning,

---

[49] Tacitus, *Histories*, II 50.
[50] Suetonius, *Life of Otho*, 12.

Otho the effeminate could still have won,
But unwilling to pay the tribute of blood to the god war,
He preferred to deal himself a sure blow to the chest.
In life, Cato had towered over Otho,
But did he overshadow the emperor in death?[51]

"Cato" meant, of course, Cato the Younger, who in 46 BC, after Julius Caesar had destroyed the Senate armies in the battle of Thapsus, committed suicide in Utica, thereby becoming a byword for devotion to Republican principles. The juxtaposition of these two figures alone was very flattering for Otho.

But the satirist Juvenal, petty and mean, could not forgive Otho that he had carried a mirror with him on the expedition and supposedly checked his appearance just before the battle began, nor that he applied soggy bread to his face, something neither Semiramis nor Cleopatra ever did—the most famous queens of the effeminate and licentious East.[52]

## VESPASIAN AT THE GATES OF JERUSALEM

The news about the outcome of the war in Italy did not arrive in the East until the second half of May, by which time noteworthy events had taken place in Palestine.

Vespasian had stayed in his headquarters in Caesarea Martima, impatiently awaiting reports from Rome and the Po. Yet, all the while, he closely observed what was happening among the insurgents, especially in Jerusalem. He was able to confirm (no doubt with satisfaction) that the fratricidal infighting in Palestine only intensified, just as he had predicted.

Simon had entered the capital at the invitation of its residents, who, though they had been able, with the help of the Idumeans, to

---

[51] Martial, *Epigrams*, VI 32
[52] Juvenal, *Satires*, II 102-109

drive the Zealots out of the city and into the Temple precinct, could not dislodge them from it. The Temple towered over the city, had powerful walls, and was equipped with various war machines captured from the Romans three years earlier. There was no shortage of food or other supplies stored in the buildings surrounding the courtyard. However, the Zealots had irretrievably lost all the riches they had accumulated by looting the houses and palaces of their opponents during the months of their rule over Jerusalem. Simon's men looted it from them within the first few hours of entering the city. They were less successful in their attack on the Temple. Showered with a hail of bullets from the temple walls, they suffered significant losses and withdrew out of range. Meanwhile, the Zealots reinforced their defenses. Having built four wooden towers, they placed them at various points near the perimeter wall and placed archers and machines in them. This allowed them to wreak havoc on the attackers whenever they tried to approach the Temple walls.

And thus, Simon of Giora, the great master of guerrilla warfare, elusive, agile, and quick, now found himself stumped: confined within the city walls and forced to carry out regular siege operations, he was unable to show meaningful progress to the sincere chagrin of those who had summoned him into the city.

Around mid-May, Vespasian decided that the time was ripe to take action: a new campaign was needed to overrun the rest of Judea and siege Jerusalem. The latest news from Italy probably encouraged the commander to go into the field, for they spoke of the successes of Otho's troops near Placentia and Cremona; they also spoke of the rapid march of the Danube army rushing to the emperor's aid. Everything led Vespasian to believe that the winner would be the emperor to whom Vespasian and his soldiers had sworn an oath of allegiance rather than the rebel Vitellius. And if so, there was no longer any reason to delay. The best season for offensive operations had just begun and he decided to lead his legions into Judea.

Meanwhile, Otho's ashes had reposed in a modest grave in Brixellum for almost a month, and the arrogant victor, Vitellius, visiting the battlefield of Bedriacum, looked with delight at the piles of dead and fought off the nausea caused by the stench of decaying corpses with generous helpings of red wine.

Advancing into Judea, Vespasian took the old power base of Simon—Accrabene—without a fight and then marched straight towards Jerusalem, taking into slavery or killing all the inhabitants who had not escaped in time.

He also sent a corps led by Cerealis to the south, to Idumea. Cerealis sacked everything Simon had not and took Hebron *en marche*, killing all men of military age and burning the town. And thus, by the end of June, the insurgents had lost everything except a narrow strip of land between Jerusalem and Masada, 35 miles in length.

It seemed obvious that the end was near. Jerusalem, lonely and locked in civil war, deprived of any hope of rescue, was going to fall, probably before the winter rains. Many thought that the mere appearance of Vespasian at the city gates would break the bravest hearts. And yet now, to universal amazement and surprise, Vespasian stopped. Suddenly, he interrupted all operations, turned back from the heart of Judea, and... hastened back to Caesarea.

Why?

Josephus says that it was only there, in Caesarea Maritima, that the general learned about the death of Otho. But both chronological considerations and the logic of events suggest that Vespasian had received the news earlier, while still in Judea, but decided to keep it secret and allowed it to be announced only when he returned to his headquarters.

This delay created the wrong impression—it fooled even Josephus—that the report about the real situation in Italy arrived only after Vespasian had reached Caesarea.


## PROPHECIES

As terrified as the people in Jerusalem had been to hear of Vespasian's approach, they were now suddenly relieved when, contrary to all ominous predictions, the Roman leader stopped his inexorable advance and—departed. Only a little later, but undoubtedly still in June, came the explanation of the Roman departure: the defeat and death of Otho. The news was, of course, very encouraging. Since the start of the war in Palestine three years earlier, two Roman emperors died by their own hand by stabbing themselves with a dagger, and a third was murdered in the Forum: three violent and bloody deaths of the Head of the Beast. Even the self-proclaimed Nero was murdered on the island of Kythnos. Everyone noted these apparently miraculous developments, not only the priests and the learned in the scriptures but also the common man. Only a blind man or a man of bad faith could refuse to see the obvious: that these deaths were the work of the Lord, who had caused the Romans to quarrel and rip out each others' entrails like wild beasts.

Thus, suddenly, a new breeze of hope blew across the land. The general thinking went something like this:

Judea had suffered terribly. Her towns and villages burned down; tens of thousands of men died in battle; their women and children were driven into slavery. What was even more painful, fratricidal massacres were taking place in Jerusalem, at the threshold of the Holy of Holies: the bravest sons of the land consumed by hate and vengeance murdered each other. It was all true. But the most important thing was not yet lost. Not yet.[53] It was still possible to believe that a miracle would come, perhaps at the last moment. Rome had to collapse, just as Babylon had collapsed before her and mighty Assyria before her.

New prophecies were heard in Jerusalem, the harbingers of the future triumphant hymns to be sung over the ruins of the fallen enemy city. In their content, style, and imagery, they sounded similar to those that had been spoken by Daniel and Jeremiah and were soon to be spoken in *The Revelation of Saint John* because all apocalyptic literature conforms to the same trope:

---

[53] The Polish reader of these words will reflect that the first line of the Polish national anthem reads: "Poland is not yet lost."

Babylon the Great has fallen, fallen! It became a place of ghosts and jackals, a shelter of evil spirits, a nest of birds unclean and disgusting because all its peoples had drunk the wine of his fornication, the kings of the earth committed fornication with him, and the merchants of various lands became rich from the abundance of his splendor. Repay him as he has paid you, doubly give it back to him according to his deeds! Give him the cup in which he used to mix wine for you, and pour out a double measure for him! For all in one day, plagues, death, pain, and famine will descend upon him, and he will be burned with fire. The kings of the earth, who had fornicated with him and took pleasure in him, will weep and wail over him when they see the smoke of his burning. And the great Angel of the Lord shall lift a great millstone and throw it into the sea, saying:

"This is how Great Babylon is lost, lost, and never to be found again. No one will hear its guitarists, its singers, its flute players, its trumpeters. No master of any skill will be found. The millstone will not whirr, and the light of the candle will not shine, nor will the joyful voice of the bridegroom and the bride be heard![54]

## VITELLIUS AT BEDRIACUM

Will the Battle of Bedriacum throw Rome into the abyss? Will Rome fall like that millstone cast by the Angel of the Lord? Will the Beast that sits on the Seven Hills be swept away? These questions may seem to us an exaggerated and pathetic metaphor, but they expressed the fear and horror of the civil war aroused in the Italians of those days. Let us remember that no one was able to predict the outcome of the war.

And the battle had been unusually bloody, as bloody as the bloodiest battles of the last civil war of a century ago: over forty thousand men died at Bedriacum. In his *Life of Otho*, Plutarch

––––––––––––––––––––––––––––––

[54] This is not a quote, but a literary invention of the author in the style of the Biblical prophecy.

describes his impressions of the battlefield:

> When many years later, I walked over the battlefield with Mestrius Florus during the civil war, he had sided with Otho, not out of conviction but out of necessity—he pointed out an old temple to me and said:

> "I came here the day after the battle and saw a pile of corpses so high that it reached to the top of the building. As I looked, I tried to understand why this place had been fought over with such ferocity, but I was not able to establish the reason. And no one was able to tell me anything certain about this matter."[55]

Otho's dead were not buried. The victors left them to the dogs and birds. They did this out of a primitive, barbaric contempt for the defeated. When Vitellius passed this way forty days later, at the end of May, the men of his entourage, legionaries hardened in battles with the Germans, could barely bear the sight and fetor of thousands of decaying corpses. But the emperor, a man of fifty-something, very tall, with a belly bloated by gluttony and a face red from constant drinking—looked around with undisguised satisfaction. After a while, he uttered words that were well remembered and repeated with horror:

> How sweetly smells the dead enemy. And how much sweeter a dead citizen![56]

But he was also feeling nauseous. So, he drank a lot of wine and ordered it to be given to his entourage. The battlefield must have seemed all the more shocking to them because they had come from nearby Cremona along a road beautifully decorated with laurel branches and rose flowers by the inhabitants servilely welcoming their new ruler. Here and there, altars had been erected where animals were sacrificed to the genius of Vitellius as if he were already divine. But all his men saw near Bedriacum were trampled fields, crops, and vineyards; even trees stood dead, stripped of their branches and bark,

---

[55] Plutarch, *Life of Otho*, 14
[56] Ibid.

and some overturned as if they too had taken part in the battle of giants.

As sometimes happens in similar circumstances, some officers who had participated in the battle enjoyed playing the role of guides. They eloquently recreated the course of the engagement. They indicated the starting positions and maneuvers of individual formations, their own and the enemy's. They led the emperor towards the places of the fiercest fighting. Everyone tried to highlight their own courage, energy, and brilliant decision-making under stress. They could also fantasize freely since their opponents lay dead, unable to gainsay them.

Yet, only part of Otho's forces died at Bedriacum. Rejoice as he may, Vitellius was unable to multiply the dead. The words that a dead enemy smells beautiful came straight from his heart because, for a month, he had been wondering what he may have to do with the defeated survivors.

They surrendered, it is true, but it was obvious that many felt irreconcilable hatred towards the winner. If not for the suicide of Otho, the surviving Prateorians and the Danube army would have continued the fight with fierce determination. They capitulated only because they lost their leader. The soldiers saw themselves as betrayed and abandoned, not defeated.

The emperor would have loved to order all these formations to be decimated, disbanded, and exiled to the outskirts of the Empire, but that was impossible, because faced with such a prospect, the defeated would take up arms again. Therefore, he needed to proceed patiently and thoughtfully.

## THE FATE OF THE DEFEATED

The new ruler of the Empire dealt with the Praetorians first. Immediately after receiving the news of the victory, while still in Gaul, he dismissed all of them from the ranks of the army. He did it in an apparently "magnanimous" way because he awarded them *missio honesta*, i.e., an honorary severance pay they would normally have received only after sixteen years of impeccable service. But that very same edict ordered them to hand their weapons to their commanding officers.

Both decisions were wise and understandable. After all, no one could demand that the emperor entrust the mission of guarding his person to people who, until yesterday, had opposed him with swords in hand. On the other hand, it is easy to understand that the Praetorians took this as a heavy blow, a humiliation, and a failure in life. Until that day, they had been the elite unit of the army. They considered themselves the chosen of the chosen, the lords of the Imperial court, the capital, and the entire Empire. Showered with favors and privileges, they hoped for an even better fate after victory.

And now, suddenly, everything changed. They were to be put out to pasture, scattered throughout various towns in Italy, despised and mistrusted, men in their prime with nothing to do, pensioned off into aimless vegetation. It is hardly surprising that they were eager for revenge and were only waiting for an opportune moment to regain their lost social position. They waited all the more impatiently because, following their demobilization, they lived in constant fear, for the new regime soon began to seek out and imprison some of them: a total of one hundred and twenty were put in chains.

Only later was the reason for the arrests revealed: letters signed by them, addressed to Otho, had been discovered in the archives on the Palatine Hill, letters in which they had demanded rewards for services rendered during the overthrow of Galba. All those thus implicated were sentenced and executed as traitors because they had broken the oath they had made to Galba, their commander-in-chief. This decision of Vitellius was certainly just. He simply reaffirmed the principle that a Praetorian must never betray his emperor, even if Vitellius himself had rebelled against him.

No one questioned the authenticity of the Palatine letters, yet many who had not written such letters soon began to fear that their turn was coming on some other excuse. Maybe even someone might fabricate such letters?

A different policy was applied to the legions. Dissolving them was out of the question because such a decision would weaken the already frayed defenses of the border. However, many centurions who had eagerly declared for Otho were now arrested and beheaded by the order of the emperor. Then, various formations began to be moved to different provinces to break up the cohesion of the units.

Three legions from the lower Danube, that is, from the then province of Moesia, had rushed to Otho's defense, but they only managed to get as far as Aquileia and never took part in the fighting. These were the IIIrd *Gallica*, the VIIth *Claudiana*, and the VIIIth *Augusta*. The news of Otho's death surprised the soldiers so much that they roughed up the messengers bringing the bad news as if they were the perpetrators of the misfortune and then tore up the banners, on which some overzealous officers had quickly inscribed the name of Vitellius. They also did not forget to loot the army's treasury.

Eventually, the disturbances were put down, and the legions returned to their camps on the Danube. However, mutual distrust and ill will remained on both sides. Ordinary soldiers, in particular, remained convinced that, in time, the emperor would take vengeance for the Aquileian riots and, above all, for the act of defiling his name.

Certain elements of the VIIth Legion, with the nickname *Gemina Galbiana,* and the XIth *Claudiana* had fought at Bedriacum under Otho's banners. After the defeat, they returned to their camps, the VIIth to Carnuntum on the Danube, slightly east of today's Vienna, and the XIth to Dalmatia, that is, to the coast of today's Croatia.

The entire *Prima adiutrix,* the Rescuer, which had been formed by Nero from the soldiers of the Misenian navy and inaugurated by Otho, took part in the battle—it was its first battle, its baptism of fire. In the initial phase of the struggle, the legion made a bold attack and broke the front ranks of the opponent, capturing the eagles of Vitellius's XXIst Legion. Later, however, it succumbed to the furious counterattack of the more experienced soldiers from the Rhine, gave ground, lost many of its battle emblems, and even its commander, Orphidius Benignus, killed in action. Now, the legion was ordered to take up service in Spain.

The XIVth Legion was sent even further away. It hadn't made it to Bedriacum in time, so the soldiers of the XIVth were loud in proclaiming that *they* had not been defeated and assured everyone who would listen that had they arrived in time, the battle would most certainly have taken a completely different turn. Directly before the war, they had been stationed in Dalmatia or Pannonia but were originally a British legion. Nero had brought them to the Mediterranean, for he wished to incorporate them into an army he planned to take East, beyond the Caspian Sea, in the footsteps of Alexander of Macedon. They owed this honorable distinction to the fame of their bravery, and they did not want to give up that reputation. They were now ordered back to Britain, with Batavian cohorts from the lower Rhine to accompany them for part of the journey.

However, in Turin, an argument between two soldiers of the two formations nearly ended in a pitched battle between the units that had hated and competed with each other for years. Fortunately, some Praetorians present in Turin and not yet disarmed came to the aid of the legionaries. This stopped the Batavians and prevented wholesale slaughter, and the XIVth Legion marched off to Britain. They left behind the smoking ruins of many private houses as a reminder of their short stay in Turin: the fire had started from their unextinguished campfires. The Batavians were soon thereafter sent to the Lower Rhine, for although they had shown exemplary loyalty, Vitellius was afraid of their untamed, truly Germanic arrogance.

In some respects, the XIIIth Legion suffered the worst fate of all the Othonic formations. It had not covered itself with glory at Bedriacum, for it retreated before the famous Vth legion, nicknamed since Caesar's times *Alaudae* ("Of the Lark"). Victorious Vitellius, mocking the defeated, now dealt them another disgrace. He ordered the men of the XIIIth to build amphitheaters in Cremona and Bononia, where he planned to stage gladiatorial games. The crowd in both cities mocked the legionaries as they carried heavy stones and beams like slaves. The soldiers endured all humiliations in silence and with helpless anger, but they swore revenge against the emperor and the townspeople. After completing the work, they left the lowlands on the Po and returned to their former camp in Poetovio.[57]

## VITELLIUS AND NERO

Indeed, the victor did not deny himself the pleasure, even delight, of watching gladiator fights; he devoted many hours and days to this entertainment in both cities. He loved watching fights between armed pairs of opponents and all other games, races, and competitions. He had spent his boyhood and early youth on Capri among the favorites of Tiberius, serving in all kinds of debauchery. This apparently helped his father's career. Then, he became one of Caligula's closest companions as an expert in the art of chariot driving. Accidentally hit by the emperor's chariot, he suffered a permanent injury to his legs. All this recommended him to Nero. This and his honest enthusiasm for the emperor-artist's music and singing talents.

However, in all fairness, we must say that Vitellius showed sympathy for Nero and his works even when he no longer needed to flatter anyone—unless he was trying to gain the favor of the people among whom Nero remained a dear memory. When Vitellius arrived in Rome, he made offerings to the shadows of Nero in Campus Martius, publicly and in the presence of a large group of high-ranking priests. And during a certain feast, he turned to a popular *kitharist* with a loud admonition:

"And now sing us some song of our Lord!"

The *kitharist* understood immediately what was required and intoned one of Nero's hymns, by which he won Vitellius's applause, soon echoed by all the present.

That lay still in the future, but already during Vitellius's slow progress to the capital, various people whom Nero had once favored—

---

[57] Today Ptuj in Slovenia

112

or who would certainly have pleased him—flocked to the victor in great numbers: actors, dancers, singers, drivers of racing chariots, jesters. And all towns along the route welcomed their new master ceremoniously. No one stinted on garlands, triumphant arches, altars, feasts, and games. And there was a good throng to welcome!

## THE VICTOR'S PROGRESS

There marched with Vitellius sixty thousand armed men of various formations plus countless henchmen, camp followers, clients, courtiers, and servants. And everywhere along the way, new streams joined this mighty human river. Senators and equites with their retinues hurried to pay homage, demonstrate loyalty, and find access to the fount of grace, wealth, and honor. None wanted to be last. The most eager were those who had good reasons to fear the new regime.

These masses now descended like locust on the various towns along the way, eating up all the resources, filling them with excrement and refuse, trampling fields, orchards, and vineyards. And it was already June, wheat was ripe, and trees were bending under the weight of fruit. But this year, the harvest was to be gathered not by the peasants but by soldiers. Most men in the army of Vitellius had come straight from the Rhine and had never seen such a beautiful country so completely developed and domesticated and terraformed into such abundantly cultivated land. Many were simply and literally barbarians, and they behaved at every step as if they were in a conquered country. They robbed, devastated, beat, and raped with complete impunity.

Discipline in Vitellius's ranks was poor. From the moment of victory, no one paid it any attention, and the situation was made worse by a dangerous incident in May before the emperor's visit to the battlefield near Bedriacum. The emperor gave a feast for various dignitaries in Ticinum, i.e., in today's Pavia, and his soldiers took the opportunity to party themselves. Two of them fought a mock duel to entertain the others, a duel from which a Gaul emerged the winner, a man from the native auxiliary, who laid flat his opponent, a soldier of the glorious Vth legion with the nickname *Alaudae*. The defeated man's friends rushed in a horde to avenge the shame and humiliation. The incident soon turned into a regular bloody battle in which two auxiliary cohorts were cut down. The fight would have lasted longer with disastrous consequences for the entire army had clouds of dust and flashes of weapons not appeared on the horizon. Someone shouted that it was the XIVth legion—the one that had fought with the Batavians in Turin only a few days ago. Immediately, hue and cry went up that the legion had certainly rebelled, turned back, and was on the attack, hoping to surprise the emperor and avenge Otho's death! Frantic, their tribunes began to issue incoherent and contradictory orders and prepare a defense against the enemy. The alarm was, of course, false. The XIVth was already crossing the Alps, and the approaching unit was the Vth's own read guard.

Thus, the misunderstanding was cleared up and the situation prevented from getting completely out of hand, but mutual distrust and hostility among the units accompanying Vitellius remained, and quarrels and skirmishes continued as they moved towards Rome. But in their attitude to the local population, the soldiers acted in exemplary unison, oppressing them ruthlessly.

This relaxation of discipline also resulted from the fact that Vitellius, after an unexpectedly quick victory, sharply reduced the size of his army, which he had enormously expanded, expecting a long war against Otho. He has now sent back over the Alps some of his Gallic auxiliaries, reduced the headcount of others in various ways and granted all kinds of holidays and leave. The general idea was correct as Vitellius aimed to reduce spending on the armed forces. However, it made it easy to leave the ranks and this contributed to the general indifference to camp discipline.

The emperor would certainly have held his people with a firmer hand had it not been for the ease of his victory, which made him feel invincible. At the beginning of June, after Vitellius's visit to the Bedriacum battlefield and the gladiatorial games in Bononia, scouts

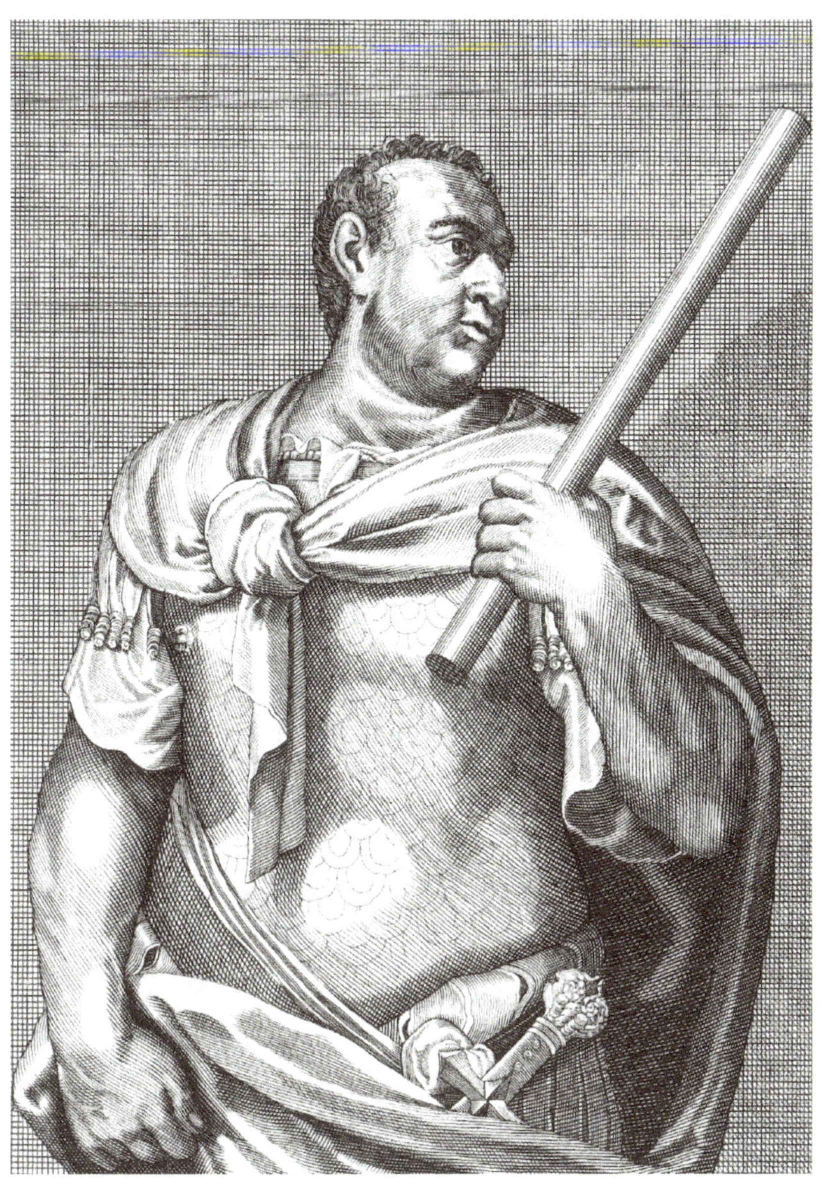

Vitellius

for special missions, so-called *speculatores,* appeared at court. They had been sent East immediately after the death of Otho; having now returned from their mission, they unanimously reported that the armies and governors of Syria, Judea, and Egypt had all, without exception or hesitation, sworn allegiance to the new emperor. Vitellius, who had been secretly worried about a possible rebellion in the East, now breathed a sigh of relief. He was now the indisputable, universally recognized, one and only ruler of the Empire. He no longer had any rivals. All provinces and armies submitted to him. He could give himself over entirely to the pleasures of power, feasts, and spectacles.

## VITELLIUS ENTERS ROME

Advancing very slowly through the towns and cities of Italy, the emperor finally arrived at the capital. It was almost mid-July. He stopped seven miles from the city at the Milvian Bridge, where the Flaminian Way crossed the Tiber. Food was distributed abundantly to the soldiers, and meanwhile, crowds of people were arriving from Rome and wandering around the camp to gawk at the terrible warriors from the Rhine. It had been a long time since the capital had seen an army this large and with so many barbarians. Some of the soldiers were dressed in the furs of wild animals and were armed with enormously long spears, never before seen in Italy. The common people, as always malicious, mocking, and hostile to strangers, did not miss any opportunity to make fun of the clumsy Gallic and Germanic simpletons. Sometimes, a wag cut off the sword belt that went across the shoulder and then asked in a booming voice, imitating the threatening tone of a centurion: "And where is your belt, private?"

But the uncouth victors from the Rhine had no forbearance for these sophisticated urban jokes. Instead of laughing good-heartedly, they grabbed their swords and hit out blindly at whomever they could reach among the circle of laughing onlookers, the guilty or the innocent. Similar scenes played out all over the city because the soldiers went in as sightseeing tourists even before the emperor formally entered Rome. They were eager to see with their own eyes the cradle and capital of that Empire, which they had served faithfully, keeping watch over its distant borders; that city whose splendor and riches were the subject of endless fantastic tales among the barbarians on the Rhine.

But the main goal of their expeditions was the Forum Romanum. Not so much because it constituted the heart of the metropolis and sported its most magnificent buildings, but because they each wanted to see the place near the Pool of Curtius, where just seven months earlier, on January 15, the emperor Galba was murdered by Otho's Praetorians.[58] For these barbarians, as for every barbarian of every era, the newest history seemed the most important, for they simply did not know any other. And, like all barbarians everywhere, they wanted to follow the famous and the celebrated, assuming that what was famous had to be important.[59]

These armed newcomers from the north, unaccustomed to the crowds of the city and even to pavements, moved clumsily, tripped on cobblestones, and slipped and fell on marble steps, sparking general ridicule. They pushed unnecessarily and brutally through the densest crowd, bumped passers-by, unwilling or unable to step out of their way. This caused arguments and fights. Frequently, patrols of peace, commanded by imperial centurions, increased the atmosphere of anxiety by interfering in ways that showed their unfamiliarity with city life.

When the day of the ceremonial entry came—it was already mid-July—Vitellius put on the purple Imperial cloak, strapped on a short sword, mounted a magnificent horse, and headed towards the capital along the Flaminian Way. This, of course, gave the impression that he meant to enter Rome as a conqueror. The sight of the emperor

---

[58] It is easy to imagine these rude barbarians taking selfies at the site.

[59] An echo of the idea that modernity is a result of a "vertical barbarian invasion."

in full military gear and carrying weapons shocked Romans, causing widespread outrage. It was an ancient and sacred custom that no one was allowed to enter the city in this way—unless in a triumph following the defeat of external enemies and with the permission of the Senate. Ultimately, reasonable arguments prevailed. Vitellius threw off his imperial cloak, unbelted his sword, and put on a toga bordered with a wide purple stripe, such as all senators wore. And the procession resumed.

Tacitus, who was at least fourteen at the time, may have been an eyewitness. In any case, it is hard to escape such an impression when reading his description of the entry in his *History*.

First came the eagles of the four legions that accompanied the emperor. They were: the XXIst *Rapax* from Vindonisia, today's Windisch in Switzerland, on the river Aar; the Ist *Italica* from Lugdunum on the Rhône, today's Lyon; the Vth *Alaude* from Xanten on the Lower Rhine; and the XXII *Primigenia* from Mainz on the Middle Rhine. Before the eagles marched the prefects of the camps, tribunes, and the highest-ranking centurions, all in snow-white tunics. On both sides of this host came the emblems of the four legions, which, although they had belonged to Vitellius's army, were now guarding the borders. Next came the emblems of the twelve cavalry squadrons, and behind them marched the dense ranks of the legionaries. Each hundred came led by its centurion, all fully armed. They gleamed with the shiny metal of their armor and helmets. They bore all the battle decorations on their chests that hung on decorative chains around their necks. The procession ended with thirty-four cohorts, recruited from various border peoples and armed in many different ways. It was an impressive display of the military might of the Empire. No one in Rome had seen so many different units in over a hundred years.[60]

The procession marched towards the city along Via Flaminia. On their left, they passed the Garden Hill and the tomb of the Domitians, where Nero's porphyry sarcophagus stood. If, in passing,

---

[60] Tacitus, *Histories*, II 89

Vitellius looked at that building even briefly, he perhaps reflected on the vicissitudes of the past twelve months. After all, he was the third successor of the man lying in that tomb in less than a year.

But if he did, he did not know—because the reports of this had not yet arrived in Rome—that on that very day, a fourth competitor entered the competition for the crown.

## REBELLION IN THE EAST: DATES

On July 1, AD 69, the Prefect of Egypt, Tiberius Julius Alexander, stood before the assembled ranks of his two legions—the IIIrd *Cyrenaica* and the XXIInd *Deitoriana*—in their camp in an eastern suburb of Alexandria. He announced to the assembled officers and soldiers that from that day on, they had a new emperor and ruler: Flavius Vespasian, the current legate and commander of the troops fighting in Judea. The ranks responded to the announcement with loud shouts of approval. An oath of allegiance to the new emperor was immediately taken. Citizens of the city made a similarly eager proclamation shortly thereafter: Tiberius Alexander appeared before them at a rally in the city's hippodrome.[61]

On July 3, as Vespasian left his residence in Caesarea Maritima early in the morning, a crowd of officers and soldiers assembled for their daily briefing greeted him with a unanimous and thunderous cry: *Salve Imperator*! They welcomed him not as a legate but by a name that belonged to the emperor alone.

Suddenly, a crowd of armed men gathered in the square in front of the command building. They were the soldiers of the XVth Legion *Apollinaris*, of its auxiliary cohorts and liaison units. Amidst their joyful cries, the title of the ruler was heard more and more loudly: *Imperator Caesar Vespasianus Augustus*. The entire legion, and a little later also the Vth, camped at Emmaus, and the Xth, holding Jericho,

---

[61] Or possibly at the Gymnasium, sources are unclear (Translator's note)

pledged allegiance to their leader as the sole ruler of the Empire.

The governor of Syria, Licinius Mucianus, was in Antioch, impatiently awaiting the news from Palestine. Immediately after he received it, he swore the resident legion, the IVth Scythian, for Vespasian. His men took the ceremony downright enthusiastically. Immediately afterwards, Mucianus went to the theater in the city, where he delivered a very eloquent speech in Greek to the leading citizens of Antioch. He announced that, from now on, Vespasian was their emperor. He explained convincingly that it had to be so for the good of the entire country and therefore, of all humanity. The governor's words were received with a thunderous ovation.

Two other legions, VIth *Ferrata* and XIIth *Fulminata*, were camped on the border of Syria. They took the oath quickly, efficiently, and willingly. And thus, all the armies of the East recognized Vespasian as their ruler before July 15. And all this happened just as Vitellius was preparing his ceremonial entry into Rome, deeply convinced that the whole Empire, from Britain to Syria, lay obediently at his feet.

Both he and Rome were to live in blissful ignorance for several weeks yet.


## REBELLION IN THE EAST: CAUSES

These events raise so many questions! First of all: how could such an unexpected coup succeed so quickly and so completely? How were so many men acting over such widespread areas—so many cities and camps—able to maintain such complete secrecy until the last moment, despite the primitive means of communication at their disposal and then able to synchronize their actions so perfectly?

Further: why did these provinces and armies turn against Vitellius only a month after swearing their allegiance to him? He hadn't been given the opportunity to show how he would rule before they decided to be rid of him.

It is obvious that the coup had been thoroughly prepared.

Various eventualities were foreseen. Various means were used to mold the mood of the army and the civilian population. The whole undertaking had to have had several determined, inventive, and energetic promotors among the most eminent people in the East. And Vitellius, unawares, had paved the way for their action.

One day, scouts from the East reported that the Eastern legions had pledged allegiance to him. However, not wishing to upset the ruler, the scouts never mentioned what seemed to be an important detail: that the ceremony had not been very edifying. The commanders uttered the words of the formula woodenly and indifferently. They asked the gods to favor the new emperor, and the ranks standing before them heard it out with deafening silence. This was especially the case in Judea, although the celebrations there were led by Vespasian, a popular general who wholeheartedly promoted Vitellius's candidacy.

Alas, his soldiers had good reasons for such ostentatious passivity. First of all, changes of rulers had become too frequent. Within a year of Nero's death, the legionaries had sworn allegiance to a new emperor three times: to Galba, Otho, and Vitellius. All of these men were equally unfamiliar and indifferent to them. The army knew full well that each of these three came to the throne over the dead body of his predecessor, all having had an equally weak claim to power.

There was also another reason for their reluctance. The first of the three emperors was initially proclaimed by the Spanish army, the second by the army of the Rhine, and the third by the Praetorians in Rome. In this situation, an irresistible question arose: were the soldiers of the army of East chopped liver that they had to accept humbly and pledge allegiance to whomever other units elected? Don't the men of the East have their own commanders and governors, as worthy to reign, as talented, as energetic, as tested in war and peace? Vitellius's men, arriving in ever-increasing numbers from Italy to supervise Eastern affairs, behaved imperiously and rudely. They were stuck-up and arrogant, even boasting about their physical size since they usually towered over the people of the East. And these Germans made it clear to all that they considered themselves victors and masters of everything and everyone.

Aat the same time, strange, colorful stories began to circulate in the East, perhaps deliberately spread, about the behavior of Vitellius' troops in Rome, about their wantonness, their rapine, and their violence.

Josephus, son of Matthias, the leader of the Jewish uprising in Galilee, captured two years earlier and held in Caesarea Maritima, overheard some of the Roman soldiers' conversations. His account, given in Book IV of *The Jewish War*, though written many years later and much stylized, still carries echoes of those simple and naive words. It seems almost as if we were hearing two guards talking to each other in front of the room where the author sits in shackles, bored by inaction and hungry for any news of the outside world. Let's reimagine his report in the form of such a dialogue: [62]

> FIRST SOLDIER: They overthrow and elevate emperors as they see fit, and what about us? We've been through so much hardship, we have spilled so much blood—our own and the enemy's, our hair has grown grey under our helmets, and what do we get for all this?
>
> SECOND SOLDIER: Oh, yes, they can do whatever they want, and we have to listen, obey, and swear loyalty to whoever they please! And is our general any worse than that fat pig Vitellius?
>
> FIRST SOLDIER: A hundredfold better, I say! And everyone has to admit it! And our right to proclaim him emperor is a hundred times better than theirs, too!
>
> SECOND SOLDIER: Damn right! Is this war here, in Judea, fun and games? They seem to think that they have a harder job with the Germans. All that boasting about how no one dares resist them because they have learned to hitch their tunics in the German bogs. But who knows who would prove the better men if it came right down to it.
>
> FIRST SOLDIER: Oh, no contest! It's clear that everyone will immediately side with us! Even if they wanted to fight, Vitellius's

---

[62] *L'Incoronazione di Poppea*, a 1643 opera by Claudio Monteverdi opens with just such a scene of two Roman guards discussing the political situation in Rome while Nero sleeps indoors.

men would quickly find out just how isolated they are. And the Senate and the people would have to be mad to prefer that glutton and degenerate over our chief!

SECOND SOLDIER: No way they would ever prefer that childless fornicator above a father of two sons. And what sons, too! Domitian is still young, true, but look at Titus! How many expeditions he has led! How many battles he has won! How bravely he has always stood! If, after he won the contest, Vespasian were to hand power over to Titus, what a brilliant emperor he would make!

FIRST SOLDIER: We have three good legions here in Judea. But those in Syria and in Egypt will immediately throw their lot with us as soon as we make a move. I know what I am talking about. More than one of their fellows has already mentioned something like that. And, you know? I have been watching all the messengers going back and forth between Alexandria, Caesarea, and Antioch. I think something's afoot! The East will stand united!

SECOND SOLDIER: And what about the legions on the Danube? Talk about hating Vitellius's guts! One word from us will be enough to get them started!

FIRST SOLDIER: That's for sure! I have heard that in April, in Aquileia, when they heard the news of the death of Otho, they refused to recognize Vitellius as emperor. They got together and consulted for a long time about whom among the governors they should elevate. But they couldn't agree on any one candidate. Only our Vespasian received praise from all. As he should, for isn't he wise, brave, and experienced in war? Nobody could say one bad word about him. But they couldn't be sure whether Vespasian would accept their decision. Still, though they were alone and leaderless, they resisted for a long time. It was not easy for Vitellius's officers to get them to swear allegiance![63]


The legionaries in Judea must have held these and similar conversations in May and June AD 69. And it seems that someone

---

[63] Josephus Flavius, *Jewish War I*, IV 10,3

encouraged them. Rumors spread about a certain letter allegedly written by Otho just before his suicide. In it, the departing emperor appealed to Vespasian to avenge his death and take the state into his hands. Copies of the letter were shown here and there, in great secrecy and only to a select few. Skeptics indeed dared to doubt its authenticity, reminding all who would care to listen that Titus was good at forging other people's writing and even boasted about it sometimes.

By the end of June, rumors suddenly spread in Syria that Vitellius intended to remove the Eastern legions and replace them with those from the Rhine. The ruler was apparently guided by certain considerations that were very important from his point of view: a more peaceful service in a mild climate and in a beautiful land would be a nice reward for the Germanic legions for their years of hard fighting in the brutal north and above all for elevating him to the throne and for their unwavering support for his cause. In their place, the Syrian legions would be moved to the Rhine. Mucianus, the governor of Syria, confirmed these rumors. He did this in a dramatic fashion at the beginning of July when he asked his soldiers to accept Vespasian's candidacy.

For all we know, he might have been "confirming" his own fabrication, but the ploy was excellent, and the project achieved the intended effect. The news about the alleged planned rotation of forces shocked both the army and the civilian population. The soldiers—even those who had come to Syria from the West in their youth—had made their home in the East by now. They founded families and acquired property, relatives, and friends. And were they now, because of one man's fancy, to leave their country and march to the ends of the world and start their lives anew in primitive conditions, among swamps and forests, suffering from frost and fog and rain, and to top it all, fighting the Germans?

Residents of Syrian towns and villages heard about the proposed rotation with equal horror. Those who had loved ones in the army would have to say goodbye to them forever, and all of them, without exception, were afraid of the soldiers from the Rhine. There have already been horror stories about their lust for gold and blood. And they hardly spoke Latin, let alone Greek! Besides, what could you expect from a people drinking in their own homeland not wine, the divine gift of Dionysus, but some sour spit made from pickled barley?

It seems obvious that if it weren't for the political skill and ingenuity of Mucianus, who skillfully manipulated the mood of the army and the general populace, Syria would probably not have declared itself for Vespasian so quickly and so unanimously. And what role did Vespasian himself play in these preparations?

## THE COUNCIL OF MOUNT CARMEL

And here is the astonishing thing: the man who should have promoted the business the most behaved strangely reservedly at first. Josephus Flavius reports the rumor—of course, made up—that the general agreed to be hailed as emperor only under the threat of the unsheathed swords of his soldiers. But the truth is that Vespasian did oppose his own candidacy at first. This was also his attitude during a secret meeting with Mucianus and his senior officers which took place at the end of May or the beginning of June on Mount Carmel on the coast of Palestine. There, he openly presented his objections:

"I'm already sixty years old. Why do I need such ambition at my age? Why should I take responsibility for the fate of the Empire upon my shoulders? After all, I can now spend the last years of my life in peace and prosperity without jeopardizing everything I have gained over the last forty years with so much hard work. Ultimately, I suppose, I might agree to risk it all for the good of the state if, indeed, as you claim, there is no one more worthy than me. An old man's fate is already sealed, so why not offer him as a sacrifice to the fatherland? But remember that I am the father of two sons, heirs of the name, dignity, and fortune. In case of my defeat, they will be its first victims, I will drag them into the grave. Especially since the younger of them, Domitian, is in Rome, and Vitellius can do whatever he wants with him. The same is true of my brother, Flavius Sabinus, whom he confirmed in the office of the Prefect of Rome. They are like hostages in the emperor's hand.

"And besides, he has not proven a bad ruler. He treats the Senate well. He doesn't get angry, he doesn't persecute his opponents, he seems inclined to peace and compromise. So, there does not seem to be any reason to start a new civil war. You say that this is what our country—Rome—demands of me. You also say that Vitellius is a slothful and depraved man who became emperor only by accident and malice of fate, and once he settles on the throne, he will reveal his tyrannical tendencies, which have been dormant thus far. But we do not know that, do we?

"You say, too, that the war will be short-lived, easy, almost bloodless because his troops aren't worth much. But believe me, I know those legions well-seasoned in wars! Even though their discipline has relaxed a bit in the capital, as soon as they face real danger, they will get their act together. And then they will summon more legions from the Rhine.

"Besides, who can guarantee that our soldiers will want to fight and remain faithful in every situation? That they won't be bribed and won't betray our cause? Believe me, our men can always withdraw from this endeavor before it takes a turn for the worse, but he who reaches for the Imperial purple can never retreat. He stakes everything: he must win or die.

"And who knows if a well-aimed blow, delivered by a sent assassin, may not be enough for this entire venture to collapse? How many times has it happened in history that the blade of a dagger has cut through the most beautifully laid plans!"

But Mucianus skillfully parried all these arguments. He spoke brilliantly, like the born rhetorician that he was. He assumed theatrical poses and struck pathetic tones. His words had the intended effect on most of those gathered, though not on Vespasian himself. Words like these:

"I call upon you, Vespasian, to take the purple! How much benefit the Empire can derive from your decision depends on you and the gods alone. Do not think this is flattery. Indeed, being Vitellius's successor is more a disgrace than an honor."

He then showed by example how every emperor to date had some personal predisposition to power: special talent or virtue, or at the very least the splendor of his family, established by a long reign, but Vitellius was entitled to neither one claim nor the other. It would, therefore, be the ultimate proof of dullness of mind and weakness of character to behave passively in a situation where the government falls into unqualified hands, which can only bring disaster to Rome. Vitellius had neither long military service nor enjoyed a good reputation. He was elevated to the purple by his soldiers' hatred of Galba and the accidental circumstance that the legions on the Rhine had no other dignitary of the senatorial rank to hand except Vitellius. And it was neither his skills as a leader nor his military superiority that defeated Otho: Otho died only because he prematurely despaired. Though, one had to admit that Vitellius had accomplished one thing in the short time he was in power: he caused the stature of Otho to appreciate to heights the man had never enjoyed when he was alive.

Then, Mucianus spoke about the demoralization of Vitellius's army. He said that whatever enthusiasm and ability it had had was subsequently lost in the Roman taverns and lupanars, where officers and simple soldiers alike imitated the sloth, drunkenness, and debauchery of their commander-in-chief. And Vespasian would have the nine legions standing in Judea, Syria, and Egypt behind him! Nine legions that had not suffered losses in wars—because their losses in the Jewish war had not been significant—and have observed a healthy and strict discipline. And theirs was an experienced soldier skilled in battle, victorious in clashes with the foreign enemy. Vespasian could also count on the navy, cavalry squadrons and auxiliary troops, and on the allied princes, who were trustworthy and eager to help in every way. And finally, there is the most reliable and powerful ally, the army of the Danube!

Vespasian finally gave in under the combined pressure of Mucianus's insistence and the arguments of all those present. He agreed to prepare a plan of when and how to elevate him to the purple.

Apparently, a significant role in his decision played the words of priest Basilides spoken when Vespasian offered sacrifice to the gods on Mount Carmel. The priest read the signs from the entrails of the sacrificial animals and said:

"Whatever you now undertake, whether to build a house, or acquire property, or increase the number of your servants, behold, here you are being given a great residence, boundless lands, and a multitude of people!"

And Vespasian, like most of his contemporaries, was inclined to believe such auguries.

This is how the meeting on Mount Carmel ended. Vespasian returned to his quarters in Caesarea Maritima and Mucianus to Antioch. And they set in motion the machinery of the plot that was to break in public on July 1 in Alexandria.


## MUCIANUS AND TITUS


Indeed, Mucianus proved to be the most ardent supporter of the cause of Vespasian, more zealous than the man himself. All of his contemporaries were to wonder why he did not make the claim himself. Why not reach for the highest prize in his own name? After all, he was a man of a distinguished family, had great talents, and certainly had plenty of ambition. Tacitus portrays the originality, even charm of his personality in books I and II of his *Histories*:

> Passion for splendor coexisted in Mucianus with diligence, kindness with arrogance, good and bad characteristics lived side by side. When time allowed, he gave himself to pleasures entirely, but he knew how to exercise great virtues when it paid to do so. Thanks to great people skills, he exerted a huge influence on his subjects and associates. He impressed with his wealth and generosity and, in every respect, stood out above ordinary mortals. He was far more skillful in conversation than Vespasian and more experienced in political affairs.

What seemed equally important (and was commented loud and wide) was that the two men had long been at odds—right down to the summer of AD 68, that is, to Nero's death. Mucianus believed that as the governor of Syria, the larger, older, more populous, and richer Levantine province, he should have authority and oversight over the business of Judea, a claim which Vespasian vehemently opposed.

So what led Antioch's proud and ambitious governor to set aside these resentments and become a single-minded supporter of his rival's claim to power?

Tacitus, who is our primary source for this part of the story (and indeed, for some of its aspects, the only one) and who knew both men personally at a later date, sums up the story in one short sentence:

> Only after Nero's death did they set aside their mutual animosity and reach an agreement. This happened in part thanks to mutual friends and in part to the trust inspired by Titus, who knew how to put aside petty rivalries and emphasize common interests and was thus by his nature eminently suited to attract a man of Mucianus's disposition.[64]

Or so, apparently, Mucianus declared to Vespasian:

> I think I am worth more than Vitellius, but I put you above me. Your house is blessed not only with military glory but also with two wonderful sons. One of them is already qualified to rule and, thanks to his previous military service, is also known to the legions of the Rhine. It would be absurd for me not to yield precedence to a man whose son I would adopt as my successor were I to become emperor.[65]

And thus, it turns out, the personality of Titus proved instrumental in elevating his father to the throne.

---

[64] Tacitus, *Histories*, II 6
[65] Josephus Flavius, Jewish War, IV 10,5

# TIBERIUS ALEXANDER AND VESPASIAN

It is understandable that a talented young man endowed with extraordinary personal charm—to which all his contemporaries attest—might have won the favor of an aristocrat already advanced in years and childless. Soberly assessing both the condition of the state and his own situation, Mucianus decided that it was more prudent to support Vespasian, a good politician and a father of talented sons who ensured the continuation of the dynasty. Besides, by placing himself in the position of Vespasian's right hand, Mucianus ensured for himself an important role and influence in the empire for years to come. All this was clear and logical.

But Vespasian was first proclaimed emperor not by Mucianus in Antioch but by someone else elsewhere: by Tiberius Alexander, the Prefect of Egypt, in Alexandria. He got that stone rolling on July 1, AD 69: the stone that started the whole avalanche of subsequent events. Vespasian's own men in Caesarea Maritima had waited for a signal from Egypt to make their move.

They received that signal only in the early morning of July 3, for even though Alexandria and Caesarea were over 500 kilometers apart, messengers riding non-stop and frequently changing horses could cover that distance in forty-eight hours. In turn, Mucianus made his proclamation in Syria only after having first assured himself that both Alexandria and Caesarea had already acted.

Vespasian remained perpetually indebted to the man behind the coup in the Egyptian capital, and he made it clear by observing July 1 as the official beginning of his reign, or, as the Romans called it, his *dies imperii*. Naturally, a new question arises here: what prompted the Prefect of Egypt to play such a decisive role in the elevation of Vespasian? What made him agree to be the first to take such a dangerous step?

After all, it could have happened—had happened before and happened since—that for some nefarious or accidental reason, his action was not followed in Caesarea and Antioch, and then, the Prefect of Egypt would have been left completely alone, helpless, and exposed to the imminent and terrible vengeance of Vitellius. Indeed, in the first days of July, it was not Vespasian who bore the full risk of the rebellion, and not Mucianus, but—Tiberius Alexander. And he incurred that risk consciously and voluntarily.

It is astonishing that our sources ignore this fact as if it were the most natural thing on earth. They give us plenty of clues to reconstruct the motives of Mucianus but leave us in complete darkness concerning the motivation of Tiberius Alexander. Even Josephus, who was then at the center of events and, as a Jew, certainly learned a lot from his kinsmen in Alexandria afterward, presents this matter only very briefly. He wrote in Book IV of his *Jewish War*:

> Because both Mucianus and his own officers pressed Vespasian to accept the imperial purple, he first turned his attention to Alexandria. He understood perfectly well that Egypt was the most important province of the East because of its regular grain deliveries to Rome. He hoped that by seizing Egypt, he might force Vitellius to capitulate, but even if that did not happen and a war resulted, the people in the capital would rebel for they would not bear starvation. Also, he wanted to assure himself of the support of the two legions there. And if, by some unforeseen and unfortunate development, his cause were to suffer a setback, Egypt would serve as an important bulwark for Palestine, which had no major ports while the port of Alexandria was easy to isolate and control, and to the west of it stretched only the waterless Lybian desert.
>
> So [Vespasian] immediately wrote to the Prefect. He informed him of the intentions of his troops and explained that if he were indeed to take upon his shoulders the imperial challenge, he would first need to assure himself of Alexander's help and cooperation. As soon as Alexander read the letter, he swore in his soldiers and his people. Both eagerly pledged their allegiance to Vespasian because they knew his virtues since he had commanded the Roman army in a neighboring territory for several years.[66]

---

[66] Josephus Flavius, *The Jewish War*, IV 10, 5

So much, Josephus.

But Tacitus describes the events of July 1 in just one sentence:

> The Prefect of Egypt, Alexander, participated in the planning of the revolt.[67]

That is all! The discretion and restraint of the Roman historian are surprising and perhaps due to the fact that—let's say it right away—he didn't like Alexander and did not want to emphasize his contribution to Vespasian's success. The following chapters will explain the reasons for his dislike.

There is no reason to doubt that there was some kind of a letter from Vespasian to Alexander. And if there was, it would have come after the Council of Mount Caramel. But it seems equally obvious that Alexander had long known about the causes, goals, and progress of the plot. Josephus' claim that the governor learned about the plot only from the letter and was somehow instantly convinced by its arguments is simply naive. The letter was only the last link in the plans developed earlier, carefully and in the greatest secrecy. It was a call sign. Who knows whether its content was not innocuous—some kind of "the eagle has landed"—just in case it fell into the wrong hands. The profound secret of the conspiracy is best demonstrated by the fact that the Prefect's office continued to date all documents with the name of Vitellius right up to July 1. In remote areas of Egypt, where news arrived with considerable delay, documents were so dated until the end of July, almost a month after Vespasian was proclaimed emperor in Alexandria. Indeed, Tyberius Alexander had gone further in his submission to Vitellius than any other governor in the entire Empire: he ordered the use of the honorific name *Caesar* in the emperor's title, even though Vitellius himself had rejected the moniker once and for all when the Senate proposed to give it to him.

At a first glance, one might assume that the Prefect decided to declare for Vespasian simply because he had no other choice: he had only two legions in Egypt, while Mucianus and Vespasian had the

---

combined force of six, not counting the troops of the allied princes. And it was obvious that no help from Vitellius would be able to reach Egypt in time if the two decided to attack him.

In reality, however, Mucianus and Vespasian would not have been able to throw all their armies against Egypt because the former had to guard the Euphrates, and the latter was at war with the Jews. And if they did decide to attack him, they would have had to march to Egypt along the coast of Palestine: a long, arduous journey on which they would be poorly supplied because of the general devastation of Palestine. The conquest of Egypt itself would not be easy either: first, at the gates of Egypt there was a chain of formidable fortifications, including Pelusium; then the many branches of the Nile now entering the height of inundation;[68] and finally, the siege and capture of the large and populous city of Alexandria. And all this in order to then commit a significant part of their forces to maintaining law and order in a vast country with millions of inhabitants.

The conclusion seems to be that Tiberius Alexander did not have to give in to persuasion to cast his lot with Vespasian and Mucianus. Rather, it seems that, at the critical moment, their decision depended largely—and who knows, if not entirely—on the decision he would make. Just possibly, the governors of Syria and Judea would never have dared to rebel if they had not had the absolute certainty that the Prefect of Egypt would support them. It was neither an accident nor some desire to honor and respect Tiberius Alexander that required him to go first.

It so happens that we have fragments of a papyrus that records

---

[68] The first indications of the rise of the river could be seen at the first of the cataracts of the Nile (at Aswan) as early as the beginning of June, and a steady increase went on until the middle of July, when the increase of water became very great. The Nile continued to rise until the beginning of September, when the level remained stationary for a period of about three weeks, sometimes a little less. In October, it often rose again and reached its highest level. From that point on, it began to subside and usually sank steadily until the month of June, when it reached its lowest level again. See Budge, Wallis E. A. *The Nile Notes for Travellers in Egypt*, London, 1895.

a speech given by the Prefect before the people gathered in the eastern hippodrome in the suburbs of Alexandria, a speech concerning the elevation of Vespasian. According to some researchers, the speech on the papyrus is the speech he gave when proclaiming Vespasian emperor on July 1; according to others, it refers to an event held several months later—a speech given to welcome Vespasian when he arrived in the Egyptian metropolis. Whatever the case, we have the words of Tiberius Alexander himself. And thus, we know that in his speech, he called the new emperor Lord, Savior, and Benefactor, and the people responded with the shouts of:

"Our Lord, Augustus, Benefactor, Sarapis, son of Ammon!"[69]

It is possible that the same words had been invoked on previous occasions, referring to earlier emperors. This was, after all, the fourth imperial proclamation in a year. So why not assume that these words were just a customary gesture of loyalty—or servility—a gesture devoid of authentic content? Yet, it is important to remember that by starting the avalanche, Tiberius Alexander was staking his life. Therefore, there is no doubt that he made every effort to make the celebration as splendid as possible and surpass all previous ones in every way. He praised Vespasian sincerely and fervently because he had hitched his fate to his wagon, for better or for worse.

It is also easy to guess that the Prefect's men did everything in their power to ensure that the crowd accepted the proclamation enthusiastically. That didn't require much effort anyway. It was enough to point out to the citizens of Alexandria the momentous honor they now attained: for the first time in history, the Roman Emperor was proclaimed by them, in their city! For the first time in a century, the Egyptian metropolis would decide the future of the entire known world. For generations, the Alexandrians had humbly accepted officials appointed by Rome, but now, thanks to an unexpected twist of fate, they will impose their ruler on the capital!

Certainly, many inhabitants of Alexandria found a deeper meaning in the unfolding events, for it was hard to resist the

---

[69] *Papyrus Fouad*, I, 8, 83

impression that some hidden power was at work, taking vengeance for the old tragedies of their country, its humiliations, and its loss of political independence.

Exactly one hundred years earlier, in 31 BC, Cleopatra, the last queen of Egypt, and her husband, Mark Antony, suffered a crushing defeat at Actium. A year later, she committed suicide, preferring a proud death to walking as a captive before the chariot of Octavian in his triumph in Rome. Octavian then founded a dynasty that ruled the Empire under the Julio-Claudian name for almost a century, but its last representative, Nero, died by his own hand. Since then, civil wars have continued to convulse the empire. And now, the mysterious hand of destiny allowed the people of Alexandria to name the new Roman emperor.

Wasn't this revenge for Cleopatra's fall? Could anyone possibly refuse to believe the prophecy, that had been circulating for several years, that the salvation of the world would come from the East?

Such considerations were consistent with the mentality of the era, which loved prophecy and divination and constantly searched for hidden relationships between various seemingly unconnected events and espied everywhere the judgments of gods, fate, and destiny. But Prefect Tiberius Julius Alexander was a coolly calculating and probably cynical man, and this was certainly not what he had in mind when he made his decision.[70]

## THE FAMILY OF TIBERIUS ALEXANDER

The future Prefect of Egypt was born in Alexandria in about AD 10. His father, Alexander Lysimachus, was one of the richest people not just in Egypt but also in the entire Empire. He was also demonstratively Jewish. Like his entire family, although they had lived

---

[70] On Tiberius Alexander, see V. Burr, *Tiberius Julius Alexander*, Bonn, 1955

outside Palestine for several generations and were deeply immersed in Greek culture, he never spared gifts for the Jerusalem temple. His brother, Philo, did not go into business but—philosophy. It earned him great fame, which has only grown over the centuries; and for good reason, for although he was not an original thinker, his writings greatly influenced the subsequent development of Jewish and Christian theological thought.[71]

The main objective of Philo's work was to reconcile the Jewish Scripture with various Greek spiritual doctrines, on which he was a great expert. On every page of his numerous treatises, we find a development or an application of ideas taken from Plato or Aristotle, the Stoics, or the Pythagoreans. Yet, this Hellenized Philo, who spoke and wrote only Greek, was an example of unbending religious intransigence, remaining faithful to the religion of his ancestors. This was why he was sent as part of the embassy of the Alexandrian Jews to Emperor Caligula in AD 39. Their mission was to plead with the ruler to release Jews from the obligation to worship his statues, as it was contrary to the commandments of their religion.

The basis of the wealth of the family was the hereditary office of the *alabarch*, that is, the collector of duties on the roads and ports of Egypt. This was the source of one of the largest fortunes in the empire. Lysimachus was also the manager of the Egyptian estates of Antonia, Caligula's grandmother. This powerful woman died in the first year of her grandson's reign and was, therefore, unable to protect Lysimachus from the Imperial displeasure that fell on him, probably in connection with the above-mentioned mission of Philo. The emperor had become so angry with the members of the delegation that he did not allow the old man to finish his speech, and Lysimachus was imprisoned soon afterward, probably on fabricated charges of financial abuse. Even their Roman citizenship, which had been granted to the family by Emperor Tiberius, did not save him. Lysimachus remained in the gaol until Caligula's death, when Claudius, Antonia's son, ascended to the throne. Thanks to the new

---

[71] Philo of Alexandria (c. 20 BC – c. AD 50), also called Philo Judaeus.

emperor, the family soon returned to their former glory. Emperor Nero proved even kinder to them.

Let us look now at the career of Tiberius Alexander starting with his boyhood days when, together with his brother Mark, he grew up under the watchful eye of his uncle Philo.[72]

# CONCERNING DIVINE JUSTICE AND THE SOULS OF ANIMALS

Philo lived at his brother's house until the end of his days and was personally responsible for the education of the boys. He naturally placed particular emphasis on what he believed to be the most important subjects of study: religion and philosophy. Not without some success: certain passages in Philo's writings show that at least one of the boys—our Tiberius Alexander, in fact—became interested in the views holed by various philosophical schools concerning the issues then current in the intellectual circles. Words that his uncle puts in his mouth in one of his dialogues show it:

"I barely slept a wink last night because the topics we had discussed yesterday have been keeping me up!"

What were these topics? Philo tells us about some of them. They may seem naïve and immaterial to us, and certainly would not deprive us of sleep. But let us remember that each era has its own magical circle of issues that are important to it but which, in the opinion of later generations, seem trivial and sometimes even ridiculous. Let us not be too harsh in disparaging what once seemed important, nor too emphatic about the matters which seem to us critical—because the time is surely coming when our own concerns earn our posterity's smile of indulgence if not pity.

Philo's treatise *On Divine Justice* survives only in its Armenian translation and takes the form of a conversation between the author and his nephew, Tiberius Alexander. The latter argues, citing many

---

[72] Josephus Flavius, *Jewish Antiquities*, XX 1,2

examples from Greek history, that those who are unafraid to resort to base means often achieve lasting success. And while they achieve their goals, the honest are forced to yield and lose. Therefore, there is no divine justice that protects the good and punishes the evil.

However, Philo, per his deep religiosity, tries to argue that justice is an indispensable attribute of the divinity that created the world and that, therefore, justice is an essential element of the cosmic order. Both men resort to Greek philosophical terminology and to arguments taken from Greek classics. If we did not know that the two men were Jews, we would never guess it, nor would we guess that the author was a zealous practitioner of the Jewish Law. Let us remember that half a century later, this very same problem became the subject of a conversation between Plutarch and his friends in the portico of the temple of Apollo in Delphi.

Another dialogue of Philo, also preserved only in Armenian, is entitled *Alexander, or whether animals have souls*. It contains a very courteous but firm rebuttal of the views of Tiberius Aleksander, expressed in the treatise in detail. The young man maintained that animals were rational beings and had souls. After all, in their behavior, they showed intelligence, foresight, and the ability to imitate, predict, and adapt to conditions. Some of them could even talk.

They could also be said to have certain virtues, for example, courage, ambition, pride, or the capacity for self-sacrifice. Again, Plutarch's Delphi dialogue comes to mind. After all, the old Pythagorean idea which appears in Thespesius' vision, that the souls of men can be reborn in animal bodies, could serve as a great argument for the thesis of young Alexander. Just as would the story of the Pharaoh Amasis reborn as a lion. But Tiberius Alexander did not use those examples, and he could not have used them for they would have run contrary to his belief that there is no divine justice, and that therefore, there were no divine punishments for evil and rewards for good, neither in this life nor the next.

Finally, it seems probable that some thoughts of Tiberius Alexander appear in another work by Philo, which has survived in its original Greek but only in fragments. It discusses the problem of the age of the world. Philo's nephew defends the claim made by various Greek philosophers that the material world has neither a beginning nor an end. Such a thesis, clearly contrary to the biblical story about the creation of heaven and earth, must have pained an orthodox Jew like Philo. It certainly made him realize that the talented young man had perhaps had too much of the Greek learning.

These echoes of the subtle and abstract disputes at the house of the Alexandrian *alabarch* between the venerable old scholar and his brash and clever young nephew allow us to understand better the sudden turn that took place in the young man's life.

## TIBERIUS ALEXANDER APOSTATIZES

Huge fortune, Roman citizenship, Greek education, Imperial favor—everything seemed to predestine Tiberius Alexander for a fabulous career open to the members of the equite class. But on one condition: he had to break with the Jewish Law as wholly and as quickly as possible.

This necessity resulted from two basic facts. First, on multiple occasions, every Roman official made sacrifices and uttered and accepted oaths before the statues of gods, especially the statue of the emperor. Secondly, every young man from a well-to-do family who wanted to climb to the higher levels of the hierarchy was obliged first to complete an officer internship in one of the military formations. Alas, the requirements of such service could not be reconciled with the principles of the Jewish religion. Sacrifices before and homage paid to statues would be a blasphemous violation of the second commandment, which states clearly:

> Thou shalt not make unto thee any graven image or any likeness of anything that is in heaven above, or that is in the earth beneath, or that is in the water under the earth: And thou shalt not bow down thyself to them, nor serve them: for I the LORD thy God am a jealous God, visiting the iniquity of the fathers upon the children

unto the third and fourth generation.[73]

And it would be impossible to serve in the army without breaking a different commandment every week:

> Remember the sabbath day, to keep it holy. Six days shalt thou labor, and do all thy work: But the seventh day is the sabbath of the LORD thy God: in it, thou shalt not do any work, thou, nor thy son, nor thy daughter, thy manservant, nor thy maidservant, nor thy cattle, nor thy stranger that is within thy gates.[74]

Not the military regulations, not the comrades in arms, and certainly not the enemy in the field would allow complete inaction every seventh day. Therefore, observant Jews never voluntarily joined the ranks of foreign armies, and in cases of necessity, they provided a replacement from among the Gentiles, paying him for his service.

But Tiberius Alexander despised the commandments of his faith, the traditions of his people, and the pious example of his father and uncle. He became a conscious apostate. During the reign of Emperor Tiberius, he served in the military, undoubtedly as a tribune with a narrow purple stripe, probably in Egypt. Then, having waited out the turbulent period of Caligula's reign, he assumed under Claudius his first civilian office—surprisingly high. In the spring of AD 42, he became *epistrategist*, that is, the administrator of Thebais in Upper Egypt. This position came with an annual salary of 60,000 sesterces. He reported directly to the Provincial Prefect, and in his district, he was the head of the civil administration and its chief judge.

Meanwhile, in AD 44, King Herod Agrippa I died. Thanks to the favor of Caligula and Claudius, he had managed to reunite almost all of Palestine under his rule, but after his death, the emperor decided to take his territories into direct Roman control. The decision was surprising because the deceased had left an obvious heir. This was Agrippa II. (He also left a daughter, Berenice, then wife of another Herod, prince of Chalcis in southern Syria). Although Agrippa II was

---

[73] *Exodus* 20:4-5
[74] *Exodus* 20:8-10

to regain a part of his patrimony in later years, those were mainly territories on the shores of Lake Gennesaret and to the east of it, while Judea, Samaria, and Galilee proper remained subject to Roman rule, as they had been before the times of Herod Agrippa I. The new imperial procurator, Cuspius Fadus, managed to restore order in the usually troublesome border regions of Palestine and to clear Judea of bandits, but he soon fell foul of the Jews.

Namely, he demanded that the liturgical vestments of the High Priest be deposited with the Roman authorities, who would release them only for the period of each service. The idea was to ensure absolute submission to the authorities, as offering sacrifices without these vestments was impossible, especially on major holidays. Jews went to Rome to complain. Thanks to the intercession of the young prince Agrippa II, who was then residing in Rome, they were able to obtain an audience with the emperor and a repeal of Fadus's decree. The delegation returned triumphant, carrying a letter in which Claudius wrote:

> A client of my house, Agrippa, a pleasant companion and a man of great nobility, introduced your ambassadors to me. They thanked me for the favor with which I have looked upon your nation, and they begged me earnestly that the ceremonial robe and headdress of the High Priest should remain in your hands, which I hereby allow. I granted this request because of my piety and because of my desire for everyone to live in accordance with their customs. I also wrote in this matter to my procurator, Cuspius Fadus.[75]

The same letter granted the custody of the Temple and its treasury and the right to appoint and remove its High Priests to Herod, prince of Chalcis, husband of Berenice, about whom the Emperor wrote in very friendly words. Following his death in AD 48, the privilege passed to Agrippa II, with whom his beloved sister Berenice now came to live.

The incident with the robe undermined the procurator's authority. Fadus had to console himself with the thought that the religious fanaticism of the Jews was simply insurmountable.

---

[75] Josephus Flavius, *Jewish Antiquities*, XX, 1,2

But soon, he came across a matter that was much more difficult for him to understand. A certain Theudas appeared among the people of Judea. He pretended to be a prophet and quickly gathered a crowd around him, which, together with all their families and belongings, set off for the shores of the Jordan. Theudas assured his followers that the waters of the river would part before them, opening a safe passage to the opposite bank, from where he would lead the faithful to a new promised land where everyone would live in peace, love, and prosperity.

Meanwhile, cavalry squadrons sent by Fadus caught up with the pilgrims camped on the Jordan. The procurator worried that the madness could become contagious and decided that the march should stop immediately. The waters of the river did not part for those fleeing. Many died by the Roman sword, many were taken captive, and Theudas, who was captured, had his head cut off and transported in triumph to Jerusalem so that everyone could see with their own eyes what fate befell false prophets.

This is how Josephus presents this story in the XX book of his *Jewish Antiquities*. However, it is interesting that the same Theudas also appear in Chapter V of the *Acts of the Apostles*. There we hear from the lips of the Pharisee Gamaliel:

> For before these days rose up Theudas, boasting himself to be somebody; to whom a number of men, about four hundred, joined themselves: who was slain; and all, as many as obeyed him, were scattered and brought to naught.[76]

First, the matter of the robe and then the strange affair of Theudas accelerated the dismissal of Fadus. His place as procurator of Judea was taken in AD 46 by... Tiberius Alexander. That was a significant promotion because the procurator of Palestine belonged to a higher category of officials, received 100,000 sesterces a year, and enjoyed great independence since he reported to the governor of Syria in only a limited number of special cases and had under his command

---

[76] *Acts* 5:36

significant armed forces: five infantry cohorts and a squadron of cavalry. Naturally, we do wonder to whom Tiberius Alexander owed this honorable nomination.

His background certainly recommended him. People in Rome seem to have come to the reasonable conclusion that a procurator familiar with the customs and mentality of the Jews would avoid clumsy mistakes of the Fadus sort. It also mattered that Emperor Claudius knew and respected his father, at one time his own mother's estate manager. There is also no doubt that Alexander's candidacy was supported, if not even put forward, by Herod, prince of Chalcis, who enjoyed the trust of Claudius. And Herod may have done this because his wife Berenice had once been formally (but only formally) married to Mark, the brother of Alexander. (The young man died prematurely, and the marriage was never consummated, but it is clear that close personal contacts existed between the great princely family of Judea and the house of Alexandrian billionaires).

The new procurator found himself in a difficult situation right away. There was a major crop failure in Palestine, followed by famine, which severely affected Jerusalem. *Acts of the Apostles* mentions it:

> And there stood up one of them named Agabus, and signified by the Spirit that there should be great dearth throughout all the world: which came to pass in the days of Claudius Caesar. Then the disciples, every man according to his ability, determined to send relief unto their brethren which dwelt in Judaea: Which also they did, and sent it to the elders by the hands of Barnabas and Saul.[77]

But Christians were still a very small group, and they only aided each other. Significant help for the broad sections of the population came from an unexpected direction, from far, far away.

---

[77] *Acts* 11:28-30

# QUEEN HELEN OF ADIABENE

The famine was just beginning when Queen Helen arrived in Jerusalem, surrounded by a magnificent retinue. Her homeland, called Adiabene in Greek, lay very far away indeed—on the upper Tigris, on the border of the Roman Empire and the kingdom of Parthia. It had a mixed population—Iranian, Armenian, Greek, and Semitic. The queen arrived in Jerusalem on a religious pilgrimage. She came to offer in the Temple a legally prescribed thanksgiving in her new role of a faithful and exemplary follower of the Jewish Law—although she had only recently become one.

By a strange coincidence, her son, Izates, had also adopted Judaism at the same time, though completely independently and without her knowledge. He had grown up far from her, at the court of a friendly prince somewhere in Mesopotamia. There, he met a Jewish merchant named Ananias and received preliminary instruction in Judaism from him. After his father's death, Izates returned home to assume power and brought Ananias with him. Only then did the mother and son realize with surprise and joy that they were on the same spiritual journey. From then on, they encouraged and supported each other.

Helen, however, was inclined to proceed in baby steps in fundamental matters, treating her religious faith as purely personal, private, and even secret. So when Izates told her that he planned to adopt all the obligations of the Jewish Law, including circumcision, she became worried and opposed the move. She warned that this could lead to disturbances in the kingdom as the population, especially the aristocracy, would not want to have for a ruler someone who, having abandoned the faith of their forefathers, adopted a foreign religion, especially one despised by many.

Izates turned for advice to Ananias. Surprisingly, Ananias agreed with his mother. He worried that if the king were to undergo circumcision, he would have to leave Adiabene because his subjects would (only naturally) expect some divine chastisement for such an act of apostasy on the part of their king.

And then he added the following significant words:

"But you can worship the Lord without getting circumcised. The most important principle of Judaism is not circumcision but observing the ten commandments."

Izates accepted the argument. But soon thereafter, a highly respected scholar of the scripture, rabbi Eleazar of Galilee, arrived in Adiabene. When he was brought into the king's apartments and saw him bent over the Holy Scripture, instead of praising his piety, he became scandalized. He said:

"By giving yourself to this study without first being circumcized, you show your disregard for the Law. It is not enough to read the Law. The point is to fulfill its every demand scrupulously!"

The King submitted to circumcision that very same day.

His mother and Ananias were told about it only after the fact. But contrary to their fears, there was no public outrage and there were no disturbances.

And for this happy development, the queen now wanted to offer her thanksgiving at the Temple in Jerusalem. Izates had given her rich supplies and a large retinue and personally escorted her to the borders of his dominions.

The story of the conversion of the royal family of Adiabene is noteworthy for several reasons. First of all, it is an example of the zeal with which Jews of that time propagated religious propaganda, which in turn allows us to understand the missionary zeal of early Christians. Furthermore, we are dealing here with a case of apostasy, i.e., of a departure from the faith of one's ancestors, but in a direction opposite to that of Tiberius Alexander. The doubts and hesitations of the Adiabene neophytes also show what hindered even the strongest Jewish sympathizers from fully embracing the Law.

Finally, we meet the puzzling character of Ananias. From the point of view of Jewish orthodoxy, he expresses a downright heretical view. Indeed, a view so unusual that some scholars have suggested that Ananias may have been an early Christian or at least been exposed to the teachings of the apostle Paul, who preached:

For he is not a Jew, which is one outwardly; neither is that circumcision, which is outward in the flesh. But he is a Jew, which is one inwardly; and circumcision is that of the heart, in the spirit, and not in the letter; whose praise is not of men, but of God.[78]

Indeed, what other words would Ananias have used if it had come to a debate between him and Rabbi Eleazar? Could Ananias have been a student of the apostle? Could Izates have been the world's first Christian ruler? And his mother, Helen—could she have been a prototype for another Helen, the mother of Constantine the Great?

Whatever the case, the arrival of the queen in Jerusalem turned out to be a salvation for the city. Thanks to her son's generosity, she had enormous sums at her disposal, and when she saw the scale of the famine, she immediately took up charity work. She sent her people to Alexandria to buy grain. She sent others to Cyprus to bring a cargo of dried figs. She then distributed the grain and fruit among the needy. And soon, King Izates sent more money for further charitable action.

Helen remained in Jerusalem for many years. She decided to prepare a place of eternal rest for herself and her family at the gates of the holy city.[79]

## HELEN'S TOMB

A little over seven hundred meters from the Damascus Gate in Jerusalem, there is an underground tomb with a dozen rock-carved chambers. As attested by Josephus, three large pyramids once stood above it. This wonderful monument, the most impressive in Jerusalem of that era, was compared by some ancient writers to the famous tomb of King Mausolus in Asia Minor, one of the seven wonders of the ancient world and the source of our word "mausoleum."

An ancient myth said that once a year, always on the same day

---

[78] *Romans* 2:28-29
[79] Josephus Flavius, *Jewish Antiquities*, XX 1, 2-3

and at the same hour, a mysterious mechanism opened the heavy marble door leading to the underground, but once the door closed again, it could not be reopened until the following year. As late as the 4th century AD, the historian of the Church, bishop Eusebius of Caesarea, reported seeing the tomb and its pyramids. The monument eventually went to ruin, mined for building material, although one pyramid remained standing as late as the 17th century. Although robbed and vandalized, its underground section remains still and impresses with its prodigious size and the remains of its truly royal decor. In time, it came to be thought of as the tomb of the kings of Judea.

Bishop Ignacy Hołowiński, a Polish cleric, translator of Shakespeare, and travel writer, saw it in 1839. The description he published is valuable because it describes the condition of the site before systematic excavations began. I quote an excerpt from his report:

> In the middle of a rocky mountainside, the traveler observes a huge structure open to the sky, like a quadrangular cistern carved in rock, into which he may enter from the eastern side through an arched gate carved in the slope. Once one enters, the cistern turns out to be a beautiful courtyard, 30 paces long and wide, surrounded by four smooth walls of solid rock, 13 cubits high.

> Opposite the entrance is a chamber carved in the rock, twelve paces long and five paces wide, leading to the underground. The decoration of the rock above this opening arouses a special delight of the visitor:

> Underneath the nicely crafted cornice is a wide panel with a bas-relief of several decorative elements repeating rhythmically: three vertical bars, a circle, a palm branch, an oak wreath, and a cluster of grapes. And beneath it, on the edge of the opening, there is a second frieze consisting of palm leaves, pine cones, lemons, and vines. They are arranged into a garland with such exquisite art that the whole may vie with the greatest works of later periods. And in the arrangement itself, one can perceive that true Eastern whimsy,

which would later produce the arabesque.[80]

We should make a small correction here. There is no lemon fruit among the ornaments of the frieze, and there could never have been one because the fruit was unknown in the ancient Mediterranean. The fruit in the fruit in question is, beyond doubt, a pomegranate.[81] The grapes, arranged among wreaths and palm leaves, are depicted on this bas-relief in the form of three bunches. Similar reliefs can also be found on other Judean monuments from this period. This leads us to suppose that perhaps we are looking at a decorative design of the Second Temple of Jerusalem. Indeed, we do know that there had once been a grapevine of pure gold above the gate leading to the interior of the Temple, and from it hung a bunch of grapes of pure gold, reported to have been the size of a man. The sculpture was a gift from Jews living in the diaspora, and it constantly increased in size because pious pilgrims continued to add something to this wonderful decoration every time they visited the holy city.

Now, the frieze in the tomb pleased our traveler, who, as his numerous remarks lead us to believe, had a good eye for decorative detail. Having entered the cave, however, the visitor saw with great sadness a picture of complete ruin:

> Down three or four steps, the traveler descends into a small square dungeon filled with standing water, refuse, and rubble. On the left, he sees the main entrance to the royal chambers, but so littered with rabble that one must crawl on his fours to enter its large, four-sided hall, from which one passes to six other rooms of unequal size. Each room has seven or eight niches along the walls. In addition, on stone benches carved in the living rock, there stand sarcophagi or stone chests cut in the shape of our coffins with lids, bearing beautiful bas-reliefs in the shape of oak wreaths. Some covers are still in place, but

---

[80] I. Hołowiński, *Pielgrzymka do Ziemi Świętej* [A Pilgrimage to the Holy Land], St. Petersburg 1853, s. 415—416.

[81] The origin of the lemon is unknown, though lemons are thought to have first grown in Assam (a region in northeast India), northern Myanmar, or China. A genomic study of the lemon indicates it was a hybrid between bitter orange and citron. They were introduced to Persia and then to Iraq and Egypt around 700 AD.

most of them are broken. In the sarcophagi, one sees small elevations, like head supports. Radziwiłł[82] saw bones still in them,[83] but today, they are empty. There are small openings in these chests for the drainage of impurities.

The last two rooms are slightly lower in the rock. One can access them down seven steps strewn with refuse. Judging by their rich bas-reliefs, these were the most important graves, but today they are quite ruined. I saw one stone chest, or sarcophagus, taken from one of these rooms in a corner of the city serving as a trough for watering cattle.

There is no element of foreign stone in this structure, as everything has been carved from the native rock. When you look at this work truly worthy of being called royal, when you see the detail and finish, the extraordinary regularity and smoothness of the workmanship, the graceful delicacy of the reliefs, you know that, despite all the progress of the centuries, they cannot be bested. But what amazed the travelers of old the most were the stone doors on hinges, of which there were still three in 1681 and one during Chateaubriand's visit.[84] Now broken into pieces, they lie forlornly on the ground, together with the stone hooks and hinges on which they had once hung.

The bishop then wonders whose ashes might have been buried in this magnificent tomb and weighs various views put forward at the time. Kings of Judea? Jewish leaders of the time of Persian rule? Or maybe Herod's family? Hołowiński completely rejects the thesis that it is a

---

[82] Mikołaj Krzysztof Radziwiłł (1549-1616), Polish traveler, author of *Pamiętniki z pielgrzymki do Ziemi Św.* [Memoir of a Journey to the Holy Land], 1595

[83] These were the traditional Jewish bone boxes (ossuaries). During the Second Temple period, Jewish burial customs were varied, differing based on class and belief. For the wealthy, one option available included primary burials in burial caves, followed by secondary burials (i.e., reburials after the soft tissue had decayed) in ossuaries. These bone boxes were placed in smaller niches of the burial caves, on the benches used for the desiccation of the corpse, or even on the floor.

[84] See, François-René de Chateaubriand (1768-1848), *Itinéraire de Paris à Jérusalem*, [A journey from Paris to Jerusalem], 1811

monument of the Queen of Adiabene, arguing as follows:



He was not alone in this opinion; many eminent contemporary archaeologists shared it. One of them was the Frenchman F. de Sulcy,[85] who in December 1863 discovered a chamber within the complex, so well hidden that it had escaped the attention of both robbers and visitors throughout the centuries, Hołowiński included. In the chamber, he found an intact stone sarcophagus. Lifting the lid, he saw a well-preserved skeleton of a person about 160 cm tall, with its arms crossed on its chest, lying in a mass of rotting remains. The bones soon crumbled into ashes in contact with the air. Only a few fragments remain: a fragment of the lower jaw with teeth, the patella of a knee, a part of the bone of one of the fingers—and small fragments of clothing and jewelry. All this, as well as the sarcophagus itself, is now in the Louvre. Sulcy, who had previously believed that the tomb belonged to the kings of Judea after David and Solomon, now had to revise his view. For there, on the side of the casket, between two rosettes and in two types of writing—Syriac and Hebrew—he found an Aramaic inscription announcing the name of the dead person: "Queen Saddah." This had been the Semitic name of the queen of Adiabene, known to the Greeks as Queen Helen. Moreover, her name was also found on a clay vessel seal discovered in the tomb's ruins.

The arrangement of the underground chambers, the inscriptions, their language, and especially the ornamentation of the rock friezes and sarcophagi clearly indicate that this monument dates not to a distant era of pre-Nebuchadnezzar Judea but from later Graeco-Roman times. Hołowiński's argument that such a huge grave would never have been made for just one person misses the point: like many contemporary tombs in Palestine, it is a family tomb intended for the eternal rest not only of Helen but also of all her relatives.

---

[85] Louis Félicien Joseph Caignart de Saulcy (19 March 1807 – 4 November 1880),

And there were many of them.

King Izates died in the country on the upper Tigris at the age of fifty-five, in the twenty-fourth year of his reign. According to our reckoning of time, it was probably AD 62, and Emperor Nero had been ruling the Empire for nine years. The Lord of Adiabene left behind twenty-four sons and as many daughters, of course by many different wives: polygamy was almost the rule in the East among the wealthier classes, and Jewish Law did not prohibit it. During his lifetime, the king sent five of his sons to Jerusalem so that they could learn the language of their co-religionists and receive a proper upbringing under Helen's care. After the Izates's death, his older brother, Monobazos, ascended the throne. He, too, was favorably disposed towards Judaism. Queen Helen, who had been living in Jerusalem for many years, returned to her homeland immediately upon hearing the news. She almost certainly wanted to take away the body of her son and lay it to rest in the family tomb, which she had prepared with so much expense near the gates of the holy city. However, she died soon after arriving in Adiabene—she was already a very elderly woman—and a procession with two coffins set off from Adiabene to Jerusalem. One of them, the queen's, was deposited in the chamber discovered in 1863.

About a dozen years after Helen's burial, the body of King Monobazos was laid to rest in the same tomb, and its three pyramids signified that it was a tomb of three persons of royal dignity.

Many other members of the family were buried here, including Princess Grapte (her Jerusalem palace, as we remember, was the headquarters of John of Gischala in AD 68 and 69). The bones of the dead were placed either in sarcophagi, fragments of which remain, or in the niches cut in the living rock described by Hołowiński.

But perhaps the most interesting object in the tomb, missed by the pilgrim from Poland, is a large round stone, the size and shape of a millstone; it was once used to block the entrance to the underground chambers. This method of closing graves was often used in Palestine: another such stone has been preserved in the tomb of the Herods, dating to the same period. Looking at these stones, we are reminded of the perplexed words of the three women—Mary Magdalene, Mary, mother of James, and Salome—who, on the first day after the Sabbath, early in the morning at sunrise, came to anoint the body in the tomb of Joseph of Arimathea. On the way, they said to each other:

> Who shall roll us away the stone from the door of the sepulcher? And when they looked, they saw that the stone was rolled away: for it was very great. And entering into the sepulcher, they saw a young man sitting on the right side, clothed in a long white garment; and they were much affrighted. [86]

## TIBERIUS ALEXANDER AND THE ADIABENITES

The tomb built by Helen has survived to this day as one of the most precious monuments of Jerusalem architecture from the period immediately preceding the outbreak of the First Roman War, but the costly gifts that Helen and Monobazus had placed in the Temple have disappeared. Monobazus donated gold handles for liturgical vessels, and the queen donated two large gold objects. One of them was a mirror, placed above the gate of the vestibule of the temple in such a way that the first rays of the rising sun would be reflected in it and illuminate the tabernacle faced with polished stone, causing it to glow like the second sun. Another gift from Helen was a large tablet inscribed with the elaborate commandments of the Law concerning the method of punishing unfaithful wives. It seems noteworthy that a woman should have selected that text as the most worthy of immortalization in precious metal.

The royal family of Adiabene spared neither gold nor blood for Jerusalem. The princes of the family volunteered to join the struggle as soon as the Jewish War broke out. They fought in the Jewish ranks from the very beginning, starting in AD 66, distinguished themselves with extraordinary courage in the battle in which Cestius

---

[86] *Mark* 16:3-5

Gallus was repulsed at the walls of Jerusalem, and they persevered to the very end, sharing in the suffering of their co-religionists, even as it grew ever more severe as the Roman legions tightened the screws of the vice of destruction.

By the end of August of AD 70, the legionaries had already captured and burned the temple, but the insurgents were still occupying parts of the city, preparing for a desperate fight. Then Titus spoke to their leaders from the other side of the ravine that separated the Temple from the Upper City. He called on his opponents to surrender immediately and unconditionally. He shouted:

"Oh, you unfortunates! What do you still hope to accomplish? Your nation is a corpse. There is no temple. The city is at my mercy. Your souls are in my hand. Do you believe that by dying in this way, you will gain the fame of heroes? I shall not argue with your madness. I'll only say this: if you lay your weapons and surrender without any preconditions, I will spare your life!"

They replied that they would not throw themselves on his mercy, as they had sworn by all that was sacred never to give up. However, they begged him to allow them to leave the city with their women and children. They said they would leave the fortifications, go far away into the desert, and leave to him without a fight all of Jerusalem and all the treasure gathered there.

Titus became furious: these people were on the point of death and dared to dictate conditions as if they had won!

He ordered his heralds to announce:

"Very well. Henceforth, I will no longer accept surrender. You can no longer count on my mercy. I will not spare anyone. Fight with all your might and try to save yourselves if you can. I will now act according to the law of war."

And he turned to his men, saying:

"Sack the city."

Which, of course, excited a great zeal among the troops getting ready for a final attack. The next day, the legionaries entered the district of Acra. It had burnt down in a fire that had started at the archives of the district of Ophel. The fire reached as far as the palace of Helen, which stood in the middle of Acra. Its houses, tightly packed about its narrow streets, full of corpses of those who had already died of hunger, wounds, and disease, blazed in a huge conflagration. That's when the sons and brothers of King Izates presented themselves to Titus, together with a handful of the most prominent citizens of Jerusalem. They begged the chief to show them mercy. And he, although full of anger because his offer of mercy had been rejected the day before, gave way and spared their lives. However, he ordered everyone to be put under guard, and later, he took the sons and cousins of the King of Adiabene to Rome in chains. There, they remained as hostages to guarantee the loyalty of the country on the Tigris, which had often vacillated between Rome and Parthia.

There seems little doubt that the princes of Adiabene owed their salvation to Tiberius Alexander—for he was there in AD 70, the highest-ranking Roman officer in Titus's army. It is easy to guess that he would have advocated for the supplicants: he must have remembered that twenty-odd years earlier, he—then the procurator of Judea—had received significant help from their mother and grandmother, Queen Helen.

## JUDEA, ARMENIA, EGYPT

Historians have recorded another significant event from the time of Tiberius Alexander's procuratorship of Judea. Religious fanatics again attempted to take advantage of the suffering of the population to stir up sectarian riots. But the procurator quickly quelled the uproar with a heavy hand. He crucified the two leaders of the rebellion. They were brothers Jacob and Simon, sons of Judah the Galilean, the founder of the sect of Zealots.

Herod, prince of Chalcis, the husband of Berenice, died in AD 48. Tiberius Alexander left office shortly thereafter, probably still in the same year. It is possible that there was some connection between these two events because the death of the prince changed the political calculus in Palestine: Roman authorities decided to entrust the administration of Palestine to new men. But the successors of Tiberius Alexander—mostly petty, brutal, and greedy men—resorted to ruthless methods of oppression, provoking the population to resistance and rebellion, which, in turn, triggered more Roman repression in a vicious cycle of ever more vicious cruelty. It had to end in a catastrophe sooner or later—and it did in AD 66.

We don't know where Tiberius Alexander served after leaving Judea. We catch a glimpse of him again in AD 63, in a land very distant from Palestine, on the upper reaches of Euphrates and Tigris, near Adiabene. A powerful Roman army assembled there under the command of Domitius Corbulo[87] in preparation for war against the Parthians. It consisted of four legions and many auxiliary cohorts, totaling some 60,000 men, and Tiberius Alexander served on its general staff. But the planned war never happened because King Tiridates proposed negotiations. Tacitus writes in his Book XV of his *Annals*:

> On the appointed day, Tiberius Alexander, an excellent Roman knight, assigned to Corbulo as war commissioner (*minister bello datus*), and Vinicianus Annius, Corbulo's son-in-law, who had not yet reached senatorial age but already served as a deputy legate of the Vth legion, presented themselves at the camp of Tiridates, to honor him and to reassure him that he did not need to fear treachery.[88]

This short mention shows how high this nephew of the Jewish philosopher of Alexandria had risen among Roman dignitaries. But three years later, he climbed even higher: in the spring of AD 65, he attained one of the highest and most powerful positions available to people of his class, the equites: Emperor Nero appointed him the Prefect of Egypt. And thus, Tiberius Alexander returned to the

---

[87] Gnaeus *Domitius Corbulo* (AD 7–67) was a popular Roman general, brother-in-law of the emperor Caligula and father-in-law of Domitian.

[88] Tacitus, *Annals*, XV 28

country of his birth to become its ruler. This nomination was all the more significant because Nero—it was widely reported—intended to travel to the Nile right after completing his Greek journey, to lead a military expedition far south, beyond its cataracts, to discover the mysterious sources of the great river and the causes of its annual flooding. The Prefect of Egypt would have played a very significant part in these plans. The emperor had certainly considered various candidates, looking for a conscientious, energetic, and trustworthy man.

When King Agrippa II, then ruling various territories on Lake Gennesaret, heard about this promotion of Alexander, he immediately hurried to the capital of Egypt to congratulate him personally. His sister, Berenice, widow of Prince Herod of Chalcis, though she usually did not leave her brother's side, remained in Jerusalem. A pious woman, she wanted to perform certain religious rites in the Temple related to her Nazirite vow. Here, she witnessed the arrival of the procurator Gesius Florus and the bloody incidents that followed. The disturbances, gradually gaining strength, soon led to the outbreak of the war, which is our subject here.

The bloody events in Jerusalem soon had an echo in Alexandria, a city with hundreds of thousands of Jews. There were riots, but the Prefect, though a Jew himself, suppressed them mercilessly, sending his two legions against the mostly unarmed population of the Jewish district. His uncle and tutor, Philo, had not lived to see it.

Two years later, in June AD 68, Alexander stood before the same two legions as they swore allegiance to their new emperor, Galba. Seven months later, in February 69, he swore them in to Emperor Otho and, three months after that, to Emperor Vitellius. And throughout that turbulent period, Tiberius Alexander remained unshakably loyal to the capital of the Empire, calmly and without hesitation accepting all orders from Rome. He had tied his fate to Rome, for better and for worse, and there was only one Rome.

And then, suddenly, on July 1, AD 69, that same Tiberius Alexander became the first man in the Empire to dare to take an arbitrary, audacious, and rebellious step with possibly incalculable and irreversible consequences. Despite what the Senate had already decided and what all the provinces and armies had humbly accepted, despite his and his legions' recent oath, he refused to obey the emperor already residing on the Palatine and elevated against him someone who, from a purely legal point of view, was only a usurper.

## TIBERIUS ALEXANDER AND BRENICE

Once we become familiar with the outlines of Alexander's biography, we are inclined to think that he championed Vespasian's candidacy for the sake of his own insatiable ambition, an ambition which had led him to break with the faith of his forefathers, adopt a Roman identity, and rule his kinsmen with a heavy hand. Evidently, he now calculated that he could expect no further advancement from Vitellius, who didn't know him. If, however, he chose to support Vespasian, he would be taking a huge risk, yes, but also opening great prospects for himself. For if Vespasian were to win, Tiberius Alexander would become one of the most important men of the Empire, a member of the inner ruling circle, ranking right after Vespasian, Titus, and Mucianus. It was a gamble, but a gamble worth taking.

Thus, let us accept that Tiberius Alexander decided to betray Vitellius out of self-interest. Yet, for that to happen, there must have been someone who had forewarned him that a revolt was brewing, someone who had been privy to the plans of Mucianus and Titus from the very beginning, who enjoyed their complete trust, and at the same time, had direct access to the Prefect of Egypt and could tell him about the business without fear of betrayal. Only one person in the world at that time met all these conditions: Berenice, sister of King Agrippa II.

Both Berenice and Tiberius Alexander were Jews, even if they differed in their attitude to religious tradition. She performed all the rituals devotedly while he openly ignored the most basic commandments of the Law. Yet, they both belonged to a small group of extremely wealthy families in the East and, like most such people in Eastern countries, were completely Hellenized. They thought and spoke Greek. Although short-lived and never consummated, Berenice's former marriage with Mark, Alexander's brother, connected them in a family bond, which meant a lot in those times. And, of course, the Prefect knew perfectly well—because who in the East did not?—that Titus loved Berenice. To the mind of Tiberius Alexander, this had to be an additional and extremely important reason to support Vespasian. For it was as clear as daylight that Titus would soon stand to inherit from his father, a man already advanced in years, and that, in turn, meant that Berenice, by his side, would be able to ensure a bright future for her family and friends.

And there was one more reason for these two to work together. The Prefect of Egypt, the nephew of a Jewish philosopher so passionately devoted to the traditions of his people, and a Jewish princess, great-granddaughter of the great Herod, the king who had regenerated Judea economically, strengthened it with fortresses and honored it with the magnificent expansion of her Temple had another cause in common: the fate of Judea. They both condemned what they saw as the sheer madness of her inhabitants and did their level best to help the Romans suppress the uprising. At the same time, they shared a sincere desire to save Judea, especially Jerusalem and its Temple, from destruction.

The planned acclamation of Vespasian as emperor would lead to a new civil war in the empire. Vespasian's generals, setting out against the legions of Vitellius, would lead significant forces away from the East, and this would greatly de-escalate the hostilities in Judea and postpone the final attack on the holy city.

Both Berenice and Alexander may have hoped that during that interval, the Zealots would fall or come to their senses or that more moderate and cautious elements would come to the fore, fed up with the blasphemies, rapine, and fratricidal murder. Finally, they may have hoped that the Romans would become more lenient and more understanding. And that the delay might thus deflect the mortal danger that hung over the country. In any case, the most important thing at the moment seemed to be to gain time. And what could possibly accomplish that better than putting forward a new Imperial candidate?

Are we allowed to attribute such thinking to Alexander? This is, of course, nothing more than a guess. And yet, we should recall a significant fact, which seems to support the view that Philo's nephew wanted to save the greatest sanctuary whose cult he himself rejected. That, despite his apostasy, he tried to save it at the last moment, in its last hours.

## DEBATING THE FATE OF THE TEMPLE

In the second half of August AD 70, Roman legionaries stormed the perimeter of the Temple from the side of the already captured Fortress Antonia, entered the outer courtyard (Court of the Gentiles), and set fire to its magnificent colonnades with their wooden ceilings. Despite this, the insurgents, locked in the inner courtyards, did not give up. The porticos burned the whole day and the whole night, but in the morning of the following day, Titus ordered the fire extinguished and the area near the gates cleared of rubble: he wanted to make room for his troops, who were about to storm the sanctuary.

Simultaneously, he summoned a council of his officers. In attendance were: Tiberius Alexander, the legates of the three Judean legions, the Prefect of the Camp of the two Egyptian legions (they had been transferred to Judea a few months earlier), the procurator of Judea, Antonius Julianus, several tribunes, and various procurators of various districts and agencies. Titus turned to them with a clearly formulated question:

"We have to decide what to do with the Temple. Should we spare it, or should we destroy it?"

Immediately, several voices spoke up, saying:

"Destroy it, for such is the law of war. Destroy it, too, because the Jews will never submit and will continue to raise revolts as long as the Temple exists. For it is not just a center of worship but a gathering place for fanatics from all over the world."

Others were of a different opinion, thinking that it was reasonable to save the Temple if the defenders agreed to lay down their arms. But if they continued to defend it, the Temple would have to be burned down like any other fortress, for, in such a case, the sin of sacrilege would fall on the Jews who forced the Romans to attack it.

Titus agreed with the latter view. Indeed, he went even further and declared:

"I will not take vengeance on inanimate objects, even if the Jews persist in fighting. No, I will not allow the destruction of such a magnificent temple—its loss would be a loss to Rome, too. But if the Tempe survives, it will be a jewel of our Empire forever."

Tiberius Alexander seconded this opinion. Two other senior officers did the same: Haterius Fronto, Prefect of the Camp of the Egyptian legions, and Sextus Cerealis, the legate of the Vth legion.

So that was it. Titus closed the meeting and ordered his men to rest before the attack. Only a few cohorts were detailed to put out the fires and clear the approach to the sanctuary.


Such was the course of the meeting according to the account left to us by Josephus in Book VI of his *Jewish War*.[89] He was at the Roman camp and enjoyed the complete confidence of Titus and his officers because of how ardently he served their interests. He had even approached the walls of Jerusalem, exposing himself to slings and arrows, and loudly called upon his compatriots to surrender. Josephus, of course, was not present at the meeting, but he was in a good position to learn what had been said and decided. His testimony should be reliable.

There is, however, one other account of the meeting, though it is very late, for it comes from the end of the 4th century. We find it

---

[89] Josephus Flavius, *The Jewish War*, VI 4,3

in the *Chronicle* of Sulpicius Severus, a Christian author from Gaul, writing in Latin. Taking into account the time and space separating his account from the Jerusalem of August AD 70, we would normally assume that Severus's version has little value compared to Josephus's. However, this would be a hasty judgment because Severus drew on a very early, informed and reliable source, that is, the now-lost parts of Tacitus' *Histories,* which were themselves based on the account of a participant in the meeting: Antonius Julianus, procurator of Judea. All we know about him today is that he held that office and took part in the meeting (all of which is confirmed by Josephus) and that he later wrote a book in which he blamed the Jews for the fate that befell the Temple. But it is worth noting the account of Severus because of his ultimate source:

> They say that Titus, having called a council of war, considered first whether to destroy the Temple. For it seemed to many that a building, which was so holy and more famous than all other works of man, should not be destroyed. Preserved, it would stand as testimony to Roman moderation but destroyed—as testimony to Roman cruelty. Others, including Titus, spoke against this. First of all, Titus believed that the temple had to be destroyed in order to eradicate the religions of Jews and Christians. For though these two were opposed to each other, they had come from the same since Christianity came from Judaism. And if you strike the root, the branches will wither.[90]

This remark about Christianity causes many scholars to dismiss Severus's account as false. They argue that in AD 70, the new religion was still too insignificant for the Roman general to think of it on par with Judaism—if he had heard about it at all. Such an attitude, they say, could only be justified much later—in the third or fourth centuries—when the followers of Christ became a powerful force within the Roman Empire. However, defenders of the thesis that Severus's account preserves the original report of Tacitus argue against this point. They say that the writer followed Tacitus faithfully in

---

[90] Sulpicius Severus, *Chronica,* II 30

describing Titus's opinion and decision concerning the destruction of the Temple and only added an anachronistic line about Christianity from himself.

Still, you might very well ask why we should even bother with the account of Severus since we have a contemporary source in Josephus Flavius. Yet there is one circumstance that does undermine the authority of Josephus's account: he is partial in certain matters, and in particular, he always strives to present Titus—his gracious patron and protector—in the most favorable light possible. Therefore, we cannot rule out that in the case of such a sensitive issue as the Roman commander's opinion concerning the destruction of the Temple, he deliberately distorted the truth and had his hero state a view directly opposite to the one he actually expressed in the meeting. If so, the question arises who the real advocate of preserving the temple was. Of course, we will never know, but it is at least possible that it was Tiberius Alexander and Josephus merely attributed his words to Titus.

Josephus's biases argue in favor of this assumption. Josephus disliked Tiberius Alexander and never failed to stress that the man had abandoned the religion of his fathers. This information, seemingly factual and objective, had a deeper meaning in the mouth of a Jew, a meaning that was perfectly clear to any contemporary Jewish reader. For in those days, incidents of apostasy became very common, some in favor of paganism and others in favor of new, emerging cults, including Christianity. Unsurprisingly, the rabbis condemned all apostates harshly. They preached that such people would suffer a terrible fate after death—that awaiting suicides: thrown into the abyss of the bottomless pit, they would be excluded from the blessings of the afterlife. So perhaps Josephus is trying to diminish the merit of Alexander's advocacy for the temple and to burnish the image of Titus with it.

It is useful to recall that Tiberius Alexander was seen as a renegade among the Romans, also, and that, though he was showered with honors and offices, he was not respected by them. This is the usual fate of men like him in all eras.[91] The satirist Juvenal put it in a particularly nasty way. Speaking of the statues of Roman leaders set in the portico of the Forum of Augustus, he writes maliciously:

> Among them, some Egyptian, some *alabarch*, dared to put his likeness; but it deserves only a piss.[92]

Yet, in some cases, what seemed to one side an act of apostasy seemed to the other side a noble act of conversion: a discovery of the truth, a repudiation of former errors, an entry onto the right path. The heart of Christianity pulsated with the intertwining of these sensitive issues; after all, the movement was in its essence a schism of Judaism, and its communities, carrying out feverish missionary activity among Jews and pagans from the very beginning, consisted in the first generations exclusively, and in the subsequent ones mostly of—Jewish apostates.

Echoes of these heated disputes can be read in the old Christian novel we have been reading. We left it when its hero, young Clement, listened to Peter's teachings concerning syzygies in Caesarea Maritima, a sermon which concluded that Simon Magus was the conjugate—the evil and satanic counterpart—of Peter himself. And on that occasion, we heard a reference to Berenice, a pious woman from Phoenician Tyre.

## VISITING BERENICE

After leaving Caesarea Maritima, Clement, Niketas, Aquila and I arrived in Tyre, a city in Phoenicia. Following the instructions of Peter, we stayed with Berenice, who was as pious as her mother, Justa. She welcomed us warmly; she showed respect to me, whom she had just met, and true love to Niketas and Aquila. Delighted, she talked to us like a family and made us feel at home. Understanding that she wanted to persuade us to stay longer, I had to explain to her the purpose of our visit:

----

[91] No doubt a reference to the many Poles who entered Russian Imperial service during the Russian rule 1772-1991.

[92] Juvenal, *Satires*, I 130-131

"It is right and worthy of praise that you welcome us with sisterly love, but we must put the fear of God before our own comforts. We are fighting for the salvation of mankind and are reluctant to put physical comfort over of that ultimate good. We have had news about the sorcerer Simon. He held a disputation with Peter in Caesarea in which he was defeated, and now he escaped here to continue his evil work.

"He slanders Peter to everyone, and in this way, he leads a multitude of souls to destruction. Being a sorcerer himself, he claims with incredible impudence that Peter is one! During their disputation, he was forced to admit defeat on every point and fled the square ignominiously, but now he proclaims that he has won and has bested Peter. He constantly admonishes those around him not to listen to Peter's words. He pretends to be worried about people's souls, but in fact, he deceives them.

"Therefore, as soon as our lord Peter heard about this, he sent us ahead to investigate whether these reports were true; and if they are, we should write to him immediately so that he may come here and expose his slander, falsehoods, and tricks. So, you see, since we are fighting for the salvation of souls, we must set aside all concern for our own comfort. But we'd love to hear from you, who lives here, whether what they say about Simon's activities is true."

To which Berenice replied:

"Everything is just as you say. But I will tell you other things about Simon that may not be known elsewhere. He can cause terrible visions to appear in the market square in broad daylight, so the whole city lives in fear. When he goes abroad, statues he passes by move, and strange shadows seem to follow him. He says that they are the souls of the dead. Some people accused him to his face of being a sorcerer. He pretended to want to get along with them. He invited them to his place for a feast, but then he infected them with terrible disease and evil spirits. It came to the point that many people consider him a divine being. He frightens people but also attracts worship and admiration. I no longer believe that anyone will be able to extinguish this fire, which is slowly consuming our city. No one here will dare to oppose what

Simon is teaching. Everyone will rather confirm that his words are the purest truth. Therefore, I sincerely advise you not to act against him in any way. I fear that you will face terrible danger if you do not take my advice. Wait patiently until Peter arrives. Only he can oppose Simon's power. I am very afraid of Simon myself. If you had not told me that Peter had once bested Simon, I would now be advising you to dissuade him from coming!"

I reassured Berenice that Peter understood the situation. He knew what Simon was capable of but was certain of his own powers, or he would not have sent us with this mission.

Evening came, and after a modest supper, we went to sleep. In the morning, a male relative of Berenice's came to the house. He told us that the night before, Simon had unexpectedly boarded a ship and sailed away for Sidon, leaving three disciples behind in Tyre. We asked who these people were. He replied that the first among them was a certain man called Appion Pleistonicos of Alexandria. This name intrigued me, for I had once known a man with that name who was also a native of Alexandria. Years ago, he had visited us in Rome, and my father Faustus gladly welcomed him as a learned and friendly man. Was I about to meet that Alexandrian again? Here, of all places? In Tyre?

The second one was certain Anubion from the Egyptian city of Diospolis, an astrologer by profession. The third was Athenodorus of Athens, a follower of the philosophy of Epicure.

We immediately wrote down everything we had learned about Simon as completely as possible, sent a trusted messenger with the letter to Peter, and left Berenice's house. The sun had already risen high enough to take a walk around the city before it became too hot.


## MEETING APPION

After some time, we saw a large crowd walking towards us. Three men led the group. They looked very dignified. One of them, walking in the middle, looked at me carefully. He then positively beamed, smiled, opened his arms wide, and, forgetting all dignity, ran up to me. It was indeed Appion. He greeted me warmly, hugged and kissed me. He then turned to his entourage, who watched the scene sympathetically but from a distance, out of respect to the deputy of their master. Pointing to me, Appion said with great emphasis:

"This is Clement, son of Faustus, a native of Rome. How many times have I told you about this noble young man! How many times have I praised his excellent family, beautiful character, and comprehensive education! Unfortunately, while still in Rome, our priceless friend fell under the influence of a certain barbarian. And now is being deceived by Peter. Our good Clement has been possessed by him so thoroughly that he thinks and acts like a Jew! But now, look, the gods have sent him to us so we can help him. Let us try to save this young man so dear to our hearts. I'll ask him various questions. You will all stand here as witnesses and judges of this great trial. Since our noble friend is deeply convinced that he has finally found the one and only true faith, I will ask him to tell me honestly what he thinks about the following question..."

Here, he paused for a moment to think. Meanwhile, his companions came closer and gathered around us in a circle, eager to see what turn the conversation would take. As for me, while I felt that Appion's attack was downright rude, I did not attempt to back out of the situation. On the contrary, I was very glad that the opportunity for my first real duel had finally come. So far, I had only passively listened to the great debates between Peter and Simon. But now it was my chance to show what I had learned. Meanwhile, Appion found the words he was looking for:

"Answer me honestly, dear Clement. Don't you think you are committing a reprehensible crime by arbitrarily breaking the eternal, sacred order of things? You rejected the faith and gods of your fathers, and instead, you adopted some barbaric superstition, ridiculous fantasies, and very strange customs."

I replied without a moment's hesitation:

"I fully appreciate your good intentions but must point out

your ignorance. You want me to remain forever faithful to what you yourself believe is as true, beautiful, good, and useful. But it is just possible that you may be ignorant of what is true, beautiful, and good, and by attempting to guide me, in fact lead me instead astray."

Appion was greatly insulted:

"Why would you call ignorant someone who honestly loves his native traditions and in every situation thinks as it befits an honest Greek?"

I replied:

"Whoever has decided to live in accordance with God's will will no longer be able to uphold the old traditions. Such a person will observe only that which is dictated by true piety and will reject without hesitation everything that contradicts it. Does it not sometimes happen that a man whose father had lived not very honestly decides to live differently? Indeed, it is not always appropriate to follow one's father's practices!"

Appion immediately picked up on these last words. He asked me with a malicious smile, certain that he had me trapped:

"Does this mean, Clement, that you accuse your own father Faustus of having lived impiously?"

I replied calmly:

"Not at all. I only think that his religious views were mistaken. I did not say anything about the way he had lived his life."

But Appion did not give up:

"And what do you find wrong in his beliefs?"

"This: that he believed the perverse and deceitful stories which Greeks tell about their gods."

Appion pretended surprise:

"And what myth have you in mind, which is allegedly so deceitful?"

"First of all, my father had the wrong idea about the nature of the gods. He and the Greeks. If you have time, you and your students could listen to what I think about this. But if we are going to speak about such things, should we continue to do so here in the middle of the street like this?"

At this, one of the men in Appion's entourage gestured to me and suggested:

"It will get hot soon. If you would like to talk in a quiet and cool place, I invite you to my garden. It is not far from here, just outside the city walls!"

## CONCERNING THE BELIEFS OF GREEKS

They went ahead, we followed, and soon we all found ourselves sitting by a clear, cool stream in the shade of lush-green trees. We chatted a little about this and that, and then I introduced my topic:

"First, a general note. It is important to be aware of the huge difference between a faith that one has arrived at through one's own effort after diligent research and an opinion that is cultivated only because it was acquired passively, through tradition, which persists in its customary form unaltered, regardless of its truth or falsity. No one rejoices at the truth of inherited beliefs nor worries if he suspects that they may be false. Quite simply, no follower of a tradition acts on conviction so much as out of a certain prejudice, by which I mean an unexamined opinion. Does anyone ever investigate, question, or discuss what the ancestors had in mind when they established a given custom or formulated a particular dogma? Almost everyone unquestioningly approves of his own tradition and, what is more, is proud to do so! But in fact, the most he can do is hope that fate has been kind to him and that what he inherited from his parents is indeed true, good, and beautiful. Indeed, it is not easy to throw off a garment once you get used to it. Why, we often persist in wearing it out, threadbare, and even ridiculous as it may be.

"And now I come to the heart of our dispute. To put it briefly, I say that the so-called Greek learning is a dangerous and harmful invention of the Evil One. It is dangerous because it malforms human character and inclines people to act wrongly. Here's how I show it.

"Most Greeks would have us believe that the world is ruled by a multitude of gods. It is easy to guess why man would invent these creatures, supposedly immortal and powerful, but at the same time amoral and susceptible to passions. The idea is that a person committing an unworthy act need not feel shame because, in every situation, he can quote a myth in which some god committed terrible atrocities far worse than what he has just done. And if a man is not ashamed, we cannot even hope that one day he will regret what he has done and resolve to improve.

"Other Greeks believe in Tyche, that is, Fate, assigned to man at the moment of his birth and irreversible. So what we have is something similar to the previous case: for if someone truly believes that he will neither experience anything nor be able to do anything contrary to what has been determined for him, he is inclined to commit all sorts of sins, and when he sins he does not feel the slightest remorse. He says that he only fulfills the decrees of fate. And thus, "fate" is his moral excuse. He is not the perpetrator. His deeds are neither his fault nor his merit since no one can change his fate.

"Still others introduce the principle of blind chance. This means that in this world, everything happens by itself, without any plan or providence, and no one controls it. In my opinion, this is the most dangerous view of all. If no being stands above us, seeing through us and judging us, then everyone can do whatever he likes and he needs never fear punishment. Therefore, those who think this way will not come to their senses easily or at all. After all, they are unable to predict the consequences of their actions."


## THE TENTH OF AB


Let's try, at least for a moment, to understand the reasoning of the ancient readers of this novel. The more enlightened and more educated among them would have known perfectly well that in AD 70—barely a couple decades after the events described in the novel— an event had taken place that seemed to disprove the arguments of

Clement.

He was a Judeo-Christian. He had abandoned the evil deities and erroneous ways of his pagan ancestors. He embraced the teaching that the Messiah had come and suffered a martyr's death during the procuratorship of Pontius Pilate in the reign of Emperor Tiberius. Consequently, the same Clement accepted the view that the Temple in Jerusalem was the only tabernacle of the True God, a being who was good, just, all-seeing, and who providentially directed the universe. But look what happened to this temple! Many contemporaries, even among pious Jews, openly claimed that neither human nor divine agency destroyed the Tabernacle, but Fate—that is, blind chance. But Clement condemned just this view as utterly immoral!

The discussion between Titus and his senior officers concerning the fate of the Temple took place on the 9th of the month Ab. It adopted the view of Titus—or perhaps of Tiberius Alexander— that the temple should be spared. There was no more fighting that day because the insurgents, crowded in the inner courtyards of the temple, were overcome by fear and fatigue, and the victorious Romans could afford the delay. During the night, however, the Jews regained their courage, and their will to fight returned. Around the second hour of the day, that is, very early in the morning, the defenders of the Temple made a surprise sortie through the eastern gate and attacked the Roman guards camped out in the outer courtyard. The legionaries put up a brave defense, although the enemy initially had superior numbers and was in excellent fighting spirit. The Romans closed ranks and covered themselves with a wall of shields. Titus saw the clash from the walls of Fortress Antonia and quickly sent in reinforcements.

The insurgents lost several dead, pulled back, regrouped, and attacked again. The two ranks pushed back and forth across the large square, among smoke and fire, until the fifth hour of the day. Only then did it become possible to push the Jews back into the inner courtyard. The heat of the blazing sun was by now pouring down from the sky, so immediately after the clash, Titus returned to his makeshift quarters in Fortress Antonia. He wanted to rest and give respite to his cohorts so that he could launch the decisive attack with all his forces at sunrise of the following day. But fate had it otherwise. Disregarding the heat, the insurgents sortied once again and attacked those Romans still engaged in extinguishing the fire of the burning porticoes. A general melee broke out, with men fighting in disorderly small groups. At that point, one of the Romans grabbed a burning log from the heap of rubble and ran to the gilded window in the northern wall surrounding the Sanctuary. His companions lifted him up, and he threw the firebrand inside. The fire evidently hit some flammable material, for a powerful blaze exploded immediately. The defenders screamed with terror and rushed in from all directions to extinguish the fire, forgetting about the fight and not even caring about their own lives.

Writing about the legionary who threw in the torch, Josephus adds that he did it without an order and without thinking, as if pushed by some demonic power. But just these words, seemingly looking for an explanation for what happened, raise some suspicions. Was the fire really started by accident? Had no one really issued a secret order?

Titus was lying in his tent when a messenger rushed in with the report of renewed fighting and a fire threatening the temple itself. The commander immediately jumped up and ran to the place of action as he stood. Josephus tells us he was still thinking about saving the temple. He was followed by senior officers and thousands of soldiers. There was a terrible uproar and confusion, with hosts of armed men milling about the external courtyard, fighting and trampling the wounded. Many died, trampled to death, or pushed into the fire. In vain did Titus call on his men to extinguish the fire. No one could hear his voice, and no one paid attention to his gesticulation. No force could stop the rush of the human river. The soldiers who finally reached the inner courtyard now pressed around the wall of the Sanctuary, and thunderous cries broke out from the back, calling on them to burn everything. The insurgents put up desperate resistance in isolated groups, and others tried to escape, while the Romans, in battle rage, killed everyone and everything they could lay their hands on.

Many civilians had sought refuge in the Sanctuary, thinking

that the Temple was the safest place in the besieged city. In the preceding days, prophecies circulated in Jerusalem that those who took cover in the Temple would live to see the promised miracle of salvation. Yet, whole mounds of corpses had already piled up around the great altar, where sacrifices were made, and streams of blood flowed down the twelve steps of the Tabernacle. Titus climbed the stairs and entered the interior. He wanted to see the treasury and the sacred objects of worship gathered there before fire consumed them forever.

But he ran out onto the courtyard immediately, calling on his men to extinguish the fire, for he had noticed that the flames from the neighboring buildings did not yet catch the walls and ceilings of the Inner Sanctum. The centurion of the bodyguard, Liberalis, tried to drive men with his cane, but this did not work. Everyone who entered the sanctuary thought only about its fabulous treasures, determined to take advantage of the fire to seize something for himself. The soldiers expected their officers to announce that they confiscated the treasury for the state but, in fact, steal it for themselves; they assumed that they, the privates, would receive only a pittance after the final victory.

And at that moment, right behind Titus's back, someone threw a torch into the Sanctuary. The fire caught immediately, even though most wooden elements were covered with gold foil, so the fire would not have caught easily.

At the entrance to the Sanctuary hung a great, heavy curtain of Babylonian workmanship, woven with astonishing skill from threads of various colors, blue and red, white cotton and purple wool. This intermingling was said to have a deep symbolic meaning, representing the elements of the universe: red symbolizing fire, blue—air, cotton—earth, and purple—the sea. The former two, on account of their color, the latter two, on account of their origin, since cotton grows on land and purple comes from the sea. The curtain was decorated with embroidery representing every object in the sky—except the signs of the zodiac.

It should not be confused with another curtain hanging in the back and separating the first part of the tabernacle from the Holy of

Holies. Later Christian tradition held that one of these curtains—but which one?—tore apart when Jesus expired on the cross, revealing the interior and thus symbolizing that everything ancient had already come true and the mystery of faith had been revealed.

Josephus Flavius, a witness to the fire, says:

> Although the heart aches at the thought that a work more admirable than anything else seen or heard of has been wiped out from the face of the earth, a work incomparable in its immensity, splendor, and richness, in its every detail, and above all, in its meaning, let your mind be comforted to think that inexorable fate lays its mighty hand on every human work and on every place dear to human heart. And only amazement remains when the mind reflects on how precisely fate manifests itself: the destruction of the present Tabernacle fell on the same day of the same month on which the First Tabernacle was destroyed by the Babylonians. From the construction of the First Temple by King Solomon until the destruction of the Second Temple in our day—which took place in the second year of Emperor Vespasian, exactly 1130 years, seven months, and fifteen days passed. [93]

# THE CONFERENCE OF BERYTUS

Josephus was right: August AD 70, when the temple in Jerusalem burned down, was indeed the second year of Vespasian's reign, if we count, of course, from July 1, AD 69, when Tiberius Alexander proclaimed the new emperor in the capital of Egypt. This act was repeated three days later at Caesarea, in the presence of Vespasian, and then in Antioch. But those ceremonies, carefully planned, prepared, and agreed upon in advance, constituted only the formal beginning of the game, and the plotters immediately set about securing all the necessary elements of any successful rebellion: speed, resolution, and surprise.

---

[93] Josephus Flavius, *The Jewish War*, VI 4

Already by the end of July AD 69, a war council met in the Phoenician city of Berytus, today's Beirut. The deliberations were chaired by the newly proclaimed Emperor Vespasian. For he, once the irreversible step had been taken, immediately set aside his former doubts and devoted himself with his usual energy to the matters of war. Or rather, two wars: after all, he had to think both about the war in Palestine and the inevitable war against Vitellius. Titus came to Berytus alongside his father. He was accompanied by various commanders and officials of the three Palestinian legions. From Antioch came Mucianus, leading a similar procession of delegates of the Syrian army. We do not know whether Prefect Tiberius Alexander appeared in person, though it is certain that his representatives participated in the meetings. Moreover, the interests of her kinsman were, to some extent, represented by Queen Berenice, also present in Berytus. Tacitus writes, not without irony:

> She was in the bloom of her years and beauty, pleasing even to Vespasian, thanks to the splendor of her gifts. [94]

Very likely, her brother, King Agrippa II, was also present. Back in January of AD 69, he had traveled with Titus to Rome to congratulate Galba on his assumption of office. But when the two arrived in Corinth and learned of Galba's death, Titus returned to the Levant— all the more willingly since Berenice was waiting for him there—while Agrippa continued on to solicit the favor of Otho. He remained in the capital to observe further developments. He was certainly pleased to see the rising cult of Nero because he himself owed to the deposed emperor a significant expansion of his kingdom (which was why, as early as AD 55, he had renamed his capital at the source of the Jordan *Neronias*). Otho's wholesale rehabilitation of Nero's favorites augured well for Agrippa's interests. Who knows, maybe he also quietly ordered flowers to be placed before the porphyry sarcophagus in the Domitians' tomb?

Alas, the defeat and death of Otho placed the Jewish king in a

---

[94] Tacitus, *Histories*, V 81,2

rather unpleasant situation: since he had rushed to Rome fully aware of the circumstances of Galba's death, everyone understood it to mean that he approved and supported the assumption of power by his killer. How would Otho's victor, Vitellius, view this? Despite this—or perhaps precisely because of this—Agrippa decided to wait in the capital to try to ingratiate himself with the new ruler of the Empire. Meanwhile, envoys reached him from Palestine, from his sister, Berenice. They brought secret dispatches about a "great event" being planned in the East. The king wasted no time. He left Rome on some excuse and traveled back to his homeland post-haste.

Almost certainly, Sohaemus of Emessa was also present at the meeting in Berytus, the Roman client and Priest-king of what is the present-day Homs in southern Syria.[95] His estates lay too close to the center of the rebellion for him to show any hesitation in such a decisive moment. Like it or not, he had to join the cause.

The situation was slightly different for Antiochus, king of Commagene.[96] His was the most powerful and richest of the Roman client states in the East, with its own powerful religious center at Mount Nimrut.[97]

It is true that Antiochus immediately supported Vespasian, contributing men and money, but he probably did not come to Berytus. He could easily justify his absence by his advanced age and the

-------------------

[95] Emesa was recorded by Herodianus (c. AD 170-240) to have been by the 3rd-century BC the centre of a worship of the ancient pagan god Elagabalus, the original name of which is posited to have been *El-Gabal, Elah Gabal,* or *Ilah Gabal* all meaning "God of the Mountain." Emperor Heliogabalus (ruled 218-222) was an hereditary Priest-King of this cult.

[96] Corresponding to today's Adiyaman Province in Eastern Turkey.

[97] In 62 BC, King Antiochus I of Commagene built on the mountain top at Nimrut a tomb-sanctuary flanked by huge statues 25-30 feet tall of himself, two lions, two eagles, and various composite Greek and Iranian gods, such as Heracles-Artagnes-Ares, Zeus-Oromasdes, and Apollo-Mithras-Helios-Hermes. When constructing this pantheon, Antiochus drew heavily from Parthian and Armenian traditions in order to reinvigorate the religion of his ancestral dynasty, aspiring no doubt to create another cult center to rival those of Jerusalem, Pafos, and Homs (Translator's Note).

hardships of the long journey from the upper Euphrates to Phoenicia. But the Romans trusted Antiochus completely. It was clear that he had no choice but to support Vespasian with all his heart. The reason was obvious: his son, who bore the same name, was in Rome when the civil war broke out; he stood at Otho's side and fought bravely in the April battles on the Po. He was wounded in one of the skirmishes near Cremona. Although the prince managed to save himself and later returned to his homeland, the family could not expect anything good from the victorious Vitellius. And they had reasons to fear for their throne, for they had already lost and recovered it twice in the last half-century due to the endless rotation of Roman emperors.

## MONEY, ARMS, STRATEGY

Numerous embassies from the cities of Syria, Palestine, Asia Minor, and Egypt were also present. They offered to the new emperor congratulations, best wishes, and gifts customary on such occasions—often in the form of heavy wreaths of pure gold. Vespasian eagerly accepted all gifts and contributions because fighting two wars required huge amounts of money. He was bravely seconded in this respect by Mucianus, who often repeated the old adage that money is the sinew of any venture. His mint in Antioch immediately began striking gold and silver coins with the image of the new emperor and the inscription *Imperator Caesar Vespasianus Augustus*, although, for obvious reasons, the Senate had not yet granted him these titles. On their reverse, the coins featured either the head of Titus—thus emphasizing his special role at his father's side—or the auspicious figures of Victory and Courage. Following the example of Syria, other Eastern mints soon began to strike the same coin, recycling older monies they received in taxes.

Mucianus proved very skillful in squeezing money out of the population; he did not hesitate to employ the services of informers to locate taxable assets of the rich. The governor did not spare his own wealth either but refused to pay bribes or make exorbitant promises. Vespasian showed similarly commendable continence in making promises, though they are customary among all those seeking office.

All cities were ordered to produce and deliver weapons needed to arm newly formed Roman cohorts and newly raised auxiliary units. Extraordinary conscription was imposed in all provinces, and veterans settled in various countries of the East were recalled to their units. Energetic officers appointed by the new ruler traveled from the Black Sea to Egypt, gathering men and resources.

Taking advantage of the emperor's special powers, Vespasian distributed senatorial positions to various people from the equite class. Those nominated did not always stand out for their moral qualifications. In those days of urgent preparations, when there were not enough people to fill newly created positions, some achieved dignity entirely thanks to being available and ready to please. Vespasian could not be choosy because most of the representatives of the old Roman families were in Italy.

But his most important task was to establish a strategic plan and assign key commands. First of all, it was decided that Vespasian would travel to Egypt because that country was of exceptional importance as the most fertile and, in case of a setback in war, the easiest to defend. The Emperor was to stay there and make sure that no grain shipments sailed for Italy. This decision suggested that, despite everything, Tiberius Alexander was not entirely trusted.

Since the emperor was to remain in Egypt, and therefore away from the theater of operations, one might have expected that Titus would lead the army against Vitellius. But, no, this most difficult, but also the most honorable, task was entrusted to Mucianus, thus indicating that he held a special position in the new Imperial hierarchy.

Of course, his experience and authority were another reason for the decision. Titus was still too young to be able to manage operations on such a large scale. Instead, he was given the supreme command in the war against the Jews. Here, the situation was relatively simple, as it was only a matter of capturing Jerusalem and a few fortresses, and the capital of the country was still bleeding in a fratricidal conflict. Titus knew the country, its people, and its tactics. It seemed almost certain that he might relatively easily achieve the fame of a victor there. And who knows whether Berenice's presence did not also play a role in this decision?

She certainly wanted Titus to remain in Judea because only then could she keep him close and, at the same time, hope to save the holy city from destruction.

The battle order was as follows:

The two Egyptian legions were left in Egypt. They were supposed to maintain order in the vast country and constitute a reserve in the event of an unfavorable turn of events.

The three Palestinian legions were also left in Judea to prosecute the Jewish war, but their headcounts were substantially reduced, and two and a half thousand men were transferred to Mucianus. (Such temporarily separated units of the Roman army were called *vexillationes*).

The three legions stationed in Syria could be reduced even more as there appeared to be no danger from the Parthians. Their king assured Mucianus, in secret negotiations, that he would remain friendly and neutral. Rumors even spread—perhaps Mucianus himself, always full of ideas, ordered them to be circulated?—that the ruler of the Parthians had offered to send forty thousand archers to aid Vespasian, but Vespasian demurred. He was afraid that using foreign troops in a civil war would lead the residents of Italy to consider him a foreign invader.

But it is certain that Vespasian sent envoys from Berytus to both kings—of Parthia and Armenia—warning them against attacking the borders of the Empire at such a critical moment. He then apparently decided that such diplomatic action was enough and decreased the strength of the Euphrates army by about one-half, taking one whole legion for his expeditionary force and two *vexillationes* from the other two. The legion he took was the storied VIth legion, *Ferrata*, whose tradition went back to Caesar's conquest of Gaul.

In total, Mucianus's corps numbered a little over twenty thousand men. This would not be enough to defeat Vitellius' powerful army, for he had sixty thousand men in Italy alone and could bring more from the Lower Rhine. But Vespasian and Mucianus expected support from the legions on the Danube. It was a very large army, and even if its commanders were to leave half their strength behind to guard the border, Vespasian's offensive force would easily double in size.

In order to rendezvous with them, Mucianus decided to march through Asia Minor to the Balkans and concentrate his navy in Byzantium. From there, he intended to cut across the peninsula by way of Macedonia and arrive at the adriatic Sea near Dyrrachium, in today's Albania. But Mucianus was prepared to change his route depending on developments.

Another critical decision during the meeting in Berytus was to undertake fifth-column operations in Vetellius's territory. Officers in civilian clothes were sent to Italy with appropriate letters to the troops, commanders, city councils, and governors. Particular hope was placed in the Praetorians dismissed from service and disarmed. It was well-known how much they hated the new emperor, how painfully they felt their humiliating dismissal, and how much they feared repression. Could they perhaps be brought back into action?

The fate of these secret agents, sent on dangerous missions, was mixed. All experienced many dangers and adventures while traveling by land and sea—what subject for a historical adventure novel! Some managed to complete their mission successfully, but others fell into the hands of Vitellius's men and were sent back to Rome to be executed for inciting a rebellion. Still others, trailed or outright hunted, managed to hide and wait out the worst, thanks to the help of various friends.

After the congress of Berytus, Vespasian and Mucianus, and probably Titus and Berenice, went to Antioch to prepare the departure of the expeditionary force. They were accompanied by Josephus, son of Matthias, formerly a leader of the Galilean revolt, who had been taken prisoner two years earlier at Jotapata and had since been kept under guard in chains. But Josephus left the Phoenician city a free man. His chains had been broken in a public ceremony in

Berytus.

# JOSEPHUS UNCHAINED

Let us recall:

Two years earlier, at the beginning of July 67, after the Romans captured Jotapata, they pulled out Josephus from his underground hiding place. It was full of corpses, for all who had hidden there died voluntarily, killing one another, in order determined by lot. Only their leader, Josephus, survived as he was supposed to be the last to commit suicide and—didn't. He was then brought before Vespasian, Titus, and two tribunes and told them—or at least this is what he later wrote in his chronicle—that he was the herald of an important message from God. And he swore that if it weren't for the divine commission, he would certainly have killed himself along with the others.

He continued:

> I hear you want to send me to Nero as a prize. And I tell you not to do this! There is no need. Do you think he will reign for a long? No such thing! You, Vespasian, will be emperor soon. You don't believe me, it's understandable, but yet I am in your hands. Keep me under guard and then punish me severely if anything of what I am telling you today does not come to pass!

Did the captive really dare to prophesy in these words? This seems doubtful and we only have his testimony for this. Josephus maintains that his bold words had their effect and that, although he remained under guard and in chains, his captives were in no hurry to send him back to Nero. Apparently—again, Josephus claims—Vespasian somehow learned from the captives at Jotapata that Josephus had a gift of prophecy because during the siege, he had predicted the fall of the fortress after forty-seven days, which is exactly what then came to pass. In any case, from that moment on, Josephus enjoyed the special favor of the Roman general, as he later said with pride:

> He gave me rich clothes and other valuable gifts, was constantly friendly towards me, and showed me solicitude, and Titus did as

well. And on his orders, I married a certain girl, captured near Caesarea and coming from that area. [98]

But the hour of triumph came to Josephus only in Berytus. He writes about it in Book IV of his *Jewish War* with truly oriental exaggeration, praising himself in a way free of any undue modesty:

> Since more or less everything went smoothly and the whole project unfolded favorably, Vespasian came to the conclusion that he had been destined for power by Divine Justice and that Divinity had placed the world in his hands. So he remembered all the signs and omens preannouncing his reign, of which very many had happened over the years—and among them, the words of Josephus, who had dared to call him emperor while Nero still lived.
>
> And then he realized with trepidation that he still held that man in chains. Having summoned Mucianus along with other commanders and friends, he first told them about the skill and energy of Josephus, who had given him so much trouble at Jotapata, and then about his prophecy. He admitted that, at the time, he considered the prophecy a fabrication born out of fear, but time and subsequent events showed that the prophecy had been divinely inspired. So he said: "It is a disgrace that this man, who had passed on to me the word of God predicting my ascent to power, should find himself among the captives and suffer the fate of a prisoner!" He then sent for Josephus and ordered him released. All the present could thereby draw encouragement and hope of reward after seeing how gracious Vespasian was to a mere foreigner. Titus, standing next to his father, said: "We must immediately remove this ugly stigma of slavery from this man by breaking the chains." For this is how Romans liberate those who were imprisoned unjustly. And they crushed my chains with a hammer." [99]

The reader might doubt whether Josephus owed his liberation to his prophecy. Could he have owed it more to a powerful protector? If so, was it—Berenice?

---

[98] Josephus Flavius, *The Jewish War*, III 8,3
[99] Ibid., IV 10, 7

In Rome, there was a different mood, and different omens were observed. On July 18, immediately after his triumphal entry into the capital at the head of sixty thousand men, Vitellius received the dignity of *Pontifex Maximus*—the high priest. All previous emperors had held it. Accordingly, the new ruler of Rome published the customary edict on religious ceremonies that very same day.

This triggered a general consternation for July 18 was thought to be an inauspicious date. In 477 BC, that day brought destruction upon the entire Fabian clan, drawn by the Etruscans into an ambush on the Cremera stream. On the same day a century later, the Roman army suffered a terrible defeat in battle against the Gauls on the river Allia. Since then, a strictly observed tradition forbade any important public or private business to be transacted on July 18, and now the inhabitants of Rome asked each other with astonishment:

"Maybe Vitellius did not know it? Or maybe he forgot? Even if he thinks the whole business is just a superstition, he's giving ammunition to his critics. Do his advisors really work in a constant haze of wine, as their enemies claim?"

But an impartial observer had to admit that despite the possibly inadvertent mishap with the inauspicious date, Vitellius began his rule in the capital not badly at all and, in any case, much better than had been expected. He wasn't vengeful, did not launch persecutions, and he maintained an exemplary appearance of the rule of law.

He made it clear that he wanted to cooperate with the Senate. He diligently participated in the meetings of the august assembly, even when the agenda included consideration of insignificant or even trivial matters. It happened one day, very early in the reign, that Senator Helvidius Priscus dared to disagree with the emperor's opinion. At first, Vitellius was visibly upset but soon he calmed down. He contented himself with a purely formal procedural move: he called upon the people's tribunes to support him since a people's tribune had just been shown contempt. (Vitellius, like all his predecessors since Tiberius, was vested with the powers of the people's tribune). And whoever disagreed with him was thereby showing disrespect to the Roman People. The whole thing ended in Vitellius's comment:

"Of course, it is nothing new, but the most ordinary thing when two Senators hold different opinions."

He thereby signaled to his colleagues that he considered himself one of them, the first among equals. The incident made all the greater impression because Helvidius Priscus was considered a steadfast and even provocatively bold defender of republican ideals. In this respect, he was a faithful follower of his father-in-law, Thrasea Paetus, who, under Nero, paid with his life for the courage with which he defended civil liberties and people wrongly accused. And now Vitellius, as if justifying Helvidius's attitude, said calmly and with a very serious face:

"Thrasea Paetus and I have once disagreed, also."

He said it in such a way that no one could guess whether he was joking or really meant to imply that he had once been in opposition, for in Nero's times, he had boldly attacked... Nero's enemies. Some people were outraged by this statement, saying that it was downright impertinent to compare that situation with the present one and himself with Thrasea Paetus. Others, however, saw it as a backhand tribute to republican virtue.

This incident concerned only senators, whereas the favor of the wider masses Vitellius gained by appearing in the Forum alongside candidates standing for office and recommending them personally before the elections—for some elections took place in July. Of course, it was only a formality, an empty and downright absurd relic from the times of the republic, when there was a real fight for popularity, support, and votes. Now, everything was agreed in advance in the imperial palace, and the alleged elections turned into a ridiculous and humiliating demonstration of the loyalty of the subjects. Some, however, were pleased that Vitellius showed respect for the appearances of real political life because fictions do matter in public life.[100]

# FEASTS AND GAMES

But Vitellius won the most sympathy among the common people by attending theaters and the circus. He watched all spectacles with true pleasure, especially chariot races, and he had long been a passionate and downright fanatical fan of the faction of the Blues. Some said that he owed his governorship of Lower Germany to that association. Galba had granted the office to him on the advice of Titus Vinius, who was also an ardent supporter of the Blues. Soon after his arrival in the province, Vitellius was proclaimed emperor by his legions. These despised Galba, had already started a rebellion, and were only looking for a candidate for the throne with a senatorial rank. They found him in the freshly arrived person of Vitellius.

So now Vitellius supported the Blues even more passionately, believing that he owed his amazing career to them. Suetonius reports that he even punished members of the audience who dared to shout slogans against the Blues during races. But if there is any truth to this, and some people were indeed punished for rooting against the Blues, it probably happened only towards the end of the emperor's reign, when, feeling threatened by the progress of the rebellion from the East, he seemed to detect signs of disloyalty everywhere and became furious at the drop of a hat. But in his first months in power, Vitellius made every effort to be popular and appear fun and carefree.

Although there was a shortage of funds, the chariot stables were rapidly expanded, new gladiator units were brought in from other cities, and exotic animals were imported from faraway places. It seemed to the people that the happy days of never-ending games and feasts of Nero were back again.

Vitellius feasted without interruption, splendidly and

---

[100] The results of Polish elections in 1974 (like all "elections" in the Soviet Block) were also decided in advance.

elegantly. In this respect, he outdid Nero, for the world's greatest artist deprecated the pleasures of the table and concentrated on the pleasures of the bed. Suetonius gives us this description of Vitellius's gluttony:

> He always ate three and sometimes four times a day. There were breakfasts, lunches, dinners, feasts. He handled the volume easily because he had learned to vomit. He invited himself to the homes of several different people each day, and none of the hosts spent less than four hundred thousand on preparing a party for him. The most famous of all these feasts was one hosted by his brother. It is said that he served two thousand fish and seven thousand birds. But Vitellius surpassed even this when, at one of his own feasts, he presented a tray which, because of its enormous size, he labeled "the shield of Minerva, the guardian of the city." On it, he served the livers of cuckoo wrasse,[101] brains of pheasants and peacocks, flamingo tongues, and the milk of moray eels. These delicacies had been brought from the Parthian border and from the Spanish Strait by special *triremes*. Being a man of insatiable gluttony and rather poor manners, he was unable to refrain from eating at all times, either when offering sacrifices to the gods or traveling. He ate both the sacrificial meat and the spelt cake right at the altar, snatching them hot from the fire. And at roadside eateries, he grabbed food that was still smoking or the previous day's leftovers.[102]

Another author informs us that the Shield of Minerva was purpose-made out of pure silver and cost over a million sesterces. After Vitellius's death, it was preserved in the Imperial treasury for half a century until Emperor Hadrian ordered this extraordinary monument of his predecessor's morbid tastes melted down for coin.

These were difficult months for all the notable celebrities of Rome since they continually hosted the emperor or were hosted by someone alongside him. Difficult not only financially, as these feasts cost a fortune, but also because not everyone had Vitellius's ability to vomit several times a day. One of the most distinguished and richest,

---

[101] The cuckoo wrasse (*Labrus mixtus*) is a species of brightly colored fish native to the eastern Atlantic Ocean from Norway to Senegal

[102] Suetonius, *Life of Vitellius*, 13

and at the same time wittiest senators of that time, Vibius Crispus, fell ill and was unable to participate in the continuous cycle of mutual receptions. He considered it proof of a special grace of the gods and expressed it in a witty remark often repeated afterward:

"If I hadn't gotten sick, I would surely have died."

Moreover, Vitellius loved pomp and show, and not only at the table. He also wanted to live as brilliantly as anyone had ever seen. He was not satisfied even with the gigantic—although still unfinished— *Domus Aurea* of Nero. He believed that its decor and facilities were too simple. The wife of Vitellius, Galeria Fundana, criticized the modesty of the decorations.

Such tastes ridiculed the emperor in the eyes of the elites, who emphatically, although not always sincerely, worshipped the ancient Roman simplicity and self-discipline. The people, however, were pleased to see a ruler who had weaknesses, like any normal person. And even the strictest Catos had to agree that an emperor who so freely admitted guests to his table and so willingly visited his friends' houses was much preferable to someone who, like Emperor Tiberius, lived modestly but was suspicious and unapproachable. Yes, they did express the concern, both then and later, that Vitellius might eat through all the financial reserves of the Empire, so severely reduced by recent wars. (Some later calculated that during the few months of his reign, Vitellius spent nine hundred million sesterces on all manner of pleasures and luxuries). But these worries only showed ignorance of state finance. No chain of Lucullus's feasts[103] could have significantly impacted state finances, which were expressed in numbers several orders of magnitude greater. Furthermore, expenditure on *Domus Aurea* and the opening of elite houses for luxury goods revived demand in the capital and stimulated the economy.

However, during that summer of 69, something else became a

---

[103] Licinius Lucullus (117-56 BC), was famous for his lavish feasts with the most expensive and sophisticated dishes, and was sometimes described as the greatest glutton of antiquity. His feasts were sufficiently extravagant to establish a lasting place for his name as a synonym of "lavish" in the English lexicon.

real political, economic, and even—public health problem for Rome.

## VITELLIUS'S OFFICERS AND MEN

There were still thousands of troops from the Rhine in the city. No barracks could accommodate them, so they were quartered in private homes and even in public porticos and temples. Many pitched their tents across the Tiber, among the marshy fields of an unhealthy area called the Vatican. The men used to the clean water and cool but crisp air of the north, badly endured the heat and the cloudy waters of the Tiber. They became ill, many died, and the epidemic began to spread to the civilian population.

There were also constant break-ins and robberies because the wealth of the capital of the world, visible not only in the palaces of the nobles but also in ordinary middle-class homes, lured the newcomers from the border, who had previously lived in extremely primitive conditions. Due to idleness, strict military discipline broke down. No sentries were posted. There weren't even roll calls. Bands of armed men roamed with impunity throughout all districts, looking for opportunities to rape and pillage.

A recruitment campaign ordered by Vitellius for newly formed cohorts of Praetorian and Urban Guard caused additional dissatisfaction among the masses and anger among the demobilized soldiers of the former guard units. There were to be sixteen new Praetorian cohorts, as opposed to nine before, and four Urban cohorts. Each cohort was to have a thousand men. The idea was to select the most trustworthy and capable men for these guard units, taller and fitter than average. But the whole process was haphazard and lackadaisical. The best candidates often refused to join, preferring to remain with their old units, while those of little value joined. One reason for this strange state of affairs was the rivalry between the emperor's closest and most influential advisors: Caecina Alienus and Fabius Valens.

As legates, that is, commanders of legions of the army of the Rhine, both had contributed greatly to the elevation of Vitellius. Fabius Valens was the first to solemnly and publicly greet him with the title of emperor in Cologne on January 2. Both directed the military operations against Otho in the Po Valley the preceding spring because Vitellius himself was still on the other side of the Alps. Valens boasted, not without reason, that he had proved the better general in that campaign, having saved Caecina from severe straits. Caecina may have been inferior to Valens in his talents as a general and less popular among his soldiers, but he was superior in his looks (he was very tall), eloquence, self-assurance, and daring.

Their mutual resentment, barely concealed, intensified after their victory. The stakes were enormous: who would have greater influence with the ruler, and thus—since Vitellius was only interested in games and feasts—the decisive role in the government. However, the emperor was clever enough to constantly rotate his favors, now granting them, now revoking them, in a manner designed to introduce a sense of unpredictability. He understood perfectly well that the mutual hostility of the two generals best guaranteed his own safety. In his perfidy, he even went so far as to appoint them together as consuls for the year 69, starting in September.

In that capacity, Fabius Valens and Caecina staged magnificent games at the beginning of that month to celebrate the fifty-fourth birthday of the emperor. Processions, sacrifices, performances, and games lasted for two days. Gladiator fights took place on almost every street throughout the city. The fighters appeared in armor and costumes that were more magnificent than ever before.

It was then that Vitellius himself offered sacrifices to Nero's shadow. He did this not at the tomb of the Domitians on the Garden Hill because the trip seemed too far to him but at an altar erected on the Campus Martius, where it would be visible from far away.

He gathered around the altar all the ancient and venerable colleges of priests. Sacrificial animals were butchered, and the pyre on which their entrails were burned was lit by the members of the college of *sacerdotes augustales*.[104] It had been founded over fifty years earlier for this very purpose—to supervise the cult of the Julian clan. The ceremony caused a heated controversy in the city. Tacitus did not spare it a sarcastic remark:

> This thing, pleasant to the most wicked, aroused indignation among the righteous.[105]

Others said: "Vitellius did this to make plain whom takes as a role model in governing the state!"

But the ceremony had a deeper meaning, and from Vitellius's point of view, was fully understandable and perhaps even praiseworthy. For it was customary, when celebrating the birthday of the emperor, for him to honor the memory of his predecessor on the throne. But who was the predecessor to be thus honored? Not Otho, whom Vitellius had defeated as a usurper. And not Galba either, for his legions had elevated Vitellius to the throne in opposition to that emperor. Therefore, only Nero remained as the last legally reigning and universally recognized emperor of the Romans. And since he was the last representative of the Julio-Claudian family, it was appropriate that priests appointed to maintain the cult of the Julian family led the ceremony.

# SPORUS

The seemingly carefree atmosphere of the birthday celebrations was marred by an unpleasant incident: the suicide of Sporus. When we recall everything we have learned about Sporus's life, a truly pitiful picture emerges and a sense that only death could have liberated the boy-girl from further humiliations.

---

[104] *Sodales* or *Sacerdotes Augustales* (singular *Sodalis* or *Sacerdos Augustalis*), or simply *Augustales*, were an order (*sodalitas*) of Roman priests originally instituted by Tiberius to attend to the maintenance of the cult of Augustus and the Julii.

[105] Tacitus, *Histories*, II 95

A few years ago, Nero ordered him castrated to make a girl of him—only because his facial features resembled the recently deceased Sabina Poppaea. During his Greek journey, he took Sporus-Poppea to wife, and Tigellinus stood in for the father of the bride. Calvia Crispinilla, the mistress of the pleasures of love, watched over the training of the new Empress.

Certain facts seem to suggest that Sporus was truly attached to Nero. S/he stayed by him even when all the others abandoned him. S/he fled alongside her husband from Rome to the suburban villa of the freedman Phaon and stood next to him as he prepared to die. Nero, having ordered a grave to be dug to the size of his body and testing the blades of daggers with his finger, begged Sporus to begin to mourn him. Then, the sound of horses was heard: Nero's pursuers were entering the villa. There was no time to waste. The emperor stabbed himself in the neck with the help of the freedman Epaphroditus, who steadied his trembling hand. The ever-faithful Sporus was later among the handful of attendees at the cremation prepared by Acte and the two nurses.

Sporus watched the funeral pyre and saw the burning corpse but was no longer present when Nero's ashes were collected into the urn to be deposited in the porphyry sarcophagus in the Domitians' tomb. Nymphidius Sabinus, the Praetorian Prefect, had Sporus dragged away.

Nero had raised Sabinus to the highest dignity and trusted him completely, but in the decisive moment, he shamefully betrayed the emperor and greatly contributed to his destruction. He now decided to take over Nero's entire estate, including Sporus.

Just like Nero, he treated Sporus as his wife and, just like Nero, called him/her Poppaea. Was he just imitating the emperor, or had he also been one of her secret admirers? Alas, Nymphidius Sabinus died quickly and violently as soon as Galba heard the reports of his ambition to assume the imperial purple. A few months later, Sporus was taken over by the new ruler, Otho, who followed all Neronic traditions. And again, the fact that Sporus resembled Sabina Poppaea added to the relationship a certain perverse charm, for Poppea had once been Otho's wife. But Otho also ended his life tragically, stabbing himself in the heart.

Given the mentality of that era, it is easy to guess what rumor spread throughout Rome: Sporus brings misfortune! This is probably why Vitellius and his advisors avoided him/her for a long time. However, in time, they decided to use his beauty and fame in a different way. Sporus, the lover of two emperors and of a pretender to the throne, a boy-girl, a living image of Nero's deceased wife, was to appear on stage during Vitellius's birthday games to enact the role of a kidnapped virgin in a theater play!

But Sporus did not allow this humiliation to take place. S/he took his/her own life.

And thus, Sporus became the truest sacrifice offered to the shadows of Nero. But at the same time, he seemed once again to be a harbinger of disaster. For no splendid and noisy rites could make men forget what was already known in the capital: the East had rebelled.[106]

# SETTING OUT

The fact that Vespasian had been acclaimed emperor in Alexandria on July I had to have been known in Rome by the end of the month. But those countries seemed so distant that both the emperor and the population treated the reports quite indifferently. Only a new report, received at the beginning of August, drove home the true horror of the situation. Aponius Saturninus, the governor of the province of Moesia, wrote that the IIIrd legion, *Gallica*, which had once served on the Euphrates and was translocated to the Danube only at the end of AD 67, rebelled. However, the governor must have dispatched the letter in a great hurry, for it seemed strangely unclear and confusing. It is possible that Aponius had intentionally expressed his thoughts

---

[106] For a fictional retelling of the life of Sporus, see S. P. Somtow, *Delicatus: from Slave Boy to Empress in Imperial Rome,* 2023

vaguely because soon thereafter, he too went over to Vespasian's side.

Vitellius's court tried at first to ignore the whole matter, assuming that it was at most some riot in some camp and all the others remained faithful. Despite this, Vitellius summoned a general assembly of his forces and attended it personally. Speaking to his men, he harshly attacked Otho's recently disbanded Praetorians. He thundered that they were spreading false rumors about some coup in the East. He assured everyone authoritatively that there was no danger of civil war. However, it did not go unnoticed that he did not mention Vespasian's name once during the entire speech.

Shortly thereafter, soldiers were sent into the city to eavesdrop on the conversations of the civilians and immediately and brutally punish all inappropriate comments and gossip. Such methods only added fuel to the fire in a city already buzzing with all sorts of rumors. It is true that the news arrived from the East with great delay and greatly distorted since Vespasian and his men tried to cut off all communications in order to keep their movements and preparations secret. Besides, as every year, in July came the *etesias*—strong westerly winds which made navigation east to west extremely difficult.

Bracing for the worst, Vitellius decided to mobilize his troops spread out across the various parts of the West and bring at least some of them to Italy. However, he did not act with excessive urgency because the capital already had sixty thousand soldiers, and Vitellius was afraid that orders perceived as hectic would create the impression of panic and perhaps put unfortunate ideas in his legates' and governors' heads. Since the calls from the capital were not urgent, those responsible for carrying them out did not show excessive zeal. Besides, some of the dignitaries, especially those on the Rhine and in Britain, had enough local threats to deal with to want to part with their soldiers. And given the recent disorienting rotation on the Imperial throne, it seemed wiser to wait and watch the events in Italy from a distance.

Meanwhile, it became clear that all the Danubian legions had gone over to Vespasian's side. And then the rumor spread that they had seized the mountain passes between the eastern Alps and Italy in preparation for a descent into the valley of the Po. There was no more point in delaying the inevitable. At the end of September, Vitellius decided to send his Roman armies north. They were to be commanded jointly by Caecina and Fabius Valens, but since the latter had not yet recovered from a serious illness, the command was initially held by Caecina alone.

Not even three months had passed from Vitellius's triumphal entry into Rome. Let us recall once again the image of that procession:

First came the eagles of the four legions accompanying the emperor and then the prefects of the camps, tribunes, and the highest-ranking centurions, all dressed in white. On both sides of this host came the emblems—but without the eagles—of the four legions that had remained at the borders. Next came the battle standards of the twelve squadrons of cavalry, and behind them marched dense ranks of legionaries with their centurions, everyone in full, ceremonial armor, with decorations and medals on their chests. This armed and decorated column was closed by a long host of thirty-four auxiliary cohorts.

And now, along the same Via Flaminia, but in the opposite direction, dragged their feet a disorderly crowd of soldiers exhausted with heat and insubordinate from long idleness, lack of discipline, and the charms of big city life. It was still a huge host: it included four legions, *vexillationes* of seven others, and multiple auxiliary cohorts. Some of the cavalry had already gone ahead to Cremona, but none of these formations was heading for the expected battlefields on the Po with any enthusiasm. With every hour of their slow progress, their commander sank into deeper and deeper reverie. He thought secret, inscrutable thoughts. The first signal for their implementation came with the unexpected order from Fabius Valens, still sick in Rome, for his units to stop and await his arrival.

Hearing of this, Caecina decided that, given the enormity of the threat, it was unconscionable to divide the army. He ordered the main body of the army to march on in the direction of the Po while he set off for Ravenna, supposedly to deliver a speech to the soldiers and sailors of the navy stationed there.

# VITELLIUS AND THE STARS

Vitellius who had always shunned the clatter of weapons and the inconvenience of the military camp, remained the capital. He thought with concern about what turn the fighting on the Po River might take and what the end of September would bring. Finally, he received a certain ephemeral document that had been circulating in Rome for some time, containing only two short sentences:

> So say the Chaldeans. For the good of the state, Vitellius must be gone by October 1.

In content and form, it was an obvious mockery of the official edict in which the emperor had ordered the removal from Rome and from all of Italy of all Chaldeans and "mathematicians" (as astrologers were then called) by October 1.

Like even the most enlightened people of his era, Vitellius was superstitious. He maintained a witch from the Germanic tribe of the Chatti in his retinue. He had brought her from the Rhine and sought her advice in all confidential matters. She supposedly told him that he would only be able to reign long and peacefully if he survived his mother, which is why, it was said, she died soon after her son's arrival in the capital. He welcomed her at the Capitol and honored her with the title of Augusta, but when she fell ill, he forbade feeding her. Others again claimed that she had made the decision to die voluntarily. She asked her son for poison and received it surprisingly easily.

This was probably slanderous gossip fabricated by the emperor's enemies, but it was widely believed because everyone knew about Vitellius's superstitious nature. That was why the playfully menacing "Chaldean Edict" was composed. The ruler read its mocking words with barely concealed fear. What if this prophecy, though ostensibly a joke, actually foretold the future? Most people of that era accepted astrologers' judgments with fear and faith, but at the same time, they had a deep dislike and even hostility towards them, suspecting them of the worst sort of scheming. If we believe our sources, this double attitude was particularly strong in the case of

Vitellius—and not without reason.

Various stories circulated about it. One said that as soon as he was born, his parents, as was common practice at that time, turned to the Chaldeans to cast a horoscope for the child, or what was then called *genitura*. What the content of that horoscope was, many attempted later to deduce from certain facts. And thus, for example, Vitellius's father strived until the end of his days to ensure that his son would not be entrusted with the governorship of any province, and his mother despaired when he received Germania from Galba, and even more when he was hailed emperor. When she heard about it, she exclaimed:

"Now he is lost!"

His father and mother may have simply been thinking of the incompetence and weakness of their son, but their words were interpreted differently.

It was also said that during the reign of Nero, whenever someone mentioned in his presence the great skills of "mathematicians," Vitellius would reply with utter contempt:

"They're fools. They are clueless. Just imagine, they predicted that I would one day become emperor!"

These words were repeated to Nero, but he only laughed:

"Vitellius emperor? What preposterous nonsense!"

In other cases of this sort, Nero typically punished both the authors of the prophecies and their subjects as severely as possible, usually by death. He acted this way in perfect ignorance of the obvious dictum that no ruler has ever succeeded in murdering his successor (though many have murdered people who could have been good successors). To avoid such fate, young Otho, another man for whom astrologers also predicted the throne, chose a slightly different method to lull Nero's vigilance: he told everyone who would listen that it was comical to predict the reign of a man as seriously ill as he was—why, a man standing with one foot in the grave!

Now, if we consider all these stories, we would have to assume that Vitellius's *genitura* may have said something like this:

> He will receive the imperial purple when he takes a governorship, but if he does, a terrible fate will await him.

Of course, this whole story seems to be a later invention of astrologers wishing to shore up the popular belief in the power of their predictions. We, moderns, would be inclined to suggest a completely different reason why Vitellius expelled "mathematicians" from Italy. Most of them had sided with Otho, predicting a quick and shameful end for Vitellius. In the wake of being disproven, the masters of sidereal knowledge had to acknowledge that a *slight miscalculation* had taken place. Vitellius will indeed be defeated and die miserably, only a little later, and by someone else's hand.

And now imagine the sincere joy of these mathematicians when the news about the rebellion in the East started filtering in. The Chaldeans could now again stand tall before their clients and say:

"You see, the stars always reveal the truth. And the salvation will come from the East!"

In this manner, Vespasian, without any effort and without even knowing it, gained hundreds, perhaps even thousands, of zealous and very influential supporters in Italy. They proclaimed secretly, but at every possible opportunity, that his victory was absolutely inevitable because it was the will of Destiny, written in the stars. Indeed, few other people in the vast Empire were as sincerely devoted to the new emperor. Vitellius, outraged by these treasonous predictions (today, we would simply call it hostile propaganda), became livid. He exiled the practitioners of the sidereal knowledge.

Of course, in those September days, only minnows were still left in Rome. The truly outstanding, famous, and rich "mathematicians"—warned perhaps not so much by heavenly signs as by well-wishing clients—had fled the capital. One of the first to do so was Otho's court astrologer, our old acquaintance, Ptolemy Seleucus. Many years ago, he had belonged to Otho's circle. Later, he served Sabina Poppaea and thereby exerted great influence at Nero's court. After her tragic death, he again found himself at Otho's side in Lusitania and returned with him to Rome in AD 68. It was he who, having determined the position of the stars at the beginning of January 69, stated categorically that the 10th of that month boded badly for any new venture.

Which was why Galba died only five days later.

## WOMEN AND THE STARS

The mysterious figure of the astrologer Ptolemy Seleucus became legendary and remained in Roman memory for centuries,[107] the more so because he later managed to creep into Vespasian's favor. And thus, he is mentioned—although not by name—by the satirist Juvenal in his Sixth Book, written around AD 116. It is worth mentioning this matter briefly and quoting some of its fragments.

The poet wrote the satire as a warning for his friend Postumus, who, otherwise sound of body and mind, suddenly decided to get married. "You'd do better to hang yourself or jump head-first out of the window onto the pavement below or from a bridge into the river!" Juvenal exclaims, astonished, terrified, and shocked. "Marriage is nothing but an enslavement, as women are beings full of all sorts of faults, weaknesses, and vices, capable of committing the worst and most vile crimes!" In the catalog of women's weaknesses and sins, there must, of course, be mention of the unhealthy weakness of the ladies toward various superstitions and toward the secret art of the Chaldeans in particular:

> Whatever the astrologer says, they will believe it as if his words came directly from the god Ammon. In Delphi itself, the oracles have fallen silent and a cloud of unknowing obscures the future of the human race, but he who has been exiled the most times and who, through false friendship and venal charts, brought death and destruction to Otho's predecessor, passes among them for a fountain of knowledge about the future.

Since the famous oracle of the god Ammon lay in the Libyan oasis of Siwa, the poet can be taken to allude to the spread of eastern cults in

---

[107] A reputation somewhat like that of Giuseppe Balsamo/Alessandro di Cagliostro, or Aleister Crawley, or Madame Blavatsky in our times.

the West, a trend that "has silenced the oracle of Apollo." Otho's predecessor is, of course, Galba and the astrologer who makes calculations using "venal charts"—Ptolemy Seleucus.

The satirist continues his passionate diatribe:

> The secret knowledge of the master arouses trust in proportion to the number of times he has been jailed and the years he has spent in the slammer. No mathematician can become famous unless he is sentenced for high crimes at least once. And, obviously, the most trustworthy is he, who barely escaped hanging; or who has had the opportunity to become familiar with the Cyclades; or forlorny bid goodbye to the island of Seryphos![108]

> Well, consider now that your witch seeks such advice from just such a *Logos* because her mother, suffering from jaundice, is dying too slowly. But first, she'll ask about you, and then when she might bury her sisters and uncles, and whether her lover will outlive her (for what greater blessing can the gods grant?)

> And still, this inquisitive woman desires to know what the gloomy star Saturn forebodes and in what constellation Venus will be kind, what month will bring losses, and what month will bring profits.

> Oh, remember to avoid a lady in whose hand you will see a calendar worn smooth from constant browsing like an amber rosary. You no longer need to consult anyone other than her, for she's your oracle! When her husband leaves for the army camp or returns to his country home, she will not go with him on the journey unless its advisability is confirmed by calculations based on the writings of the mathematician Thrasyllus.[109] When she wishes to travel a mile out of town, her little booklet will tell her the auspicious hour. When the corner of her eye itches, she will use an ointment only after she has checked her horoscope. Even if she is sick, she will not find a

---

[108] Cyclades, Seryphos—common places of exile for minor offenses.

[109] For Thrasyllus, the astrologer of Tiberius, see Jacek Bocheński, *Tiberius Caesar*, Mondrala Press, 2023, p. 82 and following: "In the *ephebeion*—a place of training for young men—which was part of the Rhodian gymnasium, he happened to meet an extraordinary mathematician."

better time to eat than the one indicated by Petosiris.[110]

The Egyptian name Petosiris literally meant "the Gift of Osiris," just as our modern name Isodore means "the gift of Isis." Petosyris was thought to have been the author of an astrological manual, which was highly valued in the early empire.[111]

To see more clearly what astrology meant for Greeks and Romans, let us give the floor to a man with a reputation as a skeptic and mocker and a very intelligent and talented writer. We are talking about Lucian of Samosata, who lived in the 2nd century AD. He says in his short treatise *On Star Science*:

> My goal is to censure those professors who teach their students not to practice astrology.
>
> This ancient science has not appeared in our country recently. The kings of the ancient past created it, all of them pleasing to the gods. However, the people of today are ignorant, reckless, reluctant to study, and express views opposite to those of the old ways. When they find a mathematician who makes a false prediction, they accuse the stars and despise astrology. In their eyes, astrology is unhealthy, untrue, false, and vain. In my opinion, their judgment is wrong. After all, a bad carpenter does not disprove the art of carpentry, and an unmusical flute player does not disprove music. Rather, they themselves are at fault while their science stands.
>
> Our ancestors were in love with fortune-telling. Meanwhile, some of our contemporaries claim that it is impossible even to imagine any use for astrology. According to them, the science is unbelievable and false. The planets of Zeus and Ares (i.e., Jupiter and Mars) move across the heavens without giving as much as a flying care at a rolling spelt cake about human affairs and have nothing to do with it.
>
> Others say that astrology is true but unprofitable. What they mean is that a prophecy cannot change what is coming. In other words, if it is prophesied, it will happen. I can answer this objection as

---

[110] Juvenal, *Satires*, VI 553-581

[111] *Petosiris to Nechepso* is a letter describing an ancient divination technique using numerology and a diagram. It is likely to be a pseudepigraph.

follows:

The stars, indeed, do follow their own paths in the sky, but every accident that occurs among us is a byproduct of their movement. When a horse runs, birds and animals escape from it, stones fly, and dust rises, stirred up by the rushing wind. Can you possibly claim that a similar effect does not accompany the swirl of stars? We can see the light of even a distant fire, even if it does not burn for us and has no interest in keeping us warm. Shall we then assume no influence from the stars?

Astrology certainly cannot make bad things good or bring about a change of any kind, but it is beneficial for those who use it. It allows them to rejoice in advance about the good things that will come, and accept inevitable misfortunes without complaining. Because they have had the time to reflect on their fate and come to terms with it, their suffering is made bearable. Such is my view on astrology.[112]

## VESPASIAN AND THE STARS

But let us return to Ptolemy Seleucus. It is hardly surprising that he, until recently the most trusted advisor of Otho, preferred not to welcome his conqueror in Rome. He left the capital before Vitellius's troops arrived. Perhaps he traveled East with King Agrippa, Berenice's brother? We do know that he reached Vespasian and won his favor, in time becoming a court astrologer again. For Vespasian, a man otherwise sober and rational, perhaps even a bit cynical, was not free from this superstition, as Tacitus says. The historian also reports that during the Council at Mount Carmel, while Vespasian still hesitated whether to accept power, people around him began to argue that signs and constellations were auspicious, and their words seemed to

---

[112] Lucian, *De Astrologia*

Vespasian

influence his final decision.[113]

Thus, it seems that the interpreters of the revolutions of heavenly objects unanimously sided with Vespasian and opposed Vitellius. The latter, however, could console himself with the undoubted fact that, despite the prediction of the alleged Chaldean Edict, neither the last days of September nor even the first day of October brought him any harm. He breathed a sigh of relief. But the scales of the civil war—though no serious clashes had yet taken place—were already beginning to tilt against him. The astrologers weren't completely wrong.

The Emperor was still unaware of the fact even though the name of the man who was about to make the decisive contribution to his downfall was already discussed in Rome.

## LEGIO VII GALBIANA

Marcus Antonius Primus commanded the VIIth legion nicknamed *Galbiana*. It was stationed on the middle Danube, in the great military camp of Carnuntum, just a little east of modern Vienna. The legion, as its name indicates, had been formed recently, in late spring of 68. Galba, then governor of Nearer Spain, created it in preparation for his revolt against Nero. With the help of Otho, then the governor of Lusitania, he carried out hurried recruitment among Romans settled in Iberia. By June 10, he stood in front of the ranks of the legion to present its commander and centurions of the highest rank (*centurio primi pili*) with the sacred symbol of the legion: its silver eagle. This figure with outspread wings represented the guardian deity of the state and the army: the god Jupiter. In camp, it stood enshrined in its own portable sanctuary in the main square next to the headquarters building. In side niches stood the battle emblems and banners of individual cohorts. Legionary eagles were worshiped as religious

---

[113] Tacitus, *Histories*, II 78

objects, and their cult had become more pronounced since the establishment of the Empire. This caused a tart remark from a certain writer who was also an old-school officer: Pliny the Elder. In book XIII of his *Natural History*, he recalled with contempt how Otho taught Nero to smear his feet with fragrant ointments, and Caligula ordered his toilet seat to be perfumed, after which he adds:

> They also anoint the Eagles on feast days nowadays, our eagles covered with the grime of war and bristling with spears. If we could only know who first introduced this practice! For it is certain that only thanks to it they have conquered the world![114]

The day on which a legion received its eagle was celebrated annually as its holiday, the so-called *natale aquilae*, or the "eagle's birthday." Legion VII *Galbiana* observed theirs on June 10. We have discovered ancient inscriptions from a century later commemorating this holiday. By a strange coincidence, Nero committed suicide in Rome the day before, on June 9. Of course, when Galba handed over the eagle to his new legionaries in Spain, he did not yet know it.

After Nero died, the danger of civil war seemed to dissipate, and the new legion appeared no longer necessary, but the ceremony of summoning the eagle could not be undone. The youngest unit of the Roman army had been created, and it would now have to serve.

Its first assignment was peaceful and honorable. The legion accompanied Galba on his slow journey overland from Spain to Rome. However, soon after arriving in the capital, in the late autumn of the same AD 68, the new formation was sent to the far north, beyond the Alps, to Carnuntum on the Danube. It is easy to guess that the young legionaries accepted this order without enthusiasm. They would certainly have preferred to stay in Rome or at least somewhere in Italy, living safely and pleasantly in a country very similar to their homeland. They weren't exactly pining for the hardships of military camp life in the inhospitable and cold countries of the north, where their closest neighbors across the river would be savage barbarians.

---

[114] Sarcasm. Pliny, *Natural History*, XIII 23

But Galba was a stickler for the ancient tradition and thought that no regular army units should be stationed in the city—except for the Praetorian and Urban cohorts established by Augustus. He also wanted his legion, composed mainly of recruits, to gain fighting experience, which was easiest to earn on a border that was then considered less dangerous. This was rational as far as that went. But the decision to send the VIIth Legion away proved to be a disastrous move for the emperor. Had the legion remained in Rome, Otho would never have dared to attempt a coup, and the Praetorians would have remained faithful to the emperor. Galba realized his mistake too late.

But here's a surprising thing: in the war between Vitellius and Otho, VIIth *Galbiana* sided with Otho, even though he was the cause of their founder's murder! In the early spring of 69, the formation moved from the Danube through the Alps and into the valley of the Po to oppose Vitellius. Alas, it arrived too late and never took part in the fighting—only a few of its *vexillationes* managed to see action. Then the victorious Vitellius ordered the legion right back to its camp in Carnuntum.

How can we explain that these men, recruited by Galba, took Otho's side and were prepared to shed their own blood for him? There were various reasons for this. Galba, though he had formed the legion, was not popular among his soldiers. He was miserly and harsh, and above all—as was commonly said in the tents and camp barracks—he often proved ungrateful:

"He rewarded his own legion by sending it off into the boonies of the far north! He deserved what happened to him!"

We should also remember that during the ten years of his Lusitanian governorship, Otho made a good name for himself both in his own province and across the entire Iberian Peninsula. Galba's men were thus naturally disposed to accept him. Yet another reason why the VIIth supported Otho was the sense of solidarity with the other Danube legions. There was a fair bit of friendly—and sometimes not so friendly—competition between the men of the Rhine, the Danube, and the Euphrates.

But the decisive role in the whole matter was probably played by the legion's commander, the man who had received the eagle from Galba's hands: Marcus Antonius Primus.

## ANTONIUS PRIMUS

He came from Tolosa in Aquitaine, today's Toulouse in southern France. His family's position and influence allowed him to enter the Senate under Nero, and he must have held military and civil offices first. But soon, disaster struck, breaking a beautiful career. He got involved in some unpleasant scandal of a forged will of a certain dignitary, was stripped of his dignity, and sent back to his hometown in disgrace. That happened in AD 61 when he was just over forty. This was a true catastrophe for an ambitious man, and life in Tolosa must have seemed like exile. But only the narrow strip of the Pyrenees separated Aquitaine from Spain, ruled by Galba, who gradually came to the fore in the great conspiracy against Nero.

It's easy to see why Antonius was recruited into the preparations relatively early. It was well known that he could be trusted since he held a deadly grudge against the emperor and would do anything to bring about his downfall. Also, thanks to his family's influence in Aquitaine, he could be useful there. Galba restored his senatorial dignity and appointed him the commander of the new legion.

Tacitus, who probably knew Antonius personally and is definitely unsympathetic to him, characterizes him in a way that gives us much food for thought. He says that Antonius was an energetic, eloquent man, a master of the art of fomenting resentment among others, powerful thanks to the quarrels and divisions he knew how to incite, in some situations a plunderer, in others, generous; in times of peace he showed his worst traits, but in war, he was a very dangerous opponent. He also notes that he knew how to deal with commoners and gain their respect and admiration.

Describing one of his later battles, he gives him this testimony:

During that panic, he did not neglect a single duty of a commander and a soldier. He blocked the path of those who were terrified and stopped those who were retreating in panic. He was everywhere where the fighting was fiercest and where there was some hope of victory. By appearance, deed, and voice, he was constantly visible to his men. And in his battle fury, he finally went so far as to pierce the fleeing standard-bearer with a spear and, having snatched the emblem himself, turned it to face the enemy. This embarrassed some hundred fleeing horsemen, and they turned around.[115]

Antonius Primus was not just a politician and a soldier but also an erudite. He was interested in literature and supported poets. Or so, at least, the poet Martial wrote of him in later years. He dedicated his IXth book of *Epigrams* to him; Antonius was then approaching eighty. In his Book X, Martial mentions him in three places. One of them, although not his best artistically, reads in translation:

You ask, whose face is represented in this portrait, which, in reverence, I decorate with roses and violets? That's how Antonius Primus looked in his middle age. Now, as an old man, when he looks at that face, he sees himself as a youth. Oh, if only art could convey character and spirit! There would be no more beautiful picture in the whole world![116]

But many expressed reservations as to Antoninus's character. He was accused of excess ambition and political cynicism. People asked:

"Why did he start writing letters to Otho the moment he realized that war between him and Vitellius was inevitable? He made it clear that he could render an important service if only he were appointed commander-in-chief. But Otho spurned the offer. And this was why Antonius, though he had already roused his soldiers and was leading them through the Alps, suddenly lost enthusiasm for fighting."

All the same, Vitellius's victory put the commander of the VIIth legion in a bad position. While Vitellius did not remove him

---

[115] Tacitus, *Histories*, III 17
[116] Martial, *Epigrams*, X 32

from his post, it could happen any day, especially since those letters to Otho quickly became known in court circles. What was in them? It is true that Otho, during the last night of his life, burned everything that could discredit his supporters, but no one knew what papers he had with him during the campaign and what had been left in the palace archive. Since Praetorian letters to Otho were discovered, it was reasonable to expect that Antonius's letters may come to light at any moment, whether real or fake. It is hardly surprising that he lived in a state of constant anxiety. The news brought to him at the end of July that Vespasian had been proclaimed emperor in the East was a gift of heaven for him, restoring hope, self-confidence, and energy.

## POETOVIO

It was probably already late August when senior officers and civil dignitaries from the Danube provinces met in Poetovio on the Drava. The XIIIth Legion had its permanent camp there. It was that XIIIth which, in April, at the battle of Bedriacum, ingloriously showed its backside to Vitellius's Vth and was ordered to build the amphitheaters in Cremona and Bononia, to the jeering delight of the commoners of both cities. Its commander was one Vedius Aquila. Immediately after the Battle of Bedriacum, when the legion retreated to a fortified camp, the defeated soldiers blamed the disaster on Aquila, who probably did not bear any responsibility for the defeat and had discharged all his duties honorably. But the embittered men were deaf to all arguments. As soon as the commander entered the gate, he was surrounded by a crowd of legionaries, shouting that he was a traitor, a deserter, and the cause of their misfortune. He was threatened with flogging and would probably have been lynched were it not for Annius Gallus, a former consul and one of the commanders-in-chief of Otho's army who begged the soldiers not to worsen everyone's situation by murdering each other. Whatever happened, he thundered, the only chance for survival lay in unity. Thus saved, Aquila remained in his post as the commander of the legion, and when his men had completed the required construction of amphitheaters, he led them back over the Alps to their camp at Poetovio.

He was thus favorably disposed to Vespasian's cause from the very beginning because, like all those who had previously fought on Otho's side, he was afraid of impending dismissal. But he also wanted to prove his courage and demonstrate to his soldiers how unjust their insults had been after the Battle of Bedriacum.

Two provincial governors also arrived in Poetovia: Pompeius Silvanus and Tampius Flavianus. The former, who held Dalmatia, was already quite old since he had held the position of consul almost a quarter of a century earlier, during the reign of Claudius in AD 45. It was the year when a delegation of Jews from Jerusalem appeared before the emperor, filing a complaint against procurator Cuspius Fadus for having seized the High Priest's liturgical vestments. Caludius's letter ordering the vestments to be returned was dated with the names of that year's consuls:

> On the fourth day before the calends of July, during the consulship of Rufus and Pompius Silvanus (June 28, AD 45). [117]

Tampius Flavianus held the governorship of Pannonia. He was more or less Silvanus's age and had held the consulship either under Claudius or Nero. As soon as he realized that the Danube legions were leaning towards Vespasian, he scampered off to Italy. He did it out of "forethought," it seems, as he feared for his life on account of some family connection to Vitellius. However, he soon returned to his duties, having yielded to the eloquent persuasion of procurator Cornelius Fuscus, who very convincingly argued that declaring for Vespasian immediately offered excellent prospects for a future career. He probably also hinted, perhaps with a veiled threat in his silken voice, that Vespasian would naturally forgive a family tie to Vitellius as long as that stain was erased through diligent service.

And Cornelius Fuscus could be very persuasive. He resembled

---

[117] Josephus Flavius, *Jewish Antiquities*, XX, 1,2

Antonius Primus in many ways. Still in his prime, enterprising and very ambitious, he came from a senatorial family but voluntarily renounced his affiliation to this most illustrious estate. He believed, not without reason, that in the current political situation, a senatorial career brought more empty honor and pompous titles than real meaning or chance of acquiring great wealth. He was a quick risk-taker and a consummate fighter. He willingly took on dangerous tasks for the sake of the danger, and even the issue of possible material benefits seemed to fade into the background in some situations. Everything new and mysterious tempted him a hundred times more than easy profits.

At the end of Nero's reign, he sided with Galba and dragged the citizens of his hometown along with him—it may have been Aquileia. As a reward, he received from the new emperor the office of Procurator of Pannonia and Dalmatia, i.e., that of the chief financial administrator of the two Balkan provinces. Opposed to Vitellius for some reason, he allowed himself to criticize both his person and government publicly. And now he had no choice: he had to support Vespasian's cause with all his heart. Moreover, this restless spirit would probably have driven him to it without any specific reason, inspired only by his love of adventure. About twenty years later, during the reign of Domitian, this risk-taking was to bring him the sort of beautiful end that he had probably dreamed of. Having achieved the high office of the Praetorian Prefect, he died during an expedition across the Danube in the lands of Dacia, today's Romania.

The poet Martial honored his memory in an epitaph inscribed on the grave of the fallen hero. He placed it in Book VI of his *Epigrams*:

> Here rests Fuscus, defender of the holy person of Mars in a toga (i.e., the emperor), to whom was entrusted the office of the supreme commander. This stone does not fear the threats of the enemy. The defeated Dacian bears the heavy yoke of submission, and the victorious shadow of Fuscus rules the nearby grove.

# THE CONGRESS OF POETOVIO

As could have been expected, the meeting in Poetovio divided into two opposing groups right away, with two different views on the fundamental issue: whether to wait or to attack. The first group was led by the two governors, Silvanus and Tampius. Men approaching seventy, rich, enjoying honors and eminence, they stood to lose everything and gain very little. They preferred to act prudently, not take any risks, and not to initiate any aggressive actions. Ideally, they would have stopped at observing further developments. They argued:

"Vitellius has a powerful army in Italy—sixty thousand men and more are definitely on their way. His soldiers have served on the Rhine for years, are seasoned in battles, bloody-minded, and fearless. Their recent victory over Otho gave them even more confidence. But our men are demoralized by the recent defeat we suffered at their hands. Shout all we will about revenge and settling scores, these are just empty words and cannot be taken seriously: we are few, and fully one-third of our army has hardly seen any action at all. The numbers alone tell us what we should do. Let's take the Alpine passes as quickly as possible, yes, but then await the arrival of Mucianus. Only then will the odds even out and make it possible to talk sensibly about going on the offensive. We gain nothing by haste. Time will work in our favor."

Antonius Primus came to the forefront of the second group, supported with all his might by Cornelius Fuscus. The commander of the VIIth Legion did not spare his voice. He shouted so loudly that even the soldiers and officers gathered outside could hear him. He thundered:

"It's not true that the Vitellians are ready for war! On the contrary, they have grown lazy and demoralized by idleness and the comforts and debauchery of big city life. If we delay, they will have a chance to return to the strict camp discipline and will become dangerous again. Then, their auxiliaries will come from the Rhine and even Britain. They will soon mobilize enough people, money, and resources to crush us all.

"Let us also remember that Vitellius has two navies under his command, one at Misenum and the other on the adriatic in Ravenna. What if he decides to go around the Alpine passes and land his troops on the Dalmatian coast? Then, the Alpine passes will be worth nothing. And how will we fare us if the war drags on into the next year? Money is tight. Food is even worse. Our whole hope and only chance of salvation is a quick and decisive attack. We have to take advantage of the zeal of our soldiers while they remember the disgrace of their recent defeat and burn with the desire for revenge.

"I myself am ready to take on the most dangerous mission. You stay with the legions for now. Give me only the best cohorts. I will lead them over the Alps and I will open wide the gates of Italy. Then you can leisurely follow in my footsteps and occupy the country which I will have conquered!"

His words aroused enthusiasm among the soldiers gathered outside:

"Now you're talking like a real commander! Straight and clear, without buts and ifs, without delay and politicking. This man knows what he wants and whom he hates! But look at this Tampius fellow! He's just pretending he supports Vespasian, but he didn't really come back to us to help us fight but to plot treacherous intrigues and to paralyze us with doubts!"

And now all kinds of abuse and threats were showered on the governor of Pannonia. The old man became afraid. If a riot broke out, he might well be its first victim! So he fell silent, and the motions of Primus and Fuscus were accepted quickly and—unanimously. Letters were immediately sent to the governor of Moesia on the lower Danube—his name was Aponius Saturninus—with the summons for him to march with his three legions; and also to bring along the auxiliary units of Sarmatians and Iazyges from across the Danube to fight against Vitellius also (in effect) as hostages to ensure their countrymen on the other side didn't get any "ideas" during the upcoming war. Agreements were also concluded with the leaders of the Marcomanni and the Quadi. These warlike nations lived then in what is now Bohemia. Other letters were sent further abroad: to

*Adiutrix* in Spain and to Britain, where the XIVth legion had arrived by now. Just in case, eight cohorts and a cavalry squadron were deployed on the Aenus, now Inn in Austria: the river separated the provinces of Noricum and Retia, for the procurator of the latter province remained unwaveringly on Vitellius's side.

## MEANWHILE, IN PADUA AND VERONA

By the middle of September, Antonius Primus crossed the Alps, leading his cohorts and part of the cavalry. He took Aquileia and the surrounding towns without a fight, was welcomed everywhere, and then occupied Patavium, today's Padua. A little west of Este, he fell upon and scattered three cohorts and a cavalry squadron of Vitellius defending a bridge on the Po. Soon thereafter, two Danubian legions—the VIIth and the XIIIth—arrived in Patavium. The question arose where to establish the headquarters. The choice fell on Verona. The Danubians marched there without encountering any resistance and captured the town of Vicetia, today's Vicenza, along the way. The men considered this a good omen, as Vicetia was Caecina's hometown.

However, the beautiful and wealthy Verona was selected mainly because of its vast surrounding meadows. Here, they could put to good use their cavalry—they had a lot of it, and it was very good.

Meanwhile, letters from Vespasian arrived from Antioch and from Mucianus, already marching across Asia Minor to Byzantium. The two letters were very similar in content, for they both commanded the same thing: take Aquileia and stop there until reinforcements arrive. But it was too late to withdraw from Verona. The enemy was nearby. Caecina's units had set up a fortified camp in the nearby Hostilia. The two armies had already fought their first skirmishes.

And here a strange thing happened: Caecina, though he had overwhelming numerical advantage and should have attacked immediately, showed amazing restraint instead—indeed idleness. He

occupied himself mainly with writing letters addressed to Antonius
and his colleagues. In them, he rebuked the recklessness with which
they had taken up arms after having suffered defeat once already. Yet,
he also praised the foolhardy bravery of their men. What drew
attention was that he barely mentioned Vitellius, whom he served, and
did not disparage the name of Vespasian in any way.

Antonius responded by praising the new emperor and sharply
condemning Vitellius. At the same time, he assured the opposing army
that Vespasian would unequivocally confirm all their ranks, titles,
bonuses, emoluments, advancements, and privileges and advised
Caecina to abandon his master as soon as possible.

During this fascinating exchange of letters, the three legions
from Moesia arrived in Verona. And thus, by the middle of October,
the forces of both sides became about equal.


## TREASON


Meanwhile, Vitellius, having first sent Caecina north, and a dozen or
so days later, the finally recovered Fabius Valens, now also left Rome
himself. He didn't get far—and only reached Aricia.[118] The town lay
only half a day south of Rome, at the foot of the Alban Hills, and owed
its fame mainly to its ancient temple of Diana set in a beautiful grove.
The emperor encamped there, waiting to see what fate would bring.
As Tacitus says figuratively: "like those lazy animals, which, when you
throw them something to eat, just lie there in dull numbness, oblivious
to the past and the present."[119] In his defense, we should say that he
had already started to sicken.

But bad news managed to find the emperor even in his
charming hideaway. First came the news of the defection of the naval
squadron in Ravenna. Not for nothing had Caecina visited its
commander, Bassus. Bassus then managed to recruit several of his own

---

[118] Today Ariccia.
[119] Tacitus, *Histories*, III 36

officers and captains. They gathered at night—supposedly without Bassus's knowledge—in the main town square. They started a tumult, shouted slogans against Vitellius, toppled his statues, and killed a few guards who tried to put up resistance. Others soon joined the rebellion because most of the sailors came from Dalmatia and naturally favored the Danube army.

Ostensibly, Bassus took no part in the coup. He appeared in public only after all had been decided. He was then "arrested" and sent under guard to the town of Atria,[120] where, however, his bonds were soon removed. In the near future, he would receive new dignities from Vespasian because the command of the Ravenna squadron would go to... our adventurer-friend, Cornelius Fuscus. By AD 71, Bassus would find himself the legate of Vespasian in... Judea. The temple will have been destroyed by then and the city captured. He would capture two fortresses that still remained in the hands of the insurgents, supervise the auction of land confiscated from Jews, and die a peaceful death in Palestine. His successor would be Flavius Silva, who would capture the fortress of Masada in the spring of AD 73.

While this was happening in Ravenna, Fabius Valens was slowly making his way up Via Flaminia through the valleys and passes of the Apennines towards the valley of the Po. He was not in a hurry. He was accompanied by a whole squad of girls and eunuchs—he was not free from some perversions of his own. Surprised by the news of the rebellion in Ravenna, he stopped halfway and meditated on what to do. Should he continue towards the Po? He had few men with him and feared the Ravenna units might capture him. Should he retreat to Rome, then? That would cause panic in the city and bring on the emperor's fury. So, try to march on to Hostilia with just the handful of forces at his disposal? The risk was great, the inconvenience terrible, and should things go wrong, the resulting death would be inglorious. At length, he decided to demand reinforcements from the emperor.

---

[120] Atria or Adria, an ancient city in the territory of the Veneti, between the Adige and Po and today about 22 km from the Adriatic Sea, from which it derives its name (Strabo 5.1.8).

He sent messengers, and soon, three cohorts and a squadron of cavalry arrived. It was not enough to push ahead and yet too much to hide somewhere unnoticed. Besides, Valens didn't trust his people too much. So he sent them as quickly as possible up Via Flaminia to Ariminum to occupy that section of the adriatic coast while he himself turned with a group of trusted men towards Umbria. Was he perhaps looking for an alternative path to the Po? One way or another, he disappeared from view.

This vacillation of Fabius Valens and his delay in marching to Hostilia had disastrous consequences for Vitellius's cause; for now, dramatic events took place in Caecina's camp. He learned of the revolt of the Ravenna squadron a day or two later and immediately began to implement the plan he had agreed upon during his secret meeting with Bassus. During the day, as soon as his troops left camp and took up positions in the field, he summoned a dozen officers whom he trusted to his quarters. He presented them with the current political and military situation in the most unfavorable light possible. He said:

"The emperor whom we raised without regard for cost in blood turned out to be unworthy of the hopes we had placed in him. He is lazy, infirm, and dissolute. It is, therefore, necessary to rescue the Empire from his clutches, and Vespasian did the right thing by rising up. The new emperor has all the qualities of a brave soldier and a good ruler. He has accomplished great things in a short time. Without even drawing a sword, he already has in his hand the entire East, where the richest provinces are and all the provinces along the Danube, where there are so many brave legions. His troops have crossed the Alps. As soon as they did, the fleet in Ravenna declared for him. I know that the troops in Spain and Gaul will do the same.

"We are alone, with no one to save us. We and the whole of Italy are threatened with starvation because all overseas grain supplies are currently in Vespasian's hands. Fighting makes no sense at all. It would amount to suicide. Besides, for whom should we risk our heads? I consider it not only hopeless but also absurd to wage a civil war and die at the hands of our brothers in defense of this voracious beast! As Romans, we should do everything in our power to free the country from this man. Our civic duty is to stand on the side of the one emperor who is truly worthy to rule and whom the gods have already chosen.

"Long live Emperor Flavius Vespasian!"

Immediately, his men swore an oath of loyalty to Emperor Vespasian. They tore down all likenesses of Vitellius and sent messengers to Antonius Primus to inform him that the army of Hostilia decided to go over to Vespasian.

Alas, the announcement proved premature.

Only a handful of insiders had actually switched allegiance. They neither asked their soldiers for their opinion nor persuaded them, nor did they even bother to inform them about what had happened. And now the cohorts returning from the field saw, to their astonishment, on the headquarters and the sanctuary of the eagles the words *Imperator Caesar Vespasianus Augustus*, while the images of Vitellius lay broken in the mud. This Vitellius, whom they had proclaimed emperor only ten months earlier, to whom they had sworn allegiance, and for whose sake they spilled their blood on the fields of Bedriacum! Suddenly, furious shouts went up and grew more violent and more threatening with every moment: "Treachery! Treason! Caecina has sold us to the enemy! The Army of the Rhine goes into captivity without even drawing a sword! Disgrace! Disgrace!"

A riot broke out, and lonely Caecina soon found himself in chains. His soldiers elected the commander of the Vth Legion and the camp prefect as new joint commanders-in-chief.

Immediately afterward, probably on the night of October 19-20, the army loyal to Vitellius left their fortifications at Hostilia, burned the bridge over the Po, and withdrew to Cremona where they joined Ist *Italica* and XXIst *Rapax*, carrying Caecinus with them, trembling for his life.

# A NEW CONSUL

The news of these events reached Vitellius probably only on October 28. The Emperor, shocked by the betrayal of the commanders he had personally appointed, nevertheless had reasons to be satisfied with his troops. He could rely on his soldiers! Their conduct restored his energy and his will to fight.

He left the grove of Aricia and hurried to Rome. Here, the very next day, he appeared at a large public rally, giving a speech in praise of his army. A day later, he appeared at the Senate, where he delivered another pompous speech. The senators responded with flattery, condemning Caecina as a vile traitor and an ingrate—and they did so sincerely, for he was universally disliked—though they carefully avoided any criticism of any of Vespasian's commanders. Indeed, they phrased their statements extremely carefully, omitting Vespasian's name altogether. They condemned in the strongest possible words both "disloyal officers" and "mistakes," but without making at all clear which officers and mistakes they meant.

A minor humorous incident occurred during the session, though the seriousness with which it was treated gave good testimony to the Roman sense of order. As we remember, Caecina held the consulship that year, sharing it with Fabius Valens, probably starting August 1 or September 1. The dignity expired on October 31. The two were, in fact, the so-called *consules suffecti*, one of several pairs of which rotated during the year, though the year was always dated with the names of the first pair, the so-called *consules ordinarii*. And since the Senate had just stripped the traitor Caecina of all dignities and titles, he had also lost this office. Thus, the post was vacant and remained to be filled, though only for one day, that is, October 31, because, from November 1, a new pair of *consules suffecti* was scheduled to take office. A volunteer proposed himself for this one-day honor—senator Rosius Regulus. He assumed the honorary dignity only to lay it down twelve hours later. From then on, however, he had the right to be included in the list of *viri consulares* ("former consuls"), sit in the first row during the sessions of the Senate, and speak before others.

One hundred and six years earlier, during Caesar's dictatorship, a similar, and even more amusing, incident had occurred. On the morning of December 31, one of the consuls died and was immediately replaced by one Caninius. He held the office for a few hours, from the afternoon of that day until the daybreak of the following day. Cicero wrote about this in a letter to one of his friends:

> Know that during the consulate of Caninius, no one ate lunch, but also nothing untoward happened, because the consul was astoundingly vigilant: he didn't sleep a wink during his entire consulship.[121]

## THE SERVILIAN GARDENS

Meanwhile, Vitellius became seriously ill. He chose the Servilian Gardens as the place to recuperate because they were located just outside Rome, on the road to Ostia. It was a large, beautiful park with palace buildings decorated with the most splendid works of art, especially statues, which included three Praxiteles originals: the goddesses Demeter and Persephone, and Triptolemus.[122]

But in the minds of the people, something else made the garden famous: Nero had spent the last night of his life there. He had been traveling to Ostia, from where he intended to sail to Egypt, counting on the support of the Greeks of Alexandria and of the Prefect Tiberius Alexander. But that night, everyone abandoned him, even his bodyguard and his personal servants. In the confusion, they managed to steal a carpet from the emperor's bedroom and an expensive box in

---

[121] Cicero, *Epistulae ad Familiares*, VII 30, 1

[122] Triptolemus (also known as Buzyges), was a hero in Greek mythology, central to the Eleusinian Mysteries. He was either a mortal prince or the divine son of Gaia and Oceanus, or the grandson of Hermes through Eleusis. He was the ancestor to a royal priestly caste of the Eleusinian Mysteries of which Pericles was the most famous descendant.

which Nero kept poison just for such an occasion.

Lonely and betrayed, the emperor acted on the advice of his freedman Phaon and fled the garden on horseback. He didn't even have time to put on his sandals and, as a disguise, threw on a long cloak with a hood. He arrived at the villa of Phaon just past midnight, with only four people by his side, his faithful Sporus among them.

Vitellius settled in the same gardens for the same reason: they were restful yet close to the city. However, he couldn't sleep at night. It caught his attention that a nearby palace tower glowed with bright lights. He asked why. The answer was that Caecina Tuscus was hosting many dignitaries, among them Junius Blaesus. They were both outstanding and influential figures in Rome at that time. The former, Nero's wetnurse brother, held the position of the Prefect of Egypt AD 63-66; he lost it when the emperor was informed that he had dared to bathe in the baths purpose-built for Nero. (Tiberius Alexander took over the office of Prefect of Egypt after him). The other participant of the feast, Junius Blaesus, had until recently ruled Gallia Lugdunensis, i.e., the part of Gaul around today's Lyon. When the army of the Rhine proclaimed Vitellius emperor, he joined his standards immediately. Two months later, when Vitellius arrived in Lugdunum traveling very modestly, Junius Blaesus lent his services to the new emperor and surrounded him with every luxury. Apparently, Blaesus's generosity aroused the envy of Vitellius (being too eager to please is as dangerous as being deficient) which, nevertheless, Vitellius managed to disguise—until that night.

When the entourage of the emperor noticed that he was displeased to hear about the source of the illumination, the more cunning commented:

"There they are, celebrating your illness!"

Soon, the emperor's brother, Lucius, appeared in the bedroom.

He put on a truly theatrical display. He tenderly embraced his teenage son, also Vitellius—the boy was awkward and stuttered downright morbidly—then fell to embrace the emperor's feet, saying:

"Why be afraid of Vespasian, who is far away beyond the sea, when here, next door, we have an enemy a hundredfold more dangerous? Blaesus constantly shows your soldiers how generous and gracious he is, and he never lets anyone forget about his kinship with the former imperial family!"

Blaesus died that same night. He wasn't even given the opportunity to defend himself: he was ordered to drink poison. The Emperor is said to have witnessed his death and to have commented afterward:

"At least I was able to see my enemy die before me!"

That happened at the very beginning of November. It is quite possible that the messenger delivering shocking news arrived the very next morning: in the fields of Bedriacum, a terrible, bloody battle took place on the night of October 24/25, and the legions of Antonius Primus won a stunning victory.


# ON THE WAY FROM SYRIA TO EGYPT

It seems that Vespasian was informed about these events only a month later, in the first half of December. The cause of the delay was the season: autumn storms were a bad time for navigation.

The emperor had already left Antioch and traveled south through Phoenicia and Palestine towards Egypt. Immediately following the war council in Berytus, he had established his temporary headquarters in Antioch. From there, he sent Mucianus and his corps west but he spent the early autumn there because he received news of a dangerous development on the Black Sea. Messengers reported that a man named Anicetus had raised a revolt on the Black Sea. He was a freedman and, at one time, the commander of the troops of the king of Pontus. Currently, he claimed to support Vitellius, but in fact, only aimed to break Pontus away from the Empire. He took advantage of the fact that Mucianus had taken away from the littoral the better part of the Black Sea navy.

Anicetus gathered around him the usual volatile crowd of the dispossessed poor and he summoned the help of the wild mountain folk of the interior. He took the rich city of Trebizond and slaughtered the cohort stationed there. He burned all the ships he managed to capture and armed and trained his troops on the Roman model. He advised his barbarians to build their traditional boats with narrow sides and wide bottoms, which they had used before the arrival of the Romans and used them to pillage the coastline. Vespasian, concerned about these reports, sent several cohorts from Antioch under the command of an experienced officer. He himself remained in the city, impatiently waiting to see how things would develop and whether he would have to intervene himself.

However, good news soon came. The "army" of Anicetus was quickly defeated. Its remnants, forced onto their fragile ships, took refuge with a friendly Caucasian prince. Initially, he did not want to hand the rebels over to the Romans, but he relented when he was given the choice of a reward or war.

Vespasian was now able to leave Antioch and assume power in Egypt according to the previously agreed plan. He was already in the country but still some time from Alexandria when important letters were brought to him. They announced the great victory on the Po at the end of October. The six legions of Vitellius had been routed at Bedriacum in a murderous battle. Their camp fell. Cremona fell. The road to Rome stood wide open.

Nevertheless, Vespasian, as always sober and cautious, did not allow himself to be carried away by euphoria. He did not think that the war was won. He knew that Vitellius could still count on the newly formed Praetorian cohorts and other units that he had kept with him in the capital. Also, the legions from the Rhine and Britain and reinforcement cohorts from Gaul and Spain were probably still marching towards Italy. There were reports of troop transfers from Africa to Italy. The fight was not yet over.

In this situation, the emperor decided that the most urgent matter was to cut off all of Italy's grain supply, not only from Egypt but also from North Africa. He had the bold idea of marching there from Alexandria along the coast. He wanted to take Cyrenaica,

Proconsular Africa (today's Tunisia), Numidia, and Mauritania. Such a campaign posed many difficulties and Vespasian was eager to act motivated by the challenge.

But first, he had to enter Alexandria.


## ALEXANDRIA


He was welcomed with great solemnity and enthusiasm. After all, he was the first emperor in history to visit the proud capital of Egypt. Yes, in August of 30 BC, Octavian entered its gates, by then the absolute ruler of the entire Empire, but he was not yet an Emperor: he was to receive the title of Augustus only three years later. Moreover, Octavian appeared on Egyptian soil not as a welcome guest but as a conqueror and victor over Cleopatra, the last rightful ruler of the country.

Thereafter, for almost a hundred years, no emperor appeared in Alexandria. It is true that Nero had had such plans. Some preparations were even made, and a special bathhouse was built in which Caecinus Tuscus dared to bathe, paying for it with dismissal from office. However, political disturbances thwarted Nero's plans for the historical journey up the Nile. And although in the last days of his reign, he hoped to escape to Egypt, and even went to Ostia and spent the night of June 8-9 in the Servilian Gardens, it was all too late. Neither did the self-proclaimed Nero from the island of Kythnos ever reach the shores of the Nile.

But Vespasian arrived in Alexandria also as the first Roman Emperor proclaimed here. The inhabitants were well aware of the importance of the act that had taken place in their city just six months earlier, on July 1, 69. They proudly said that they had done the right thing then and that both Fate and the gods had since favored their decision. The recent victory at Bedriacum clearly proved this.

News about the victory caused genuine joy among the masses. Everyone knew well what terrible revenge Vitellius would have taken on Alexandria if he had won. But there were many reasons for sincere joy, and one was the most important among them: their emperor, who owed so much to Alexandria, was expected to shower the city with privileges and favors—and many of its representatives in particular. Therefore, huge crowds gathered eagerly in front of the eastern gate and at the hippodrome to see their chosen and give him an uproarious ovation. It was the same hippodrome in which, several months earlier, their Prefect Tiberius Alexander had announced their new emperor to them. And now here they stood: city aldermen, councilors and advisors, priests of all legally recognized cults, scholars of the Museon, representatives of guilds and charitable associations, as well as delegations from all the administrative districts across the country.

We have already mentioned the preserved fragments of the papyrus describing the ceremony. The Prefect, turning to the people, thundered:

"All power and might to our emperor!"

And to the people, he presented him as a deity who finally deigned to reveal himself:

"Here is Vespasian, our savior and benefactor, the emerging sun!"[123]

Of course, all these Greek terms: *soter*—savior, *euergetes*—benefactor, *helios anatellon*—the rising sun, had their own ancient tradition in the Hellenistic religion. They were generously and easily showered on almost every ruler because... they cost nothing. Fifty years earlier, the residents of Alexandria welcomed with those same monickers someone who was only a member of the ruling family.

He was Germanicus, appointed by Emperor Tiberius as the governor of the East. Terrified by these exaggerated titles, which could arouse suspicion on the part of the always distrustful emperor, Germanicus immediately reprimanded the flatterers with a threatening edict:

I accept the kindness you show me at every meeting. However, I firmly reject such epithets. They arouse envy by putting me on equal standing with the gods. They befit only the benefactor of all

---

[123] *Papyrus Fouad,* I, 8

mankind, my father, and his mother (Tiberius and Livia). Your acclamations are an insult to their divinity. I forbid them. And if you are disobedient in this matter, I will never visit you again![124]

These terms—savior, benefactor, rising sun—were soon to be appropriated by Christianity. They would enter the liturgical language of the Church and remain part of it down to the present. Few, beyond a handful of researchers, are aware of their lineage, the circumstances and political implications of their original meaning, and what factors contributed to their widespread dissemination in the Greco-Roman world.

Vespasian, as emperor, was fully entitled to these divine names, and for the reasons already indicated, the Prefect's invocation met with a lively response from the people. Tens of thousands of citizens of the metropolis filling the huge hippodrome responded with loud cheers and applause, loudly chanting and repeating over and over the Greek words:

*Kyrie hemon, Euerget, Sebaste, Serapis!*

That is:

"Our Lord, Our Benefactor, Augustus, Serapis!"

And Serapis was the most revered deity of Alexandria. There were also cries here and there calling Vespasian the son of the god Ammon or simply—a god.

Next, various important guests delivered short speeches, probably in Latin, since protocol contains the Latin words of the Prefect: "The Emperor says that he wishes you health!"

This line, too, was greeted with a storm of applause.


## APOLLONIUS AND THE CONVICTS

Apollonius of Tyana was not among the crowd welcoming Vespasian in the hippodrome even though he had lived and worked in

---

[124] A.S. Hunt, C.C. Edgar, *Select Papyry*, v I, II no. 211

Alexandria for some months, gaining wide notoriety. Or so at least maintains his biographer, Philostratus, who eagerly collected stories about his hero (and partly made them up).

The sage had come to the capital of Egypt from the island of Rhodes. He had been eagerly awaited because the fame of his teachings and of miracles had long spread in the country on the Nile (so deeply devoted to the worship of gods and eager for everything strange, mysterious, and foreign the Greeks of Alexandria were). A crowd of admirers and of the usual curious greeted him at the quay. He was escorted to the city center, and passers-by got out of his way respectfully as if before a ceremonial procession carrying the statues of gods. He was accompanied, his biographer notes, by more people than usually welcomed a newly arriving provincial prefect! And so even the wealth and authority of Tiberius Alexander paled in comparison with the respect commanded by this man favored by the gods.

And as they walked on, on one of those straight, broad, long Alexandrian avenues, they met a terrifying procession. Men-at-arms led twelve shackled prisoners, who walked with their heads bowed down:

"These are robbers, recently captured. They're taking them to the place of execution," the crowd explained to Apollonius.

But he, having looked carefully at the faces of the criminals, said in a firm voice:

"No! Not all of them are guilty! That one there," he pointed with his hand, "he was falsely accused and will soon be freed!"

He then turned to the guards and asked them to walk as slowly as their duty allowed and, when they beheaded the men, to leave that man for the last. His name was Pharion.

And it so happened—we are told—that when eight were already lying with their heads chopped off, a rider galloped up, shouting from a distance to stop the execution. And then he gave the order:

"Pharion is innocent. He confessed to crimes he hadn't committed and only because of torture. The testimony of others has cleared him. The prefect has ordered that this innocent man be released immediately!"[125]

A very instructive story. Its fictional aspect gives testimony to Apollonius's clairvoyance. The real-life aspect shows what horror was aroused by the tortures used at that time. It also shows how efficiently justice functioned under the governorship of Tiberius Alexander.


## APOLLONIUS AND ANIMAL SACRIFICES

Apollonius then went, as he was wont to do in every new city he visited, to the most venerable temple; in this case it was, of course, the temple of Serapis. It was located in the western part of the city, in the Rhacotis district.[126] The sage admired its gigantic size, splendor, architectural design and called it divinely inspired and rationally conceived. However, he did not approve of the fact that so much blood was spilled at the altar, sacrificing animals, especially bulls and geese. He told the priest directly that such food was not suitable for the gods. The priests, very scandalized by the odd accusation, asked him maliciously:

"Why do you say so, foreigner? How do you know how we should sacrifice?"

To which Apollonius replied with a question:

"And how do you know that this is the way to do it?"

The Priest, touched to the quick, raised his voice:

"And who are you, so exceedingly wise, that you would teach us, Egyptians?"

But Apollonius replied calmly:

"Anyone who has been to India can."

We should recall that Apollonius had returned from India by then. And now he showed to the priest how to offer to the gods only

---

[125] Philostratus, *Life Apollonius of Tyana*, V 24.

[126] About the fall of the Alexandrian Serapeum, see Aleksander Krawczuk, *The Last Olympiad*, Mondrala Press, 2023

the likeness of an animal, cleverly crafted from dough. And he could not resist this remark:

"And if you do that, you too will participate in consuming the fragrant smoke. Because, surely, you do not despise this portion since it is what the gods themselves feed on?"

He then instructed all the present that the way a dough figurine melted, as well as the properties of its flame, could be more helpful in predicting the future than the usual divinations made from the entrails of animals and from the burning logs. And finally, he added, turning once again to the priest:

"And when you understand this, you will understand also that the solar disk, as it rises above the horizon, reveals the future—just as it reveals all that has been buried in the darkness of the night."

It is not so important whether the reported conversation really took place. What is important is that it illustrates certain tendencies in the religious life of the empire. It shows, above all, the disgust with which some circles, especially intellectuals, had come to view the traditional blood sacrifices, a legacy of ancient times; and how they sought some way to replace in the act of sacrifice that which seemed to them primitive and barbaric with something more gentle and more palatable. Only against this background do the teachings of early Christianity become fully understandable, and they are by no means an isolated phenomenon.

We also see here how influential the idea had already become that India had the best and the most sublime to offer in terms of religious practice. The fascination with the mysterious East, it turns out, is as old as European culture. One could even say that it is a permanent component of our culture, omnipresent in all its stages of our development, a counterweight to the cold rationalism so typical of the European mentality.

Finally, we find in the words of Apollonius a mention of the worship of fire and of the sun. Both these ideas, Iranian in origin, were gaining currency at the time.

Then, in the same temple of Serapis, the sage from Tyana delivered a sermon. He particularly harshly condemned the

Alexandrians' passion for horse racing. This passion caused many deadly riots between the supporters of various teams. He concluded his sermon with a curse:

"May fire descend upon this city so full of promiscuous insolence!"[127]

Chariot races were held in the hippodrome located in the eastern suburbs of the city. Small surprise that Apollonius never wanted to visit the accursed place, even for a purpose as pious as welcoming the new emperor. However, he stayed away from the hippodrome for another reason, too: he wanted to make it plain that he was not to be counted among Vespasian's flatterers.

## VESPASIAN AND APOLLONIUS

The biographer of Apollonius goes on to tell us that immediately after delivering his speech in the hippodrome, the Emperor turned to his entourage and asked:

"Is it true what they say that the sage of Tyana is in Alexandria?"

They replied that he was and had already performed several miracles. Upon hearing this, Vespasian said:

"I'd like to meet him as soon as possible. There are urgent affairs in which he might prove helpful."

As fate would have it, one of the students of Apollonius happened to be nearby, a man apparently more eager to see the emperor than his master was. He somehow managed to push through the crowd and said:

"Our master is staying at the temple of Serapis. He has already expressed his wish to see you."

"Let's go to him immediately," ordered the emperor. "Let's

---

[127] Philostratus, *Life Apollonius of Tyana,* V 25.

pray to our gods and talk to the noble man!"

The biographer stops here to tell us that Vespasian had already wanted to reach for the imperial purple during the siege of Jerusalem. But he decided to seek the advice of Apollonius first and asked him to come to Judea. However, Apollonius refused, not wanting to set foot on the ground defiled by the Romans and the sinful actions of the Jews. As a result, Vespasian proclaimed himself emperor without meeting Apollonius.

Of course, the story is made up. Vespasian never besieged Jerusalem. But by telling us the story, Apollonius's biographer wanted to show us how great a man his hero was in the eyes of his contemporaries since even the future lord of the Empire sought his advice.

The stories his biographer tells us about Apollonius are often naive, exaggerated, and sometimes downright laughable. But we should remember that his representation of the relationship between the emperor and the philosopher has a deeper message because it promotes the primacy of ethics over politics, wisdom over cunning, modesty over pride. Here is an emperor at the feet of a sage! A ruler seeking the favor of a guru! This was something that the intellectuals of all ages throughout the Empire had dreamed of. They proclaimed it eloquently, persistently, and at every opportunity: the temporary power needs us!

And now, the biographer tells us that having arrived at the temple, Vespasian asked Apollonius... for his permission to rule the empire. The sage apparently took these words at face value and replied:

"I have already given you power. I have prayed to the gods to give us an emperor who would be just, noble, prudent, silver-haired with age, and flourishing with the offspring of righteous sons. In other words, I have prayed for you."

Those present nodded their approval for such words of wisdom.

But Vespasian asked again:

"And how do you judge Nero?"

Apollonius replied via a metaphor:

"He played the *kithara* well. But as a ruler, he sometimes tightened the strings too much, and at other times, he loosened them too much.".

"Do you mean to say that a ruler should always find the middle way?"

"It is not me who means it, but God who demands it!"

Having heard this, Vespasian raised his hands in a gesture of prayer and said:

"Grant it, oh Zeus, that I might reign over wise men, and wise men might reign over me!"

After this conversation, the two left the temple. Vespasian took Apollonius by the hand like a friend. They walked slowly to the palace where the emperor was to reside, and the procession followed them respectfully but not too far away since the ruler's words were heard and remembered:

"Perhaps people will think it frivolous and inappropriate of me to take the throne at the age of sixty. I will now tell you what I have in my defense so that you can defend me before others. I have never been a slave to wealth, even in my youth. I have held offices and dignities prudently and moderately. I was never too proud or too cowardly. And it never occurred to me to rebel against Nero. Yes, in my opinion, he often broke the law, but he had inherited the throne legally, and so I obeyed him for the sake of Claudius, who had once appointed me consul. By all the immortal gods, whenever I saw Nero behaving disgracefully, I recalled Claudius. "What a trollop inherited the throne after Claudius!" I thought to myself, but I bore it for the sake of the law.

"But when Nero was overthrown, things did not change for the better: the government went from bad to worse and finally fell into the hands of Vitellius. Only then did I decide to reach for power. I did this for two reasons. First, I wanted to be respected. And second, I thought it was my duty to overthrow that drunkard. Vitellius uses more perfumes for bathing than I use water. I suppose that if you wounded him with a dagger, he would shed not blood but essential oils. He drinks constantly and lives in a haze. He plays dice and trembles with fear to get the roll right. It doesn't even occur to him that what is at stake is the Empire! He throws himself on married women, and he openly proclaims that love combined with riot gives more pleasure. I'm leaving out the more disgusting things because I don't even want to mention them. I cannot stand it that such a man dares call himself the emperor of the Romans.

"Now, as emperor, with the help of the gods, I will act in such a way as to be at peace with myself. They say that you know best what the gods want, which is why I will make you my partner in my project to bring peace and security to all the countries under Roman rule. If the gods are willing, I will achieve it."

Apollonius heard him out with due attention and then, turning his eyes towards the heavens, said in a prayerful tone:

"O, Jupiter Capitoline, the highest judge! Take this man under your wing! For it has been destined from eternity that he will rebuild your temple, which was burned yesterday by wicked hands."[128]

The temple of Jupiter on the Capitoline Hill in Rome burned down during the capture of the city on 19 December AD 69. On the following day—the day on which Apollonius spoke to Vespasian—Vitellius died, and this death was terrible. Vespasian's troops took control of the city, and he became the sole ruler of the Empire.

And thus, AD 69 came to an end.

## Here ends the Jewish Trilogy of
## Aleksander Krawczuk

---

[128] Ibid., V 27—30.

Fragment of a French 19 century print, undated, unsigned,
Bibliotheque de L'Arsenal, Paris, France

# THE END OF THE LOVE AFFAIR
# OF TITUS AND BERENICE

How very perverse of Krawczuk to end his story here without giving us the conclusion of the love of Titus and Berenice. Perhaps he wanted us to pick up Cassius Dio and discover it for ourselves? But Cassius gives us very little. Four years after Vespasian seized the throne, Berenice and her brother, King Herod Agrippa II, came to Rome:

> Berenice was at the very height of her power and consequently came to Rome along with her brother Agrippa. The latter was given the rank of *praetor* while she dwelt in the palace, cohabiting with Titus. She expected to marry him and was already behaving in every respect as if she were his wife, but when he perceived that the Romans were displeased with the situation, he sent her away. (Cassius Dio, *Roman History*, LXV 15).

That's it.

Racine gives us more, imagining their good bye:

TITUS
N'accablez point, Madame, un prince malheureux ;
Il ne faut point ici nous attendrir tous deux.
Un trouble assez cruel m'agite et me dévore,
Sans que des pleurs si chers me déchirent encore.
Rappelez bien plutôt ce coeur, qui tant de fois
M'a fait de mon devoir reconnaître la voix.
Il en est temps. Forcez votre amour à se taire,
Et d'un oeil que la gloire et la raison éclaire,
Contemplez mon devoir dans toute sa rigueur.
Vous-même contre vous fortifiez mon coeur.
Aidez-moi, s'il se peut, à vaincre sa faiblesse,
À retenir des pleurs qui m'échappent sans cesse.
Ou si nous ne pouvons commander à nos pleurs,

Que la gloire du moins soutienne nos douleurs,
Et que tout l'univers reconnaisse sans peine
Les pleurs d'un empereur, et les pleurs d'une reine.
Car enfin, ma Princesse, il faut nous séparer.

BÉRÉNICE.
Ah cruel ! Est-il temps de me le déclarer ?
Qu'avez-vous fait ? Hélas ! Je me suis crue aimée.
Au plaisir de vous voir mon âme accoutumée
Ne vit plus que pour vous. Ignoriez-vous vos lois,
Quand je vous l'avouai pour la première fois ?
À quel excès d'amour m'avez-vous amenée ?
Que ne me disiez-vous : Princesse infortunée,
Où vas-tu t'engager, et quel est ton espoir ?
Ne donne point un coeur, qu'on ne peut recevoir.
Ne l'avez-vous reçu, cruel, que pour le render
Quand de vos seules mains ce coeur voudrait dépendre?

Which we, the moderns, might render along these lines:

TITUS
Do not kick, Madame, a man when he is down.
Let's not wallow in self-pity.
It's cruel enough that this pain devours me
And robs of my strength.
Please, rather, remember that I have always
Obeyed the call of duty.
Now, such a time has come, and our love must end.
Let us view objectively
My duty in all its cursed harshness.
Do rise above your own grievance and try to help me.
Strengthen my heart, drive away its weakness,
Stem the tears for once they begin to flow, they may never stop.
Or if we cannot stop our tears, then at least
May our pride of our own virtue sustain us in our grief.
Let all the world intuit unseen
These tears of an emperor and of his queen.
My Princess: we must part.

234

BERENICE
Oh, cruel man! How you wound my heart!
What have you done? I believed you.
I believed that you loved me! My soul delighted in
Your sweet presence and lived only for you.
Where were your Roman laws then
When you first told me of your love?
Did you say: "Oh, unfortunate Princess,
How naïve are your hopes! Do not be deceived,
Do not give a heart that cannot be received."
Did you receive it only to throw it away so
Without warning me?


*Tom Pinch*
*Ardennes National Park*
*Luxembourg*

# Seven Against Thebes

Before the Trojan War, there was the Theban War. Who fought it? Why? What does archeology tell us, and what has survived of ancient the epics?

# The Last Olympiad

Serapeum destroyed! Emperor murdered! Pagans raise a revolt! Read leading lights of their time (389-395 AD) as they debate everything from bathing to demon possession.

# A Meeting in Oea

Meet Apuleius, Rome's all-time best-selling author, a Platonic scholar, a part-time magician, and a dowry-hunter, as he works on his treatise on Plato at night and schemes to marry a rich African widow by day.

# Herod, King of the Jews

A half-caste, killer, self-made king.

# Titus and Berenice

The fate of the kingdom of Israel hung for a while on the outcome of the love affair between the middle-aged Jewish queen Berenice, granddaughter of Herod the Great, and the 12-years-younger son of Vespasian, the emperor of Rome.

Jacek Bocheński

# Tiberius Caesar

Terror is normal.
The horrifying tale of Tiberius Caesar, the second emperor of Rome: the man who normalized political terror. A moral, intellectual, emotional zero whose only skill in life was to grab and hang onto power. At any cost. A dizzying look into the great void of an empty soul.

Joe Alex

# The Ships of Minos 1-5

A Bronze Age Saga.
1600 BC. A Minoan ship sails to the ends of the earth in search of the sources of amber. Days without night, water turning to stone, monsters of the deep, peoples who sacrifice their kings to their gods and build great stone circles to worship the sun. And god's face upon the waters.
One of the greatest exploration sagas ever written.

Zbig Nienacki
# Mr. Wheels the Intrepid Art Detective

A great fan franchise, comparable to the British Sherlock Holmes and the French Inspector Maigret, the Polish Mr. Wheels---the bumbling art detective with his iconic self-built car--has been solving art mysteries for sixty years. The humorous tales with a delightful procession of quirky characters concern theft and fraud in the art world and the villains are usually gentlemen (and gentlewomen) thieves. And usually, there is a great historical tale in the background.

Arkady Fiedler
# The White Jaguar 1-5

AD 1726. An uninhabited Caribbean island off the Spanish Main. A Polish-Virginian renegade. Pirates, Runaway slaves. Colonizers. Cannibals. The great saga of the mysterious White Jaguar, a white man named John who became a war leader of the Orinoco Indians in their wars against the Spanish.